PHOENIX
GIRL

HOW A FAT ASIAN WITH BIPOLAR FOUND LOVE

PHOENIX GIRL

A MEMOIR

MICHELLE YANG

FIFTH
AVENUE
PRESS

Fifth Avenue Press is a locally focused and publicly owned publishing imprint of the Ann Arbor District Library. It is dedicated to supporting the local writing community by promoting the production of original fiction, nonfiction, and poetry written for children, teens, and adults.

Printed in the United States of America

First Printing 2025

Cover design: Yvonne Chan
Book design: Nathaniel Roy
Editor: Hannah Beresford

ISBN: 978-1-956697-33-9 (Paperback); 978-1-956697-34-6 (Ebook)

Fifth Avenue Press
343 S. Fifth Ave
Ann Arbor, MI 48104
fifthavenue.press

PRAISE FOR PHOENIX GIRL

"This stunning and searingly honest memoir peels back the layers of what we think of as an individual's mental illness to show its making through one woman's life history, and through generations of trans-national migrations. With compassion and tenderness, Yang exposes many kinds of violence – the violence of assimilation and displacement hidden behind tales of immigrant striving and American opportunity, domestic violence disguised as love or normalized as cultural difference, and the everyday violence of fatphobia. *Phoenix Girl* is at once an elegy for the wounded and a blueprint for collective healing."

—GRACE M. CHO, Author of *Tastes Like War*

"Not since *The House on Mango Street* has a coming of age story of a girl trying to simultaneously honor and escape her roots been rendered so vividly. The arc of expunging bipolar and body image shame undergirds the memoir; but it was the additional interwoven strands of physical, sexual, and verbal abuse that really got to me. Michelle's journey is spellbinding and transcendent."

—ANDY DUNN, Author of *Burn Rate* and Founder of Pie and Bonobos

"*Phoenix Girl* is clear, appealing, and poignant. Michelle Yang's descriptions of the intoxicating highs and profound lows of bipolar are vivid and spot-on. As her relationship with her body evolves and blossoms, she learns to embrace other fundamental parts of herself, too. This memoir is going to help a lot of people."

—ELLEN FORNEY, Author of *Marbles: Mania, Depression, Michelangelo, & Me*

"There are not enough books like Yang's memoir, which focus on the lived experiences of mental illness and fat phobia while also writing with clarity about our attempts to love each other and reach for joy. This is a book about the pasts that what we carry in our bodies and how storytelling, whether through writing or speaking aloud, can be a way to repair and recover, and to find ourselves in each other's stories."

—GRACE TALUSAN, Author of *The Body Papers*

To my loves: Reno, Baobe, and Phoenix.

Author's Note

"If there's a book that you want to read, but it hasn't been written yet, then you must write it." – TONI MORRISON

I am of the countless authors who have been inspired by this quote from the legendary author.

When I was diagnosed with bipolar 1 and admitted to a psych ward, I didn't know if I had a future anymore. I didn't know if I would ever feel myself again.

I turned to the library, my safe place, for comfort. I wanted to find others, real people, who have not only survived my condition but have thrived with it. But in 2001, there wasn't much on the shelves, let alone anything by BIPOC authors or anything from an immigrant point of view.

The landscape of mental health memoirs has since diversified and grown, but I still wanted to share my story—one that has a happy ending.

Though I have changed the names and identifying details of many people to protect their privacy, this story is true to the best of my recollection. I fully acknowledge that human memory can be faulty, but this book is my truth.

Thank you for reading and hope that it makes you feel less alone.

PART

—

CHAPTER 1: Heaven

AGE 7 – INCHEON, SOUTH KOREA

I stretch my tall for a seven-year-old body as long as I can and a yawn escapes, releasing the previous night's dreams into the air. A long narrow scroll of brush-painted bamboo trees comes into view, and the low white ceiling hovers above me. I rub my eyes of the blurriness. Next to me sleeps Didi, my tanned and rascally little brother, whose thin, wiry figure is the opposite of my soft, plump one. Then lies Mama, who places her tired glasses above her pillow every night. She is extra beautiful and elegant without the bulky 1980s plastic frames and her wild perm hiding her face. Furthest from me, my strong, enormous Baba snores like a bear next to Mama, guarding the bedroom door.

This is how we sleep. We have two other small bedrooms in our apartment in the Chinatown port city of Incheon, South Korea, but my parents never imagine us apart.

Our morning begins with the four of us on the floor around a small folding table low to the ground. We eat a hot breakfast prepared by Mama: white rice, a fried egg, and a simple savory soup with a side of kimchi. Baba and I walk, hand-in-hand, two miles to the Chinese school, which is especially pleasant on a spring day like today. With Baba always nearby, I am protected. Who would pick on the daughter of the hefty, six-foot-three teacher who is also the school discipline director?

The school for the Chinese community here is on top of a steep paved hill. There's a small back gate painted blue through which Baba and I enter each morning instead of the grander front entrance on the other side of the school flanked by a pair of stone lions and a million stairs. Once we cross the threshold into the schoolyard, I skip to the right, toward the historic, two-story building that houses my third-grade classroom, past the sandbox and chin-up bars. My ponytail bounces against my backpack as I wave goodbye to Baba. He heads to the office he shares with another teacher in a small rooftop structure atop the staff and admin building. On occasion, Baba will take me and my best friend off campus for lunch, but most days, Mama packs me a lunch or gives me money to buy a cup of instant ramyun at the corner store and I won't see him until the end of the school day when we'll walk home together again.

The school was founded in 1912, the same year the Republic of China (better known as Taiwan) was founded by Sun Yat-Sen, our school's namesake. The building is dusty, dark, and smells of old wood. I turn left into a classroom filled with rows and rows of desks. For each grade, there is one class of about fifty students, ruled by a single teacher with a ruthless wooden stick. Once assigned, we classmates stay together from grades one through twelve, which feels like for life.

I spot my well-worn desk in the middle of the room. All desks, in neat rows, face the chalkboard at the front of the room behind the teacher. I settle in for another day of memorizing and recitation.

But midmorning, Baba abruptly opens my classroom door.

"Hello, Teacher Chang," his voice booms authoritatively, "I need to speak with Beautiful Jade."

Baba looks big and powerful in his business suit as I see him through the eyes of my peers. The suit is tailor-made because Baba cannot find clothes that fit him here where most people are much, much smaller than him. Only Mama, Didi, and I know of the long, frustrating shopping trips to Itaewon in Seoul, near the American army base, where Baba must go to acquire clothes and shoes big enough for foreigners. These are the only clothes that will fit him.

Baba beckons me to come to him. I stand up awkwardly and walk, aware of the hundred curious eyes on my back, without any idea what this could be about. Once I step into the dark hallway and the door is closed, Baba drops his official tone. He bends down to me and says quietly, "I need to show you something."

What could this be about? Baba takes my hand again and leads me out a dozen steps to the entryway of the building. He kneels behind me, his breath warming my right ear. Baba points to a large wooden placard with columns of names in calligraphy gleaning in dedication. He whispers again, "Yang Fu Jio. See? That is your Yeh-Yeh's name. Your grandfather helped build this school. He was a revered leader in the community. He made things happen."

As an adult, I will see a black and white photograph of Yeh-Yeh at the school groundbreaking, towering in front of the other men even as he leans on a shovel. All of Yeh-Yeh's seven children, and most of us grandchildren, will inherit his impressive height and build.

Though I am a small child, standing under that placard with my Baba, I understand the gravity of what Baba is imparting, and my skin tingles into goosebumps. I puff my little chest and stand taller, swelling with pride.

When you're seen and not heard, you can get away with listening to what you're not supposed to. "She's too young to understand," Baba says when the adult conversation takes a mature turn, but nine times out of ten, I understand exactly what is said. I feign innocence though with a blank, sweet look in my eyes, and a slight shrug of my shoulders.

I learn that Baba applied for us to immigrate to the United States by eavesdropping. He applied before I was born, when Mama became pregnant with me. My Second Aunt, who had moved to America in the 1970s, filed a relative petition for our family, but the application had been such a long shot, everyone had all but forgotten about it.

But here we are, ten years later, and the application is miraculously approved. Suddenly, Mama and Baba have a decision to make. "How would you like to move to Mei Guo, Beautiful Jade? What about you, Didi?"

My brother and I have no answer to give. We are all sitting in the living room of our cozy apartment watching television. This time my blank expression is genuine. Having never been outside of Korea and Taiwan, my entire life lived in our little corner of Chinatown in Incheon, I have no idea what "moving to Mei Guo" means. Neither do my parents, really, but the opportunity is too great to pass up. It is like we won the lottery. You don't turn it down when you win the lottery.

Mama and Baba met in college in Taiwan. Though both are fluent in Mandarin and Korean, neither speak English. Baba was used to commanding a certain level of respect in the Chinese community in Korea, in part because of his natural charm and imposing stature, but also due to the reputation of his father, my Yeh-Yeh, an enterprising owner of several large businesses. Baba would be giving that up to immigrate. In the U.S., he'd become yet another lowly cook in Chinese restaurants.

"America is heaven for children. You should be so excited. All kids love America," Baba and Mama take turns assuring Didi and me, looking upon our scared faces.

I am not convinced and neither is Didi, but he is young enough not to raise too many questions. *What was wrong with our life that we had to move across the world?* But I don't ask questions or complain either. I have more sense than that.

"Ai-ya! My friend's children are so excited about moving to America," Baba continues. "Why can't you be more like them?"

The evening before we depart for America, Baba sits cross-legged on the bare linoleum floor of our small, now empty, apartment living room. I am in the adjacent tiny room, which had housed my second-hand upright piano without room for much else until the day before. When my parents sold the instrument I was forced to practice since age four, I thought myself indifferent, relieved even. But yesterday, when four men came to carry it away, struggling with it down the building's staircase, I found my face drenched with tears.

This night before the biggest trip of our lives, I am lurking in that empty ghost-piano room eavesdropping. Baba is speaking to his mother, my Popo, on the phone. "Yes, Ma. Please don't worry...No, no, we will be fine. No, I don't need money."

As soon as the call ends, Baba heaves in a large gasp of air and snatches a dirty rag from the floor nearby. I squeeze my eyes tight and ball up my body, preparing for the hollering explosion that is Baba's sneeze, while wondering why in the world Baba would use that rag.

When a moment passes and the room remains still, I peek. Baba sobs silently into the stinky rag. His shoulders tremble like dragons breaking out of mountains.

This is the first time I ever see Baba cry. He cries for a long time.

CHAPTER 2: Lost in Translation

AGE 9 – ATLANTA, GEORGIA

"Do you know any words in English, kids?" asks Second Aunt smiling her generous lipsticked smile. She is watching Didi and me in the rearview mirror after picking our family up at the airport in Atlanta, Georgia. I'm a little bit cold on this dark October night in 1990. As we zip on the freeway, I can't see much outside but the big road and big cars.

This is the first time I recall ever meeting Second Aunt, and instantly, I'm in love. She is perhaps the tallest and biggest Chinese woman I've ever seen. She is also beautiful like a technicolor movie star, glowing with warmth. She spotlights Didi and me with her focused attention in a way we're not accustomed to, and it feels luxurious.

"I do! I do!" six-year-old Didi exclaims excitedly. "I know '-O-Q'"

"'O-Q?' What's 'O-Q?'" Second Aunt chuckles, charmed, and tosses her head of short curls.

We all laugh at Didi's hybrid of "okay" and "thank you."

Next, Second Aunt teaches Didi and me to count in English. She is patient as we repeat after her. "Yi is 'one,' er is 'two,' san is 'three' … repeat after me."

When I mispronounce "six" as "sex," the grown-ups in the car boom with laughter. I furrow my brow in confusion at what they think is so funny. Before we reach our destination though, I can count to ten in English.

"I think Beautiful Jade may have a gift for languages," says Second Aunt, who also knows of my fluency in Mandarin and Korean. Like a kitten in sunbeam, I bask in the compliment.

I am nine years old when my ethnic Chinese family immigrates to America. The trauma of immigration is rarely acknowledged here. Here, the loudest narratives are dreams come true: montages of hard work and perseverance, makeovers and love stories, wealth, success, and Hollywood happy endings.

But when my family leaves the tight-knit enclave of Chinatown in Incheon, I lose my grandparents, my friends, my home, and the innocence of childhood. I lose all my toys, my piano. I never regain the innate sense of belonging after that, no matter where I go.

In my bustling hometown harbor city, I was a child who needs no introduction. Everyone recognized who I am and to whom I belong, for generations back. Grown-ups I don't know would giggle and tease, "Your face is a carbon copy of your Baba's. You could never get lost around here."

But in America, I will be an outsider, adrift. Gone are the carefree days roaming the streets and playing house with my friends. Instead, I will shoulder the weight of responsibilities beyond my years. A stone to never cause trouble. A boulder to validate our immigration with quick assimilation and gold-star achievements. An anvil to care for my younger brother. And a mountain to work like a grown-up alongside my exhausted parents.

Second Aunt exits the freeway cautiously, and I look about curiously to see what I can make out in the night. The streets are wide, and there is no one around. This is a stark contrast to the sprawling, neon-lit metropolises to which my family is accustomed.

"It's so quiet here," says Baba. "And so dark. It's eerie. I'm a little scared." He laughs nervously.

"You'll get used to it," assures Second Aunt.

Then, I see our destination: WAFFLE HOUSE.

The big, bright yellow and black lights beckon us with their bright artificial glow, like a beacon in heavy fog. I stumble out from my aunt's station wagon, overtired but wired with excitement. At around 2 a.m., the restaurant is empty inside and wafting with the scent of fried eggs, slightly burnt toast, and what I will later learn to be the fatty, salty aroma of bacon. I've entered another world.

We are guided to a booth with hard, cool seats and a slightly sticky tabletop. After some discussion, Second Aunt orders for us in fluid English, the twisted language. Before long, hot plates of food arrive, most of which are unlike anything I've ever seen. There is a round, patterned pancake of some kind. It is called a "waffle" and is the namesake of the restaurant. The waffle is served with a miniature jug of warm, brown sugary liquid, called syrup, and a creamy scoop of butter, something else I am not accustomed to eating.

"You take this syrup and drizzle over the waffle," says Second Aunt. "Americans love this stuff."

As always, we eat family style: everything is shared so we can all have a taste. The golden-yellow waffle is spongy at the center, crispy on the edges, and curious all around. The flavors and textures remind me a little of hotteok, a brown sugar-filled pancake that is my favorite winter street food back home, but not quite as good. I like the waffle too, though.

Second Aunt spends some time explaining to us what grits are, but I still don't understand. When it arrives, it looks like a sort of sandy gruel alongside Baba's chewy steak. "Is this like American xifan?" he asks while sucking the unfamiliar texture off the roof of his mouth, comparing it to the silky-smooth rice porridge we eat often at home.

All of us get to try the steak too, which Second Aunt drenches in A1 Steak Sauce. After this meal, Baba will always keep a bottle of A1 Steak Sauce in our fridge because this is how Americans eat steak.

Didi, the picky eater, relishes the ham. Luncheon meat or hot dogs scrambled with eggs over rice has always been his favorite, so he is happy to find something familiar.

My favorite is the hashbrowns—shredded potatoes fried crisp— that I douse with ketchup.

Mama eats quietly. "Everything is good," she says agreeably.

The distinct sterility of those diner fluorescent lights tints my early memories of immigration, but restless motions in my gut do not go away.

Back when our airplane began its initial descent into Los Angeles International Airport, panic rumbled in my belly. No one in my family could understand the in-flight announcements. Didi and I were scared and weary the entire long, long flight. Baba and Mama must have felt the same.

When the clouds dissipated past our plane, my guts protested. I looked to Baba with eyes wide.

"I have to go to the bathroom," I said.

"Can it wait?"

I shook my head no.

"Go ahead, hurry!" he said in a faux whisper. Nothing about my father is quiet.

I scrambled down the narrow aisle and squeezed myself into the awkward bathroom, folding shut the cold metal door and securing the latch. My suspenders with my acid-wash jeans were complicated to undo, and even my pigtails, weighted down with cherry-shaped plastic charms, were a nuisance.

An urgent pounding on the door interrupted my business, followed by alarmed voices uttering words I could not comprehend. *Geez, wait your turn. Are all Americans so impatient?*

As quickly as I could, I finished and stood up to pound back on the door. This was a signal used back home to communicate, "Someone's in here, leave me alone." But apparently, that doesn't work here. Certainly not on a flight during descent. There was more hollering. A flight attendant finally opened the door with a key. Nine-year-old me, suspenders undone, looked to them in confusion at the commotion. *What's this big fuss about?*

The attendants sighed in relief and motioned me back to my seat. My cheeks burned as all of the passengers stared at me down the aisle on my walk of shame.

As we approach Second Aunt's house in the suburbs after leaving Waffle House, the same pre-landing uneasiness plagues me. The darkness and quiet of the deserted, expansive streets make me feel exposed and alone, even in this car full of people. All I've known is the constant white noise of a crowded city. Didi and I stare out silently out the car windows, taking in the monstrous trees and ghostly houses on big plots of land.

"These look like parks, not houses," says Baba, speaking for all of us.

The rumblings in my stomach do not go away. They are a reminder that I don't know anything here. My parents—who have been my guides, my teachers, and my protectors in this world—also know nothing here.

CHAPTER 3: Three Tongues

AGE 9 – ATLANTA, GEORGIA

"Write your name for me, won't you, hon?" asks my new fourth-grade teacher loudly in a Southern drawl on my first day of school. Her shoulder-length hair is golden like the hair on the one Barbie doll that I own. (My Uncle Johnny brought her back from America for me. She is the only Barbie I own. At the time, I preferred my Korean Mimi dolls with anime eyes and did not understand why all the grown-ups made such a big deal over the genuine American Barbie doll.)

My new teacher is bubbly and kind. She smiles at me, flashing her big white teeth, but the overall effect, with her volume and height, makes me cower. I don't know what to do.

She slides a crisp, white piece of paper toward me and slowly and repeatedly mimes writing in the air, "Your naaaammmmee?"

Baba says the schools are why we moved across the world. With Second Aunt's help, my parents chose the most affordable apartment available in an upper-middle-class suburb of Atlanta in a good school district. To my aunt and my dad, "good" translates to "predominantly white."

My American public school is a sprawling one-story building surrounded by vast, grassy fields. As soon as I step inside the brightly lit building, it is hard to feel like I belong. I notice the lack of the dusty smell of old wood and powdery chalk that I associate with my school in Korea. At this new school, everything is shiny, nice, and new. Even the bathrooms are clean and do not stink. There is a gym that doubles as a cafeteria and it serves hot food for free. The teachers excitedly greet students, and none of them carry a stick. It is a great school, but no one knows me here. No part of this school is built by the sheer determination of my Yeh-Yeh. I can't feel his sweat, his tears, his bones.

The fall term is already months underway, so my sudden arrival draws plenty of quizzical stares.

"Naammee?" I shrink as my teacher's request becomes louder and her gestures more exaggerated. I understand perfectly what she wants me to do, only I have not the faintest idea how to write my name in English.

Back home, Mandarin is taught in the classroom but Korean is the language on the playground. English classes don't begin until the fifth grade. Our immigration was sudden. My parents hadn't added after-school English lessons to my years of piano, abacus, and art classes. Amid the flurry of moving and trying to make a living in a foreign land, teaching me to write my name had fallen off my parents' list of priorities. All of Baba's friends and family had told him, "Kids always learn English so fast. You need not worry about them."

I am in a silent stare-down with my lovely, well-intentioned American teacher. I blink as my mind draws a blank, trying not to let out the tears threatening to escape on my first day. I am already failing at my first task.

I don't think to write my name in Chinese or Korean to convey that I understand the instruction. Instead, I freeze.

Soon, the entire class comes to my desk to pantomime the concept of "name" around me, like a group performance. They giggle and point at each other and then at the paper, slowly and loudly narrating their actions as they write out their own names in skits. My face remains placid as I hold back tears, wishing I could disappear, wishing I was home in Korea. My classmates soon grow frustrated at my non-responsiveness. They roll their eyes as they give up. Shaking their heads before walking away. A few of them utter, "So stupid."

I stumble off the impossibly big and loud school bus that drops me very close to the neatly painted door of our apartment. As soon as I run inside, I take off my shoes and drop my backpack on the beige carpet. "Mama, can you teach me to write my name in English?" I ask with urgency.

"Michelle" had been chosen by Baba's friends for me because it sounds similar to the Mandarin pronunciation of Beautiful Jade. The idea of keeping my original given name never crosses anyone's mind. We are here to adapt, not to stick out. If it means better odds at success, we all bend with the current.

Mama starts rummaging through drawers and finds a stack of junk mail. She never throws anything away, so scrap paper is always handy. On the back of an envelope, she carefully prints "Michelle Yang" at the top and hands it to me. With a cheap plastic pen on the cream-colored laminate kitchen countertop, I copy it over and over in neat rows. When I fill that envelope to the bottom, I start another and another. Soon, all the spare scraps of paper I can find have my American name scribbled on them. I am determined never to lose my name.

Though I can write my name after that first day, my life doesn't get easier. Winning over fellow fourth graders when you can't speak the language and don't understand the culture is basically impossible. My ill-fitting clothes (all purchased intentionally too big so I can grow into them) are foreign, often printed with nonsense English words, and purchased from noisy stalls in outdoor markets where the enticing scent of tempura, udon, and spicy rice cakes permeate the air. They are a far cry from the Esprit shirts with coordinated bright-colored cuffed socks my classmates don proudly, acquired from sparkling shopping malls with indoor fountains and Orange Julius in the food court.

My pigtails, lovingly braided by Mama each morning, are all wrong too. The cool fourth-grader girls have already moved onto oversized bangs with industrial-strength hairspray, but I still operate in cutesy.

One frosty morning during the first weeks at my new school, I wait for the bus at my stop. The apartment grounds of our complex are beautiful, with aged, gnarled trees and landscaped bushes. But there are no children here. The bus only comes to pick me up alone. When Didi and I play on the weekends, it's just us. By contrast, in Korea, there were hordes of children with whom we ran wild, literally lighting things on fire sometimes, but here, all is quiet and peaceful.

I roll gravel underneath my shoes until the rumble of the bus comes down the winding path. With a loud long squeak, the bus comes to a stop in front of me. I wave goodbye to Mama and climb on the giant steps. Once I sit down, I see there is a hole in the back of the brown pleather seat in front of me that has been patched over with silver duct tape. A long strand of blond hair shimmering in the morning sun sticks out of it. The hair and its natural sparkles cast a spell over me. This is my first up-close encounter with genuine blonde hair, and I am mesmerized. Slowly, I run my small fingers across the length of the enchanted strand, wishing I could stash it in a treasure box. I don't know why I'm so drawn to it. I just am. I hold the strand between my thumb and forefinger and slowly feel it from end to end. I think I feel chills.

"Hey you, Black boy!"

My reverie is interrupted. Other words are spoken but my English is very limited and these are the only words I understand. I turn around to see a child about my age spitting words at another kid who looks scared and is several years younger.

The younger boy has round, dark-brown eyes, and thick lashes. His smooth, brown face is pointed stiffly forward, pretending not to see or hear. Tears pool in his eyes, but he is fighting them. The act makes his large eyes look even bigger, though he is trying to shrink himself like I had on my first day.

I didn't know Black could be used to describe a person in America. Back home, Yeh-Yeh called all Westerners Dai Bi Zi, which means "big nose," or Lao Wai, which simply means "foreigner." I didn't know people could be categorized or insulted by color in America, where everyone looks so different. American people could have hair that is red, yellow, brown, or black. Their eyes can be green, blue, black, and everything in between. We didn't have this diversity in Korea or Taiwan, where just about everyone had black hair, dark brown eyes, and similar skin tones. I am confused and powerless to protect the boy.

In 1990 Atlanta, Confederate flags hang everywhere—on bumper stickers, windows, and shirts. I don't know what the flag means. We live about ten minutes from Stone Mountain, and I have no clue that it is America's largest Confederate Monument and a sacred site for the Ku Klux Klan. I don't know anything about the gruesome history of my new home.

When Baba and his friends (an uncle who's not related to us and his wife) take us on a visit to Stone Mountain, we're excited for the outing and marvel at the natural beauty that surrounds us. We're all bundled up on this crisp autumn day. The leaves on the towering trees are changing color and the forest floor is soft and moist beneath my steps. We find a wooden picnic table, and Baba sets up the small red gas camping stove in its center. Once the round grill pan heats up, Baba uses wooden disposable chopsticks to roll a piece of beef fat around the surface. The smoky, rich smell instantly draws hunger pangs from my belly. My parents open the containers of sliced beef and pork and begin grilling. There's an entire rice cooker full of rice that Mama brought along with a big container of kimchi and other side dishes. This is the only way we've ever barbequed, and it is the best.

A man with a small boy wanders by and peers over at us.

"What are they doing, Daddy?" asks the little boy, who looks to be about five.

"They're having a picnic," he explains loudly. "Chinese people eat with those wooden sticks called chopsticks."

Uncle, who has been in Atlanta for years, looks up at the man and waves politely and nods. Then in hushed Mandarin says, "We're not a zoo exhibit." He and Baba laugh.

Once I've gorged myself on sizzling meat on cloudy rice with perfectly tart, spicy kimchi wrapped in lettuce leaves, I explore my surroundings more.

Stone Mountain looks like its name, an enormous mountain made of stone, but in 1972, likenesses of three Confederate leaders were carved into its north face: Jefferson Davis, Robert E. Lee, and Stonewall Jackson on horseback, holding their hats over their hearts. It is one of the largest rock-relief carvings in the world and the most visited site in the state of Georgia. But I'm nine, and I don't know that. "Who are these men, Baba?" I ask.

"I don't know," he answers. "They must be important soldiers in American history."

Second Aunt's husband is a portly, good-natured man of few words. My aunt has a dominating personality, and my uncle recedes into the background. They've lived in Atlanta since the 1970s and raised six brilliant and gorgeous daughters while attempting for years to produce a male heir. The Beautiful Six are famous in town because they are quite a sight to behold, especially as they wait tables together at New Chinatown, Second Aunt's family restaurant, which is where Baba and Mama are to work as well.

Didi and I begin to spend hours in the backroom of New Chinatown too. The room is nothing fancy—walls lined with shelves of cluttered restaurant supplies and a big round table fills most of it—but it's space for us to eat, do homework, *live* in private, away from the gaze of customers demanding us to be always on.

In this back room of New Chinatown, Mama and Baba get their first lessons on how to survive in America. Relatives and colleagues perpetuate fear, speckled with urban myths.

"Before you get into the car at night, check the back seat," whispers one uncle. "A Black man may be hiding there, waiting to attack you." Baba, all six-foot-three of him, shudders.

"If a car rear-ends you at night on an empty road, do not stop," warns another. "Instead, drive to the nearest police station." Baba shrinks.

"A Black man is waiting to attack," they seem to whisper in unison.

If any of the Beautiful Six are in earshot, they scream, "That's so racist!"

They slam their heavy textbooks and slam the door. One of the twins, the one who would later become a lawyer, gets especially irate. All of them groan. I don't yet know this word, "racist."

Second Aunt shakes her head at her beautiful daughters, smiling as you would at an adorable toddler. "Their sense of racial equality is quite admirable, don't you think?" she says to Baba. "They're so naïve."

Baba nods with a blank expression, trying to play it cool. It is a lot to absorb. I sense Baba's fear in dark parking lots. He bristles in defense around Black men. Baba takes his protector role seriously and his job becomes much harder after we move to America.

Before we immigrated, Mama lulled me and Didi to sleep with descriptions of America that seems like Disneyland everywhere, all the time. None of us are prepared for the reality, the quiet and mounting fear.

"America is heaven for children," she promised. "You'll see."

Throughout the school day, I am instructed to copy everything the student next to me is writing. My letters are an illegible, jumbled mess at first. I haven't learned the concept of spacing or any rules of grammar. My first assigned classroom guide is a top student with doe-like eyes and pretty, thick brown hair. My snail-like speed at copying prevents her from using the backs of her papers because I am never done by the time she is ready to flip the page. She grunts, rolls her eyes, and slams books to express her displeasure. I think she hates me and wonder why she volunteered to help me in the first place.

"Where are you from?" I am asked a lot.

"I'm Chinese, born in Korea," I become practiced at saying. "I was born in a noodle factory," I embellish when my English improves, even though it isn't true. I was born in a hospital, like most people, but my first childhood home had been the family compound at Yeh-Yeh's noodle factory. The backstory is exotic enough to satiate the curiosity of my suburban classmates, painting me as the freak attraction they think me to be.

During the long, lonely days at school, art class is my respite. My first passion has been drawing and painting, ever since I could hold a pencil. But at my school in Korea, art had been a throwaway class. Baba said it was a fine hobby as long as it didn't interfere with real schoolwork. The homeroom teachers who taught art at my old school in Korea didn't know or care much about the subject, but my art teacher in Atlanta seems to live for art, and it shows. I love making her smile with my vibrant, controlled brush strokes that breathe life into the arranged fruit on my paper. I sculpt a turtle with an organic curvature, relishing the feel of the precious clay and the scent of the richest soil between my fingers. The kiln transforms my turtle into a sparkling keepsake, and it's nothing short of magic.

Other kids take the lessons for granted, but I live for those hours. Art is the only class I can excel in without English. The teacher holds up my work to be admired in nearly every class. She chooses them to adorn the school display cases and entranceways.

I spend an hour a day in English as a Second Language class. Besides art, it is my other source of release. ESL allows me to engage actively with a mishmash of children from all of the world, who are equally as rootless as me and in various stages of assimilation. I count down the minutes each day to ESL and come back to life there.

ESL is held in a classroom adapted from a large trailer behind the main school building. There are rows of these trailers in that back lot. When I walk in, I'm surprised at how spacious it is inside. There are two ESL teachers every day. On my first day, the teacher with short grey hair and a crinkly-eyed smile, guides me over to a skinny, tanned Asian girl.

"Michelle, this is Patty," she says. "She is in the fifth grade and came to us from Taiwan about four months ago."

My ears perk at the word "Taiwan." Could it be true? Another soul who can speak Mandarin? Someone I can talk to?

"Hi Michelle," Patty says shyly.

I'm so excited, I'm afraid to meet her eyes at first.

As soon as the teacher leaves us, I have endless things to say. We giggle and chat and are instant best friends. I worship her. Patty's English, better than mine, sound masterful to my ears. She is my translator, my voice, and she has my undying gratitude and devotion.

About a month passes. Every day, I check the clock repeatedly until cafeteria meals, recess, art classes, and my precious hours with Patty. Then, one day in ESL, a new kid shows up. He is tall for a fifth-grader. His collared, striped shirt is perfectly crisp, likely some high-end brand I do not recognize. With his gelled hair and bright face, the effect is immediate. I blush and turn aside.

"Everyone, meet Min from Seoul, South Korea," our teacher says. My heart beats then. Someone else I can talk to. He is seated next to me and we regard each other shyly.

"I'm from Incheon," I say in Korean. "I've been in Mee-Gook a month."

"Thank goodness you're here," Min says, his smile lighting up the room. "No one else speaks Korean here."

I melt, just a little.

"Are you in fifth grade too?" he asks.

"...Um...Yes, I am," I answer. I feel guilty about lying to him. I am only in fourth grade but I did not want him to ask me to call him "Opa," a term of respect reserved for older brothers and older male friends, sometimes boyfriends. I can't even think about that without blushing. I don't want to go there. I prefer us to be equals, so I lie.

Patty, Min, and I form a funny triangle. Patty and I are the only Mandarin speakers, while Min and I are the only Korean speakers. Patty is the only one who's even semi-fluent in English, so every day involves rounds of multilingual telephone.

Min draws a picture that has me and Patty giggling.

"What's so funny?" asks our teacher.

We show her the picture but she doesn't understand.

"Bang-goo," says Min proudly.

"Fang-pi," I tell Patty, giggling into my hands.

Patty is laughing pretty hard by this point. "How do you say 'fang-pi' in English?" she asks me, scratching her head.

I think long and hard while our teacher looks at the three of us giggling. And then I am hit with a stroke of genius, and I remember what I think is the word. I say loud and proud, "Gaa-ss! Gaa-ss! He has gas!"

Our teacher bursts out laughing, and the three of us are already hysterical.

Every day at ESL, Min and I are clearly so excited to see each other that the other kids take notice. I'm excited to see Patty too, but they don't give me a hard time about this.

"Do you *love* him?" asks a skinny girl with long brown hair from Czechoslovakia. She smiles teasingly.

A short, stout boy who speaks Spanish wraps his hands around his own back and makes kissy faces at Min and me when he sees us.

The kids don't mean to torment us. They are envious that they don't also have someone from home, but it embarrasses me just the same. Sometimes, I try to distance myself from Min, but not for long. I like Min too much. It is wonderful to feel needed, not just helpless. I am his Patty. Together, the three of us, we spread roots.

My six cousins, the Beautiful Six, are a vision in their uniform periwinkle blouses when they work at New Chinatown. Cousins are called brothers and sisters in Chinese culture, and I love my six new sisters like a collection of real-life dolls I've always wanted. Second Aunt is as stunning as her teenage daughters. I hate being told I'm the spitting image of Baba. *How can I look exactly like him when I'm a girl?* But I like being told I look like Second Aunt. She is warm and nurturing. She looks like a Chinese Doris Day with her soft-painted face and perfect curls. Second Aunt is round and gregarious, her voice like red silk, smooth but loud. Second Aunt is such a contrast to Mama, whose delicate features and shy frame I could never emulate, as much as I want to.

Second Aunt is a woman in charge. She is unapologetic both at home and in business, while Mama is obedient and passive. To model myself after my slender mother seems like an uphill battle given my extra-large size and dominant features, but I can glimpse my possible future in Second Aunt. I like what I can almost see.

Mama was a stay-at-home mom in Korea. She busied herself with cleaning the apartment and preparing meals while keeping herself pretty enough to please Baba. Mama's job, in addition to caring for me and Didi, was to be at the ready with a plentiful and enticing table for Baba and his friends whenever they decided to drop in unannounced to drink. Collecting Baba at all hours when he was too intoxicated to find his way home was also a part of her wifely duties. She hated this life but accepted it as the common fate of most women she knew.

In America, Mama works at New Chinatown like Baba, an apron tucked neatly around her slim waist. Because she doesn't speak English, she busses tables while Baba cooks in the kitchen. She prefers her life in America immediately.

"Is it tiring?" asks her mother, my Lao-Lao, on the phone from all the way in Daegu.

"No," answers Mama. "I like working and making money," she says with a quick flourish of her graceful hand, a motion only I see.

Mama now earns minimum wage, but for the first time, her productivity can be measured monetarily. She loves this. In Korea and around the world, stay-at-home parents are not afforded this metric. In America, her life becomes markedly more peaceful and predictable, and her worth more tangible to herself. Though Baba often complains of boredom, Mama is a silent and diligent worker ant. Our new life means Baba is separated from his drinking buddies and a work culture that mandates alcoholic outings where he too often would lose control. His new, physically demanding job leaves him dead-tired each night after full days of manual labor. Didi and I, at ages six and nine respectively, begin to fend for ourselves after school in our sparsely furnished apartment for unprecedented amounts of time.

When Mama leaves us at night to go to work, I can feel her worry envelop us.

"Don't let anyone in," warns Mama. "If I call or Baba calls, we'll make sure to speak first before you have to so you know it's us. Never tell anyone you're home alone. That's illegal here."

I'm nervous and a little scared of all the instructions, but soon, it becomes the norm. When she and Baba come home, Didi and I will be asleep. "Listen to your sister," she reminds Didi as she closes the front door and enters the night.

And then the apartment is ours. We are glued to the small television, puzzling over *The Simpsons* which makes little sense to us. We gasp, eyes wide, when Homer and Marge kiss in bed naked, shocked that this is allowed on a cartoon on television.

Second Aunt gifts us excess chicken wings from the restaurant to incorporate into home meals. Sometimes, Mama deep fries the wings on the small red camping stove in the storage shed outside, afraid that cooking indoors with so much oil will jeopardize our cleaning deposit. Other times, she marinates the wings in soy sauce, garlic, and crushed chili. She learns to roast them in the kao shiang, the Mandarin word for oven, which literally translates to "roasting box." We never had an oven in Korea, most people don't, and it is so foreign to us. Those wings are lip-smackingly delicious. Mama is so good at making these meals that we never realize we're eating scraps.

She also fashions makeshift end tables out of cardboard boxes and covers them with worn tablecloths that smell of years of set-in grease—more cast-offs from New Chinatown. I'm not sure what color the tablecloths were originally, but now they are a light-orange sorbet color. You can't tell that they aren't real furniture just by looking. The fake furniture is fine to hold a remote control or even a cheap lamp, but when Didi and I get too comfortable, Mama warns, "Don't lean on these, they're unsteady."

All of us sleep on soft sleeping mats on the floor together in one room, like we did in our apartment in Korea. American-style beds are not missed. Though it is the first time our family struggles financially, I don't know it. There are too many changes at once to notice the material changes. What I cannot help but notice is the fear and exhaustion in my parents, who fight more and more.

Baba does not like Atlanta. He does not like having to answer to Second Aunt or her husband at New Chinatown. Starting with his first job out of college, Baba struggled with bosses. He does not follow orders, he gives them, so mixing family with work is trouble. To Second Aunt's dismay, Baba quits his job at her restaurant and finds another cooking at a competing Chinese kitchen a couple of months later. Still, he is not content.

He complains to whoever will listen. Sitting in our dim apartment, he drones on, "Who's ever seen trees this tall? It's unnatural! They cover up almost the entire sky. I can't live like this."

Soon, his complaining takes on an urgency. Baba's mood dominates every room. I can taste the fear and bitterness in the winter air as the days grow colder. Baba sits on the floor, arms and legs folded; his face, the picture of despair. "Do you know that I have to drive by a cemetery on my way home from work?"

I nod.

"Do you know how pitch black it is? And how tall the trees are?"

I nod again.

"If someone murders me and buries me in those woods, no one would be able to find me." He looks like he is going to cry.

I don't know what to do or what to say. I get very afraid too.

In Korea, Baba always knew what to do. When he got mad, which was often, it was always directed at someone or something. It is different in America. "I can't breathe when I can't see the sky," he says. "I never see daylight. It's pitch black when I leave for work in the morning and pitch black when I come home. This is no way to live."

I try to disappear into the walls. I feel sad for Mama too, who doesn't know what to say. "But we can't go back to Korea," Baba says to Mama. "No, we can't go back defeated with our tails between our legs."

We packed up our whole lives there. That can't be so easily undone.

Big, fat, feather-like snowflakes greet Didi and me one morning. We've never seen snow so beautiful and pristine. It feels like a celebration, a cleansing, a starting over. At night, I hear Mama on the phone, who uses her calling card to call her brother long distance in Lincoln, Nebraska. Like Second Aunt, Uncle Johnny also immigrated to the U.S. in the late 1970s. He was the one who brought me my one treasured Barbie doll. By the time Baba and Mama tell Didi and me, they've already decided.

"Your Uncle Johnny is opening a restaurant in Lincoln, Nebraska," Baba says. "Mama and I will go help. We will all move there"

We've scarcely been in Atlanta for five months. Patty, Min, and I have just become a happy trio. I've grown to like my school, but now I will have to say goodbye to it all again.

My fourth-grade class makes me a goodbye card and everyone signs it. I tell Patty. She is disappointed, but she will be fine. Her English is already so good, and she will have many friends. But I don't have the words for Min. I avoid, avoid, avoid. My last day in school is here and still, I haven't told Min I am moving away. I don't want him to know how important he is to me.

At my final recess at this school, Min shuffles toward me while I am on the swings. He stands there in jeans, another crisp shirt, and gelled hair, waiting for me. I jump off and walk toward him. We don't say anything.

He breaks first. "I hear you're moving away," he says softly. "Why didn't you tell me?"

I shrug and say nothing. I can't let him know I care.

"Goodbye and good luck," he says without meeting my eyes and begins walking away, but not before saying. "What will I do without you?"

I tell myself I don't care. With a sassy smile, I skip away, as if I wouldn't miss him for years to come.

CHAPTER 4: *Tumbleweeds*

AGE 10 – LINCOLN, NEBRASKA

For the second time in less than a year, my family is all packed up to leave. The empty apartment is meticulously cleaned. My parents even cover over any push-pin made holes with toothpaste. Their work (mostly Mama's) pays off, as the entirety of our cleaning deposit is returned to us, and my parents are happy about that.

When we immigrated, we packed our lives into fourteen suitcases. This time, all of our belongings are shoved into the back of my dad's new pride and joy: a maroon and silver Ford Dixie van. Second Aunt advised Baba to purchase a sensible, Japanese-made minivan for the family, but after test-driving several models, he chose the most American of them all. Second Aunt does not approve, but Baba is pleased as a Georgia peach.

"Even I can stand up in the back of the van!" he exclaims. "Imagine that!"

Back in Korea, Baba was forced to crouch in doorways and rooms where he did not fit. Here in America, he now owns a vehicle where he can stand up straight. Didi, Baba, and I also all love the small, grainy television in the back. To Baba, this half-camper, half-van is part of why he moved here. It makes no sense to him to buy a Japanese car in America. He is here to access all things American.

The four of us file out of our apartment on the wintry morning, and we are about to climb into our van when a crow caws from atop a tree near the driveway. Without a word, Baba picks up a rock, takes a few steps forward, and hurls it as hard as he can toward the bird. His sudden determination and movement is startling. I walk up next to him, looking up at the trees. "Why did you do that, Baba?"

"Crows are bad luck," he answers, sounding afraid again. "We don't want any of that."

I nod, bundled in my warmest coat, as if his behavior is normal. Baba was never unsure of himself in Korea. He was always the ringleader, the life of the party. Here, he never relaxes.

I climb in the van first. My seat is an upside-down five-gallon Kikkoman soy sauce bucket wedged between the driver and front passenger seats. There are rags on top for padding. Didi sits on Mama's lap. The rest of the van is so full we can't see out the back window.

After driving for hours, Baba pulls over at a rest stop. Climbing out of the van, we each stretch our bodies. I feel the phantom ring around my bottom from the soy sauce bucket, which will haunt me for the rest of my life. Didi and I, full of pent-up energy, run about on the grass. At a water fountain, we both take a long cool drink. As I finish, a crow lands on the cinderblock barrier next to the fountain. It tilts its head at me, its eyes posing the question, "Are you friend or foe?"

I shoo the crow away, certain I have done Baba proud, but when Didi and I get back to the van, Baba is stern-faced. "Why did you scare away that crow, Beautiful Jade? It was just thirsty."

The shame burns my cheeks and my palms. I hadn't thought of the bird needing water. I only wanted to chase away bad luck like Baba. I did it to please him. "That was unkind, Beautiful Jade."

My words stick in my throat like charcoal lumps. *Never talk back* ruled my upbringing. I know better.

Mama pulls out the rice cooker full of rice she had made back at the apartment. We eat this rice for lunch and dinner with kimchi and a can of spam. On other days, we make meals out of rice she cooks at a rest stop while we wait around, sharing a can of Dinty Moore beef stew. We eat both Spam and the beef stew cold, glossy with fat, and straight from the can. We don't eat at any restaurants, fast-food or otherwise. We are moving across the country on a budget of a hundred dollars.

As we near our destination, amber wheat fields stretch around us, as far as I can see into the horizon. Baba is aghast. Lincoln, Nebraska, is a small town. We only see one major street. Uncle Johnny, the oldest of Mama's three younger siblings, opened one of the largest restaurants there. Pulling into the parking lot of the standalone building, I see a big yellow and red marquee: Wang's Chinese Restaurant.

The new interior is just as impressive with new carpeting and gleaming light. There is no set-in-grease smell of old restaurants in the air. The space is bright and airy. "Welcome! Welcome!" Uncle Johnny and Aunt Jennifer greet us warmly.

Here, in America's heartland, are more of my relatives that I never really knew before. Aunt Jennifer is quite a bit younger and Korean, and this sparks a lot of talk.

"Koreans don't know how to save money," my parents gossip at night about my new aunt. "They dress so well and drive fancy cars, but it's all about appearances."

Despite the sometimes less-than-kind things my parents say about my new aunt, I admire her. She immigrated as a teenager and attended an American college—something uncommon in my parents' circles. She can speak English, and language is power.

Uncle Johnny recruits another uncle, a second cousin, to work in his big new restaurant. This distant uncle also has a Korean wife and two American-born children around my brother's age. Both of our families are new to town, and we move into the same sprawling apartment complex. For the first time since we immigrated, we have cousins as playmates and a relative's home where we are welcome to walk to any time. Immediately, we are folded into a community. There are green lawns and winding, neat paths aplenty, and multiple playgrounds invite us to explore and imagine. We also make friends with other kids in the complex, even though we don't speak much English yet. A neighbor girl with curly brown hair hangs a beautiful basket of candies on my door for May Day. She and I ride our bikes all over the complex. She is wild, flipping over large rocks. Once, we find a coiled black snake, hissing and slithering. We scream and run away, giggling.

Because Didi and I need ESL, we can't go to the same elementary school as our American-born cousins and neighbors. Instead, we are bussed over an hour to an elementary school downtown, where the school district pools its ESL resources. Because of this program, it feels like my downtown school is made up of mostly students of color and many refugees. The commute is inconvenient and bumpy, but I am grateful to learn English all day instead of just for one hour a day, as I had in Atlanta. The teachers are excellent and caring, and my language skills improve dramatically. I'm in the latter half of my fourth-grade year, but grade level doesn't seem to matter in ESL, as we are all learning English.

One day, the school realizes they have forgotten to teach me math for months. I have not had a single math lesson since I started there. The teachers panic, but, turns out, it doesn't matter. The math I had learned in Korea is still far ahead of where they are teaching.

Even with all the good things about life in Lincoln, I'm swallowed whole by loneliness. I miss Patty and Min. I miss Ying, my best friend in Korea. I miss my grandparents and everything familiar.

Each night, I hide my tears in my pillow. I don't want my already struggling parents to worry about the homesickness burning a hole in my stomach. They would only tell me to be grateful for my new life anyway, the same thing they are telling themselves.

Only a few months later, about as long as we lasted in Atlanta, Baba's complaining returns. "How could a capital city in an American state be so small?" he asks of my distant uncle, who smiles and nods in his good-natured way.

Baba has a small circle of drinking partners here, but they are not enough for him. "Ne-bu-las-ka? More like 'tu-ze-bu-la-se-ka,'" he says and then cackles with his buddies. "A rabbit wouldn't bother shitting here."

"There's not even a decent Asian grocery store here!" Baba laments. "We have to drive an hour to rent Korean videos. There's no fun. It's stifling." I'm nervous about the impending change in the air.

Baba and Mama both had spent their lives in big cities. Incheon, where we lived, and Daegu, where Mama grew up, are two of Korea's largest cities, each with about two million people in population. My parents both attended universities in Taipei, an even more giant metropolis. Life in Lincoln has been an adjustment, but the real issue is that Baba does not like answering to anyone, let alone his wife's younger brother.

"I need to be my own boss," he says. This is something he is proud of.

Once again, we pile into the Ford Dixie van—packed beyond capacity with a soy sauce bucket seat for me—on a cross-country road trip with an uncertain destination.

CHAPTER 5: Swap Meet

AGE 10 – ORANGE COUNTY, CALIFORNIA

Baba receives a tip from a Chinese family from Korea that they make a good living selling socks at something called a *swa'mee'* in Orange County, California—and that's where we venture next. It's a business with a low cost of entry where Baba could be his own boss. He is excited about going to a place with a big Asian community, and his bright mood is contagious.

The air is warm and dry. The sun is fierce even against the beautiful sunset when we step out of our van into the driveway of Baba's friend's home. Winding through the neighborhood to the house, all of the houses are brown. The family steps out to greet us kindly. They have a chubby son, a few years older than me, and I regard him shyly. He is all hip-hop—a basketball jersey, cocked baseball cap, and gold chain. His skin is as brown as his parents' from baking in the sun at parking lots where the *swa'mee'* tents click into mazes.

Inside the house, cardboard boxes filled with socks tower floor to ceiling in the living room, dining room, and in every conceivable corner. The dad shows us the garage, which is also full of their inventory. All of us, including six-year-old Didi, sit on the beige carpet floor in front of the television. We all learn to fold the socks into bundles of five or ten for sale. "We do this every day of the week," says the dad with a warm, leathery smile. "Then, we'll be ready for the weekend *swa' mee'*."

We kids grow antsy and are dismissed to go play outside. "What do you guys want to do?" the son asks in broken Mandarin. "Do want to play *kick the can?*"

"We don't know that game," I answer. Didi is eager to play anything. Soaking up any attention from playmates of any age.

"It's easy," he says. "I can show you how to play." He produces a scrunched-down soda can from out of nowhere and begins to kick it. We chase him. Soon, the neighborhood kids of all ethnicities, more diverse than Didi and I have yet encountered in America, join the game. With sweat dripping down our faces, laughing and running on the hot asphalt, I smile my first genuine smile since we hit the road. For a moment, I forget to worry.

Mama wakes us up the next morning when it's still dark out, before the day's heat descends. The uncle's vans are loaded up with the bundles of socks we spent hours folding and we head to our first *swa' mee'*. Until we get there, I don't understand what a *swa' mee'* is. We pull into a large parking lot, where vendors are beginning to set up. Didi and I try to stay out of the way as our parents assist their friends unfold long tables under white tents. I don't quite know where to stand to be out of the way, but I enjoy the sweet and savory scents curling through the balmy breezes. Later, I'll identify the source as something wonderful called kettle corn, but not until I am a teenager. In those early days, my parents would never spend money on something so frivolous.

As my parents get comfortable and busy with the sock selling, they send Didi and me away, giving us free rein to explore. I hold Didi's hand as we weave in and out of the shoppers, who are buzzing with excitement in their colorful visors and sunglasses. Didi and my favorite booth is run by an older Korean man who is mic'ed up and commands a large crowd each time as he demonstrates his kitchen tools. "*Beck-n-fo'*. . . *Beck-n-fo'*. . . *Beck-n-fo'*. . ." he raps rhythmically, running a cucumber back and forth over a mandolin with his gloved hands. The audience gawks appreciatively as he holds up translucent slivers of cukes before he moves on to spiralizing a carrot easily into a delicate slinky.

The days blur together. I don't know how many weeks Baba and Mama shadow this family at the swap meets, but I wander and wander and wander as the days get hotter and hotter and hotter. My skin, too, browns like cardboard under the intense sun. Most days, the breeze is gone and I breathe in stale, humid air as I crane my neck at the wares: jewelry, shell art, sneakers, and sandals. Meanwhile, Baba and Mama are busy trying to learn the business at the sock tent. There are one or two other sock stands, many selling t-shirts and bedazzled clothes with puffy paint and plastic gems. I covet the too-expensive perfumed soaps shaped like shells and crabs. Instead, I start a collection of plastic rings for t-shirt tying, one orange and one red, that I buy for a quarter each. The rings, with a thin bar through the middle, remind me of no-smoking signs. They feel solid and big in my little hands as I pull a tail of fabric through it on the front right side of my shirt. This makes me feel cool.

For weeks, our family of four have been nomads, crashing at the brown house, or with this acquaintance or that. We always sleep together in one room, like we had in Korea, but we want a space of our own. On days when there is no swap meet, my parents try to look for housing we can afford. We tour many shabby rentals. The one that we come closest to signing a lease for is a small house next to a busy freeway with chipped stucco greyed from pollution. A chain-link fence enshrouds its dead grass and dandelions. Old shoes are strewn about the threshold. "You get all of this, it's a steal," the agent showing the place tells us in Mandarin. "Just know that the owner may come over from time to time to use the downstairs room that's off-limits."

"What?" Baba asks, surprised by this unusual arrangement.

"Yes, no big deal," the agent says. "He may come to change clothes or something sometimes. Not often."

My parents look at each other in silent disbelief. Places like this easily rented for four times as much as our tidy apartment in Nebraska had. How many socks would we need to sell to make rent?

Turns out that question would never have to be answered for our family. After weeks of training, Baba and Mama notice a shift in tone from our kindly hosts. On drives to the swap meet and during quiet times at the tent, his friend starts saying to Baba, "You should sell t-shirts instead of socks."

"But why?" Baba asks, confused.

"No folding! It's so much easier," he says. "More variety of merchandise. Higher profit. It's better-la."

"They don't want the competition," Baba whispers at night to Mama while we're all settled in for the night in the guest room. "They don't want us selling socks."

I eavesdrop and wonder why our friends didn't think of this before my parents shadowed them for weeks. I wonder if they didn't think Baba and Mama would be serious about the swap meet business? I'm numb and the panicky feeling grips me. It has been less than a year since we immigrated, and there have been too many changes.

Mama and Baba have spent weeks learning to sell socks, not t-shirts. Without guides, and without knowing how to speak English, without vendor connections, such a switch will not be easy. They don't know what to do.

"Ni kan ze ba. You do what you think is right," Mama whispers back to Baba, as she always does. She is too afraid to make any decisions.

Days pass in this cloud of uncertainty. We still go to the swap meet, not sure of what to do. Finally, one scorching afternoon, in the privacy of our Ford Dixie van, Baba makes a declaration, "I don't have a good feeling about Los Angeles."

Baba has no trouble making monologues, while Mama prefers to listen, nod, and follow. "I worry the kids might xuehui in this city," he says. "Do you see the teenagers of our friends? They all act like they don't listen. They look like little gangsters."

Baba shakes his head in disapproval. It is true. The Asian kids here have swagger and confidence that I didn't detect in Atlanta or Lincoln. The teenagers here have their own lives, and I hardly see them at home. Even the boy who had taught us kick-the-can is quickly aging into being too cool to be seen with Didi and me.

Baba does not want Didi and me to be rebellious. He wants us obedient for life. He wants to live where we'll be easier to control.

We climb back in the Ford Dixie van and head southeast, Phoenix bound.

CHAPTER 6: Valley of the Sun

AGE 10 – PHOENIX, ARIZONA

Years ago, when Uncle Jerry—Baba's childhood friend who had immigrated to the U.S. as a teenager—came back to Korea to visit after being gone for decades, Baba showed him a good time. It must have been a *really* good time because now, in return, Uncle Jerry and his family become our gracious hosts. All of my memories of Uncle Jerry and his two smart, funny kids are as sweet as the red bean pastries—golden egg-washed and finished with a delicate sprinkle of black sesame seeds—that Mama learns to make from Aunt Lily, his lovely wife.

The Golden Phoenix Oriental Express is a small Chinese takeout restaurant owned by Uncle Jerry's family, who owns three other "Golden Phoenix" sit-down restaurants around Phoenix. During a time when everything seems risky, the pull toward the restaurant business is strong for my folks. For generations, both sides of their families have operated restaurants or peddled noodles in one manner or another.

"A restaurant is still the safest bet," Baba nods to himself. "People always need to eat."

We look at the restaurant, which occupies the corner two units of a strip mall on the far end, facing the street. The fast-food style tables and chairs are orange with white trim and mounted to the green, carpeted floors. The register countertop is also the same orange. The space is not too big. There's no table service. With Mama and Baba's hard work and the help of a few employees, the business seems like it would be manageable.

Baba purchases the Golden Phoenix Oriental Express using the entirety of the inheritance from Yeh-Yeh, which he had refused to touch until this decision.

As part of the sale, Uncle Jerry agrees to share all of their recipes with Baba, including the secret sauce for their famous House Special Chicken. Uncle Jerry and one of his brothers train my parents for the next month leading up to the takeover, both in front and back of the house. There is a lot to learn for Mama and Baba. Didi and I sit at a table to the side and watch. But, as the month goes on, the lunch rushes start to pick up and dinner rushes become a thing, too. Customers line up out the door, and to-go bag after to-go bag is prepped, ready for orders.

"Did you see Jerry's face?" Baba says on our drive home, in the privacy of our van. "He was surprised at how busy it got. I don't think the place has been that busy in a long time. His eyes were red when Jerry looked at his brother!"

Baba is pleased.

The next morning, Baba steps outside and takes a deep breath. "Look at the skies here! Have you ever seen such magnificent blue?"

"No, Baba, I haven't," I say, squinting up at the truly immense skies. "And the clouds, they look closer in Phoenix. Almost close enough to touch."

I stretch and point at the light, swan-white puffs.

Every evening, the big wall-to-wall windows at Oriental Express perfectly showcase the hypnotizing beauty of the fiery, vast sunsets, distracting us from the scorched, cracked earth burning our feet.

CHAPTER 7: *Skin*

AGE 10 – PHOENIX, ARIZONA

Our house in Phoenix is pink, like all of the houses in the upper-middle-class suburban subdivision. In lieu of grass, the landscaping is also done with pink rocks. The house is rented from Uncle Jerry's friend, who is moving out of state and gives us a good deal.

The elementary school Didi and I are to go to looks clean and welcoming. I'm excited that it is so close to my new home, but during the first week, the teachers realize my English is not good enough. Didi's neither. We have only been in the U.S. for almost a year. We are both transferred to Greenbrier Elementary, taking us out of the wealthier part of town. This school looks more normal—it's still a good school, just not as sparkling new and dripping with privilege.

I'm in fifth grade and determined to make friends. I spend days working up the courage to tell a joke to a classmate to make her my friend. Greenbrier is my fourth school in America in a year. I want to make this one work. My friends in Korea love this joke.

When the recess bell rings, most kids run to the playground or fight over the two tetherball stations, but there is a girl who sits in the shade on top of the picnic tables. She always sits there, content to hang out by herself. She's my mark.

I shuffle up to her. "Why does a flamingo stand only on one leg?"

The girl with perfect brown ringlets squints at me in confusion. She doesn't say anything, but her eyes seem to communicate, *why are you talking to me?*

Undeterred, unwilling to forfeit the punchline, I continue. "Because, if the flamingo stood on no legs, it would fall!" I laugh at my own joke while looking at her expectantly.

She wrinkles her nose and hops off the picnic table, shrinking as if she might catch some airborne contagion. The girl who would never be my friend scurries away, shaking her perfect ringlets in her wake.

In those early days after our move to Arizona, Didi and I stay home alone watching *Saved by the Bell*, *Family Matters*, and *Step by Step*. But soon, Baba turns perpetually angry. He calls home to check up on us regularly but is bothered if we are doing fine.

"Why am I working myself to death if I can't even see my own kids?" he snaps at Mama and at us. So, now, Didi and I are brought to the restaurant after school, every day. We must sit quietly at a table in the corner until we close at nine o'clock. The earliest we can leave the restaurant after clean up and tallying is nine-thirty, which means it's around ten when we get home. After that, we eat a late supper and watch Chinese or Korean dramas with Mama and Baba. We don't have a bedtime. We never have. Didi and I don't get to bed until 11pm, midnight, or later. We struggle to wake up for school in the mornings and often miss the bus, which makes Baba angry. But Baba means well. He wants to keep us close. He does not want us to xuehui. Baba is perpetually paranoid that Didi and I will xuehui—that Didi will turn into a drug-addicted gangster while I will be impregnated as a teen. He is afraid of the shame.

At ages seven and ten, Didi and I can't sit still in the corner of the restaurant. We grow antsy during the long days. Didi has always been hyperactive, and he wants my attention nonstop. We either bicker and poke at each other or play too loudly. One day, we're trying to play tag while seated in our corner of the restaurant. We get louder and louder. Baba sees us acting up from the small window to the kitchen, which is the handover plane for the takeout containers. During the next lull between customers, Baba barges out. Didi and I know we're done for.

"Get in here!" Baba yells as he shoves us into the lime-green hall-way—a color chosen because of the sale on the paint. The hallway leads to the kitchen and the bathrooms, out of sight of customers. He is sweaty and covered in grease under his paper rectangular cook's hat. Baba wears a stained white apron over the wide leather belt meant to support his lower back. He is heaving, his eyes terrifying.

"This is a restaurant. Not a playground," he roars. "Why can't you two ingrates just sit and behave?"

Sometimes, he simply hits us, with his hands or a stick. Each powerful blow to our buttocks is measured and counted to disguise it as a prescription. Didi and I both cry instantly when receiving our punish-ment, often before the blows even start. We rub our palms together, begging. "Bu gan la. Bu gan la," we say. We won't dare anymore. Wher-ever each blow lands, it throbs. Didi and I cry to show Baba he has caused us pain. He has taught us his lesson. He has exerted his control.

Other times, Baba orders us to hit ourselves while he watches. "Harder. Hit yourself harder," he says. "You're not worth my strength, but if you make me do it, you'll regret it."

Didi suffers this method of punishment the most. As an adult, reflecting back, Didi finds this punishment most debasing.

When Baba feels more lenient, he commands us to fa zhan—stand in punishment in the hallway for our crimes with our arms up, or on our knees, or both. For as long as it takes, until he is satisfied. Sometimes, he gets busy and forgets to dismiss us from our fa zhan.

In Phoenix, Baba is finally his own boss, but there is no longer an authority figure to blame when things go wrong. And there is so much work. Mama and Baba work seven days a week, from about ten in the morning to ten at night. My parents then stay up late watching Korean and Chinese television dramas rented on VHS from Seoul Market, seeking comfort in the familiar. Baba flounders in everything that is out of his control and expresses all his frustrations, fears, and exhaustion the only way he knows—with anger. He picks fights with Mama every day. There is always something we're doing to offend him. Baba pulls Didi and me down the hall by our ears, again and again, jabbing our heads with his index finger.

"America is heaven for children," Mama had told us years ago, before we got on the plane. "It is illegal to hit children there."

After we arrive in America, Mama and Baba are perpetually afraid. My father, especially, is afraid of everything. He listens to all the stories, whispers, and Chinese tabloid news—a man arrested for innocently patting the bottom of a neighbor's baby...

"Surely, it must have been a misunderstanding," Baba says, confused and horrified that a man could be arrested for such an act.

He listens to the testimonies of his friends and acquaintances whose uncontrollable, Americanized teenagers called the police on them for beatings, and the possibility of the police getting called to our house keeps him up at night. Baba is a man conflicted, for he believes it his duty to beat us.

One day, when we come home after school, Baba is waiting to show us a newspaper article. A Chinese father in California had chained his teenage daughter to a tree in the backyard for sneaking out.

"He was treating her like a dog because she was acting like one," he says with a laugh. "A bit harsh, but I get it. The neighbors called the police to free her."

Each time a story like this pops up, it is also a warning for Didi and me to never call the police.

"If you tell anyone that I hit you, they will call the police, and Mama and I will go to jail. Do you want that? And you will be taken to live with strangers, and Mama and I will be forced to pay them for your care. Do you want that?"

"No Baba, we don't," Didi and I promise.

Mama is a tireless worker carrying out orders. The ability to make decisions or weigh in with opinions had been beaten out of her long ago. "Ni kan ze ban ba" is her answer to Baba for everything—do whatever you see fit. The importance of the decision doesn't matter—whether it is ordering lunch or deciding to immigrate—Mama is debilitated by having to choose. She long ago forfeited her power and her voice in exchange for the freedom from fear of being held responsible. Mama cannot protect us, or herself.

"Why do you two look so dark and dirty? You look like Mexicans!" Baba frequently yells, "You are not my children!"

Under the intense Phoenix sun, my fair skin turns brown like craft paper, and Didi's several shades darker than mine. The over twenty minutes we walk and stand on the hot sidewalk beneath the merciless sun waiting for the school bus each day is enough to darken our skin.

Though Baba's fury lands on us all, Didi is the boy and the outward rebel. He bears the brunt of most beatings. Didi is hyperactive. Nothing seems to calm his energy or mood, except when he is actively being pummeled by Baba. Didi recovers quickly, like a puppy eager for love and acceptance, even from the harshest punishments. He forgets yesterday's beating and makes the same mistake again the next day. He never learns and never fears Baba's rage until it is too late, which infuriates Baba more. The terror cycles daily.

I earn straight A's. I work at the restaurant and translate for my parents. I do everything I am asked. I am the Golden Child. I am Daddy's Little Girl. Still, Baba gets angry with me for my clumsiness, and for being in his presence when he's frustrated, but I develop a pout that sometimes makes him soften and chuckle. The pout is effective at defusing Baba almost half of the times he's angry at me. One night, Baba is punishing Didi in our van outside of Oriental Express. They are in the back seat. Under the parking lot lamps, Didi tries the pout for the first time. He sticks out his lower lip, tilts his chin, and opens his teary eyes wide. Didi has watched me do this enough to know how to mimic me perfectly.

"What are you doing?" Baba yells and smacks Didi in the back of the head. My father fakes a gag. "Wipe that disgusting look off your face. That doesn't work for you. You're making yourself more despicable."

I remain silent from the front passenger seat. When Baba roars, every cell on my body quivers and every follicle stiffens. I always stay silent. I am not brave enough to come to my brother's aid. I only want to save myself.

When Didi was still a toddler, he took the beating of his life for me. There was a large wardrobe in our small apartment in Incheon, in the room where we all slept. Each morning, Mama would fold up our bedding and neatly stack them inside the wardrobe. Hidden in the bedding was a Casio camera with a big, fancy lens that Baba bought secondhand and used on special occasions—Didi and I were strictly forbidden to touch the camera.

One morning, when Mama was busy in the kitchen and Didi was playing in front of the television in the living room, I let my curiosity get the best of me. The clickety-clack of the mechanics, that soft whirl and whine of the camera called to me like a siren's song. I padded into the room where we slept and opened the wardrobe doors, quiet as a mouse. Digging under the layers of bedding, I pulled out the camera, and relished its weight, importance, and magic in my six-year-old palms. Holding the forbidden article, I positioned it to my eye and began pressing all the buttons. Suddenly, the back of the camera flipped open, exposing the 35mm film. Startled, I dropped it and then quickly stuffed it back into the wardrobe, hoping my crime would not be discovered.

I was not so lucky. Mama found the evidence the same day. She pushed her big plastic glasses up towards her furrowed brows. Her big permed hair bobbed at Didi and me. "Who did this?" Mama demanded, holding out the camera at us both seated in the living room.

"It wasn't me," Didi and I echoed each other, looking up at her.

Mama did not dole out punishment in our family. She never

hit Didi and me, not once. No, that she left to Baba. When he came home that day, she told him one of us touched the forbidden camera as soon as he walked through the door. Any sign of warmth drained from Baba's eyes, and he swatted my skinny little brother with his thick, fleshy palms—one hand gripping Didi's shoulder and the other swinging into his bottom, again and again.

"Who broke the camera?" Baba interrogated.

"It wasn't me," cried Didi.

"You dare lie to me!" Baba fumed, hitting him harder. "So small and already a liar." He ordered Mama to bring him the long plastic shoe-horn that hung by the front door.

I knelt nearby watching. When one of us is punished, the other usually watches. We are a family who is always together. There is nowhere to hide. Witnessing a beating is a warning of what could happen if we, too, misbehave. On that day, I flinched each time Didi received a lashing that should have been mine. Feeling lower than scum, I tried to work up the courage to stop my roaring bear of a father. *Please Baba, Stop. It was me. It was me. I'm sorry. I'm so sorry.* But the words never came out.

I wavered through the excruciating minutes trying to confess, but three-year-old Didi broke first. As rivers of tears ran down his toddler face, he started nodding. "It was me, Baba. It was me. I'm sorry. I won't dare do it again. Please don't hit me anymore." He knelt on his knees, rubbing his palms together up and down for forgiveness like we were both trained to do. "Bu gan la. Bu gan la."

CHAPTER 8: Becoming American

AGE 11 – PHOENIX, ARIZONA

"What's bitch?" I ask. They didn't teach this word in my sixth-grade ESL class at Greenbrier Elementary School.

"It means a female dog," answers Michelle DeAngelo, the new girl from New Jersey, who had just called a classmate a bitch.

Michelle and I hide from the blistering Phoenix sun on top of the picnic tables in the shade. Today's playground vocabulary lesson on the curious word that rhymed with "itch" has me pondering.

"A female dog can't be so bad, Michelle," I say. "Does it mean a pregnant dog? A pregnant dog has reason to be angry and protective, right?"

My new friend crinkles her brow, which is a tinge darker than her wiry, walnut-brown hair. A crooked smile plays on her full, pink lips. There is a twinkle in her big blue eyes, as big as I'd ever seen and tiny brown freckles dotted all over her peachy skin.

Michelle's arrival means I am no longer the newest, strangest, or fattest one in the grade. The bullies have a new target. In her first week, Michelle raises her hand and asks to go to "the lavatory." The class breaks out in uproarious laughter and she is teased mercilessly ever after. She is as stuck with me as much as I am with her, but we're grateful for each other.

As sixth-grade girls in the 1990s, we take telling each other how much we hate the way we look very seriously. It is then the job of one friend to tell other, "No, you're so beautiful, I'm the ugly one. Just look at my..." *Fill in the blank*. And the cycle continues. If one does not actively announce how much one hates the way they look, they're quickly labeled "stuck-up" and ostracized.

Dutifully, I am learning to engage in this norm. Michelle is far better practiced at it. Sitting on swings next to each other, I say, "My dad says my skin is getting too dark, and I'm so fat, I wish I could lose weight."

"Only your face is a little fat," Michelle responds. "Your body is fine."

I don't believe her. Michelle continues, "Besides, your almond eyes and olive skin are beautiful."

"What do you mean my eyes are shaped like almonds?" I wasn't sure if I should be offended. I have never had my eyes compared to nuts before. Not to mention—olive skin? What does that mean? I don't even know what an olive is.

"It means your skin underneath is green," she says. "It means your eyes are pleasantly slanted."

I bristle at the word "slanted." I don't like that word. I jump off the swing and start walking away. Michelle follows me.

"It's a compliment!" Michelle says.

I shrug and shake my head. I don't understand, but I let it go.

When Michelle enters my life that year, my days become brighter. We bond over having the same first name, being transplants against our will, being fat and unpopular, and having pesky little brothers. When she invites me to her house, I greet her mom the way my dad trained me. "Hello Mrs. DeAngelo. Nice to meet you."

"Oh, no. Don't call me Mrs. DeAngelo," she guffaws. "Call me Gail. Mrs. DeAngelo is my mother-in-law."

This is so strange to me. In Korea, such disrespect would mean a slap was coming, or worse. In Arizona, adults genuinely prefer kids to call them by their first names, as if we are equals.

With dyed red hair and a very loud voice, "Gail" is not shy. She loves to brag in her thick New Jersey accent, "My dow-ter, she looks like Lyndah Cah-tah."

I stare at Michelle blankly, awaiting translation. She rolls her eyes at her mother, sighs and explains, "You know, *Wonder Woman*?"

I don't know. I have no idea. *Wonder Woman* is one of countless pre-1990 American pop culture references entirely lost on me.

Michelle is my first white American friend. Before Michelle, my friends have all been recent immigrants themselves, as transient as me. I am in awe of my new friend. Sixth-grade-me has never before met anyone so openly boy crazy. Michelle talks about boys (and men) incessantly, fanning her face with her hand, feigning swoons at all the guys she finds hot. She shows me pictures of shirtless men in teen magazines. Antonio Sabàto, Jr—the Italian Stallion—is her favorite. My cheeks burn just imagining my parents catching us. It's a thrill to be around her.

In Korea, none of the kids spoke about romantic crushes. Children are not supposed to have such thoughts. Though as early as pre-school, I had a crush on a Korean boy with permed curls and a chipped front tooth, I knew to keep it to myself. Michelle's openness is a defiance I admire. Around her, there is no need for secrecy.

Michelle likes the sporty boys while I shyly hold my breath around the nice, nerdy ones. The smartest boy in class is the one I admire from afar. I never dare wish for a boyfriend though, which is strictly forbidden by my parents. "No dating until college!"

I can dream though, and for years, I dream. I dream of a platonic friendship that will blossom into the best kind of romance—when the time is right. I want a Gilbert Blythe to my Anne Shirley. A Dawson for my Joey. Every book, TV show, and movie I love are variations on this main plotline. I have not found a friend like Min—who could make me blush—since Atlanta. I yearn for this more than anything.

Friendship with me comes with unexpected complications for Michelle. Her life is so carefree compared to mine. She can't understand why I am not allowed to come over to hang out very often, let alone sleep over.

"Just ask your dad, Michelle," she says. "Maybe he will say yes this time."

I am afraid to get my hopes up. "Baba, Michelle is asking if I can come to her house to play this weekend?"

His face, always greasy from the kitchen, turns stony. He hates being asked. "If you go to your friend's house, then we will be obligated to host them, and we can't do that."

Our house is too messy. The grown-ups are never home. How can we reciprocate? Baba and Mama are never convinced when I say we don't have to have Michelle over, that her family's okay with it.

When Baba finally says yes, after months of my begging, I don't know what changed his mind. I'm too thrilled to ask questions. He doesn't say anything to me. He is quiet during the drive.

When our minivan pulls into Michelle's cul-de-sac in the neighborhood of pink houses, Baba says suddenly, "Didi is coming with you."

"What?" my brother and I are both shocked.

"You heard me. It's not fair that you get to play at your friend's house and Didi doesn't," he says with finality. "Both of you, get out!"

Didi can't believe his luck. Quick as a flash, he undoes his seatbelt and jumps out. I can hear his thoughts: *Anything but another day at the restaurant.* As soon as our feet hit the pavement, Baba peels off.

"Well, come on!" Didi says as he sprints to Michelle's front door. I groan.

Michelle lives in a new cookie-cutter house in the Phoenix suburbs with shining white walls and Astroturf-green carpet. She has the perfect average American family—two parents and two and a half kids, if you count their black Labrador retriever as the half. Didi starts ringing their bell repeatedly.

I try to stop him, and we're in the midst of struggling when the door opens. We freeze. Gail, Michelle, and Michelle's younger brother

Mikey look out at us. I don't want to explain, but I must.

"My dad said my brother had to come too," I say, looking sheepishly at their porch.

Gail peers behind us at the empty curb. Baba had long gone. "Well, come in then," she says.

I let out a silent breath of relief. Michelle leads me upstairs to her room. Michelle and I get right to painting each other's nails, gossiping, reading magazines, and giving each other makeovers. Meanwhile, Didi runs amok in the house, like a caged animal finally freed. He jumps on furniture, rough-houses, and shrieks. Soon, Mikey, who is a couple of years younger than Didi, is in tears, screaming, "Mooooomm!" over and over again.

No one can control Didi. He will not listen to me, but I do my best. I want to savor this day of freedom.

Dinner at Michelle's house is Didi and my first white American family meal. Unlike when we eat at home, the television is off. The DeAngelos sit in the neat, brightly-lit dining room. Each person has their own plate, instead of a meal served family-style. Amid the chaos, Gail manages to shape plain ground beef into five lumpy patties and pops them in the oven. As a side, we have microwaved frozen broccoli. It isn't fancy and lacks seasoning, but I am grateful to Gail for making anything at all and for feeding us.

We begin to eat, and Didi opens his mouth, "What *is* this?"

I hold my breath.

"Hamburger," Gail answers, all out of patience.

"Where are the buns, then?" asks Didi, who doesn't know when to stop.

"We. Have. No. Buns." Gail grimaces as her red hair begins to frazzle at the ends.

"Well, do you have any ketchup?" Didi says, without missing a beat.

Michelle and I shoot each other worried looks. Why does my friendship have to come with such baggage?

Nevertheless, the rest of the meal is uneventful. Didi loved not being violently forced to eat his broccoli. (At home, this is a big problem. Didi often vomits on the table while attempting to swallow his greens.)

Baba is hours late to pick us up, far past Mikey's bedtime. Bedtime is a concept that does not exist for Didi and me. Was this Baba's plan all along? To make it go so badly that we would never be invited back?

I am invited back, though, and the DeAngelos become our friends. In turn, Baba supplies the DeAngelos with plenty of free food from the restaurant, including Sesame Chicken, which is their family favorite.

Some months later, we are invited to our first American backyard barbeque and pool party at their house. Mama can't come, as one person always has to watch Oriental Express. Baba doesn't like to hang out too long either. He has too much pride to struggle with English in public. Didi and I are very excited though. My brother runs off immediately, splashing around in the pool.

As soon as Michelle comes up to me, she asks wide-eyed, in a conspiratorial tone, "Have you ever had tiramisu?"

"Tira...what? No, what's that?"

"It's an Italian dessert. It's sooo good," she says. The DeAngelos are very proud of their Italian heritage.

At first bite, the creamy coffee flavor swirls on my tongue. "Wow!" I light up as the slight burn hits my throat. "I've never tasted anything like this."

"There's rum in it," Michelle cocks her eyebrows devilishly.

"Oh."

I consider this. Michelle seems to think this was important information. "What is rum?"

Michelle smacks her forehead in disbelief. Being my friend must feel like having to explain the whole world, sometimes.

With her boy drama and pop culture lessons, Michelle is a provider of distractions I so crave. She knows little of what happens at our house, but she helps me brush off the teasing at school and emboldens me to rebel a little.

When Spirit Week at school calls for a "Twins Day," we are excited to pair up. Gail drives us to Walmart to shop for something that we can both wear. We choose plain pink t-shirts. Gail pays for my shirt without hesitation, and, as an eleven-year-old, I can't believe her generosity.

To this day, I still have a picture of me and Michelle from that Twins Day in a photo album somewhere, grinning ear-to-ear with our arms around each other.

Chapter 9: Chocolate

Perhaps influenced by the DeAngelos with their black lab, Baba bursts through our garage door one afternoon, letting in a gust of hot desert air. In his hands is an adorable black Labrador puppy from the Phoenix Humane Society.

"An all-black dog to ward off evil spirits and bring us luck," Baba holds up the pup, beaming with pride.

Didi and I shriek with excitement. He is the cutest, softest, sweetest thing I've ever seen. Though I've always wanted a puppy, I've never even played with one before. Didi and I jump around each other, quibbling over whose turn it is to hold him and who gets to walk him first.

Neighbors stop us outside to fawn over the lively addition to our family. "Look at his big paws," they coo. "He's going to be a big boy!"

Michelle is so excited for me. "What are you going to name him?"

"We are thinking Chocolate or Cocoa?" We are going back and forth.

"Well, which one is it?" Gail snaps. "You have to choose one and stick with it or you're just confusing him."

We end up going with Chocolate, though it is a mouthful. And we are clueless as to how to train him. Baba, who also knows nothing about dogs, is unprepared for how large Chocolate grows. Within a few months, the dog can knock over adults, and his growth shows no sign of slowing. Without proper training, he grows unmanageable.

"We can't keep Chocolate. He is too big and too badly behaved," Baba says, one day.

As abruptly as Chocolate appears in our lives, he departs. Baba returns him. The guilt eats me up. Chocolate is proof that we can't maintain or nurture joy.

In our family, he only suffered. For Chocolate, our love also meant having to endure neglect, being chained in the backyard under the hot Arizona sun. And, ultimately, our love led to abandonment. We robbed this beautiful puppy of a charmed life with a good family. Now, he is an untrained adolescent, back where he started. The guilt keeps me awake at night. I pray that he will be adopted still.

"Chocolate looked so well-behaved once he was in a cage again," Baba says upon his return. His shoulders are hunched over and his face sags—he feels guilty too but he cannot control his impulses.

CHAPTER 10: Takeout Kid

AGE 13 – PHOENIX, ARIZONA

"Oriental Express, how may I help you?" Hesitation and a soft laugh answer my greeting.

"Hello?" I try again.

The customer clears his throat and half snorts. "Aren't you a little young to be working? How old are you?"

Dodging his question, I go on, "May I take your order?"

I am relieved that he drops the matter of my age and places his order. Starting at age twelve, in addition to the responsibility of maintaining excellent grades, I begin working front-of-house. I take orders at the cash register and by phone and package to-go orders. When the restaurant is slow, I collect the plastic trays, wipe, and dry them before lining them with Chinese zodiac paper placemats. I refill soy sauce bottles, clear tables, and take out the garbage. I train newly hired teenagers when others move on.

My parents pay me a ceremonial three dollars an hour for my work and then deposit it back into their bank accounts. Most of the time, I don't mind. I like working. Endorsing checks makes me feel grown-up, powerful, and official.

But, as I get older, resentment brews. I work most Fridays and Saturday nights when the restaurant is busiest, which makes any social life near impossible. On Sundays, I am assigned to manage the restaurant on my own while my parents and brother take the day off to run errands and eat dim sum or dine at a Korean restaurant. Most of the time, I understand. My labor is the only way Mama and Baba agree to take a day off; they are too frugal and untrusting to pay for someone else to cover the shift. But I am also a teenager, and I feel left out of the leisurely family outings. I am starved for downtime, too.

On Sundays, my parents rush out of the restaurant in a flurry of excitement like children

"Call us if it gets busy, Beautiful Jade!" Mama says with her sweet smile, miming a phone with her hand to her ear.

Many of those Sundays are uneventful with a slow trickle of customers, and I don't mind it much. I sit behind the counter on an upside-down soy sauce bucket and read a library book. But, on occasion, a sudden onslaught of hungry customers lines up behind the register at the long orange counter. Sometimes there are so many of them that they don't fit inside the restaurant. The front door gets propped open as the line snakes out the door in an L-shape. Trying not to panic, I move as quickly as I can. Some customers are kind, but others are frustrated and angry at having to wait. One laughs and remarks, "You're here all by yourself? You should have more help!"

I sneak in a call to my parents, as soon as it looks like the rush is not going to die down. "Mama, it's so busy, I need help!"

The phone is passed to Baba who says, "We're too far away, Beautiful Jade. By the time we come back, the rush will be over. Mei Ban Fa. You will have to handle it."

There is no arguing with him. How does he know how long the rush will last? He doesn't, but they're not coming. I am on my own.

With no backup on the way, I become increasingly scrambled.

A group of young men arrive at the front of the line, and the

tallest of the bunch squints at the long paper menu and asks, "Uh…
Do you have tacos?"

"No, but we have Mu Shu dishes which come with pancakes
that are like tortillas," I say without skipping a beat, fully in solution
mode. "Or there's a Mexican restaurant just . . ." I start to point, but
it's no use. He and his buddies burst out laughing. I was too frazzled
to recognize he was playing a joke on me.

Panting, I run up and down the long narrow space behind the
orange counter. Taking orders, packing them, filling drinks. The
phone rings incessantly with more phone orders. Sometimes, I have
to let it go unanswered. The food cartons pile up. Tables on the other
side of the counter need to be cleared and wiped. I dash out when I
can as impatient customers glare.

Mei Ban Fa. There's no other way. My family brings back a styrofoam box of cold dim sum leftovers as a consolation. I feel like choking
on them.

By sixth grade, I was the best English speaker in the family. I transition
from being an ESL student to earning straight A's. But English is still
challenging. Book reports and other larger projects make me panic
and keep me up at night with stress dreams and nightmares. Though
I love reading at my own pace, the idea of reading an assigned book,
writing to summarize it, and presenting it in front of the whole class
terrifies me. I procrastinate, not wanting to face this fear, until mere
days before the due date. Tossing and turning, I can't breathe at night.
I loathe myself for procrastinating so long.

My parents can't help me with homework. They don't read or
write English, so Baba asks the teenagers who work at the restaurant
to help me with my book reports while they're on the clock. These
teenage employees save me on many occasions through middle school,
but I feel rotten. I feel like I cheated because I hadn't earned my
grades by myself, because I needed help. I get into self-hate spirals.

When Baba says, "You need to do ten times better than your white classmates to get equally as far in this country, Beautiful Jade. You are Chinese and an outsider," it means he's had a rough day at the restaurant. These are most days. "It's not fair, but it's the reality. You can't fail your mother and me. We've sacrificed too much."

In my early teens, the shopping center is bought out by a new property management company. We receive a letter that I translate for my parents; it says our rent is about to increase forty percent. Oriental Express entrees cost only about $3 to $4 each, despite heaping portions of quality ingredients. In this business of low margins, that kind of rent increase could kill us. My parents are beside themselves. "Ze Ma Ban? Ze Ma Ban?" What will we do? they sigh to one another. Mama tsks in despair

We need to do something. A determined Baba orders me to follow him outside on what is another glaringly bright day. We drive southbound on I-17 until the buildings change from newer construction to the brown, older buildings in between the suburbs and the city center, until we arrive in the downtown area of tall corporate buildings. Other than the too brief winter, it's always hot in Phoenix, and this day is no exception. I'm wearing a scruffy Stussy t-shirt, jean shorts, and flip-flops. My hair is pulled back in a messy ponytail. Baba has on his work jeans and a collared shirt, which is nicer than he dresses on a normal work day, but inside this glossy high-rise office tower his outfit looks ragged. We had no idea we were coming to a place that looks like this.

A receptionist, in a fitted, professional navy dress and clackity heels, shepherds us into a large conference room, where we sit freezing from the air conditioning. The icy, soft, black leather of the high-backed chairs raises goosebumps on my skin. The black marble table takes up most of the room and is the longest and shiniest I have ever seen. This room could easily host thirty people and, already, I am intimidated. Baba is, too. I can tell because he is uncharacteristically quiet, building up the courage to face what's next. Even though the room is empty, he speaks to me in a whisper. "We have to convince them. We have to." Our livelihood depends on this meeting.

We wait. The air becomes colder and more constricting by the minute. Eventually, we hear the door open. A tall, lean man with neatly combed silver hair wearing a perfectly tailored suit enters. He doesn't smile, but he greets us politely and shakes Baba's hand, then mine. His long fingers feel cool and smooth. The man sits down at the head of the table.

"Tell him," Baba says to me in Mandarin, with a slight lift of his chin.

I clear my throat and inhale, looking up to meet his eyes. I can't read them. They are a color called "hazel." We did not have this color in Korea.

"I'm here to translate for my dad," I say. "He doesn't speak English very well."

Baba straightens up and turns to face me. "Tell him this rent increase will make it impossible for us to do business," he dictates with authority while raising his thick right arm up and down, the side of his hand hitting the cool marble table top again and again.

I tuck a loose strand of hair behind my right ear and try not to tremble or shrink. I know better. I am trained by Baba. "We received this letter about our rent increase . . ." I unfold it before us.

The man nods and still betrays no emotion. The rest of the meeting is a blur, but it goes quickly. I ask if it's possible for us to keep paying our original rent. I am nervous but firm.

There is a pause. The man says yes.

Baba and I are shocked. "Thank you, thank you," Baba says.

We shake hands again. The man's hand feels warmer this time.

Baba is delighted and cannot stop smiling. "It was because you were in there with me, Beautiful Jade. He must have had a soft heart. And you always bring me luck!"

Most of the time, when I have to translate for Baba, it doesn't go as well. I hate making calls. Baba gets impatient and yells at me because he is unable to hear any of what is being said on the other line. "Say what I'm saying, just say what I'm saying!" he screams at me in increasing intensity.

If I try to block him out to listen to the phone company representative, insurance salesperson, or whomever I'm ordered to call that day, he becomes irate. He yells so loudly that I can't hear anything. I can't dispute the bills or think straight. He wants to fight, but he can't turn me into the type of fists he needs. Panic sets in and I want to disappear.

The worst is when I can't decipher what he wants me to translate. All the fine print. Talking to his friends, Baba decides to invest in mutual funds. Friends can help sign him up, but they can't be counted on for ongoing help. That responsibility falls on me. Each time a thick envelope of documents arrives in the mail, my stomach begins to cramp.

"Beautiful Jade, translate these for me," Baba says casually, tossing them onto my textbook as I'm doing my homework at Oriental Express. "What do they mean?"

Sighing, I take out the documents and try. I really, earnestly try to understand what I am reading, but I'm only a kid. I don't even know what a mutual fund is and do not understand what any of the fine print or policy changes mean.

"I don't get it, Baba. I can't understand."

"Why not?" he says. "You can read English. It's in English. You are smart. Read it again. You will figure it out."

"But I can't."

"You can, and you will. This is important." Baba is stern, making an authoritative gesture with his right arm, his hand hitting my book.

I'm about to cry. I hope he might soften, seeing my anguish. His voice is gentler, but he says, "Take it slow. Read it again. You will get it. You want what is good for our family."

With that, Baba stands up from the corner table that is my usual spot and goes into the kitchen. As with all things in my life, failure is not an option.

Every night, I toss and turn. I have recurring nightmares of making mistakes on forms I fill out incorrectly for Baba and Mama: they are arrested and our restaurant is shut down because of me.

By middle school, I am determined to free myself. I know what I must do. I have to earn a full scholarship to college. This is the only way to take back my future from my parents. According to Baba, my career choices are either to become a doctor or a lawyer, but I want more options. I want to travel the world. I want to act in plays and take art classes. I want to be free. To have freedom, I must pay my own way. If I am financially beholden to him, he will control me forever. Academic success is my only key to freedom.

CHAPTER 11: Fear of Water

AGE 13 — PHOENIX, ARIZONA

Fast as lightning with comebacks and naturally charming, Didi has a sweet smile and is quick to make friends, but he is not one to focus on schoolwork. His report cards contain B's, C's, even D's and the occasional F's starting in elementary school. This is not acceptable for Baba. "Why am I here selling Kung Pao Chicken? Did I come to America to watch my son become worthless?"

Failure is not an option. Every time report cards make their way home, a sense of danger fills our house as it deflates of any joy—it is something that can be detected by instinct, like when animals sense a predator crouching. Baba often punishes Didi in private, in the master bedroom. He orders Didi, or sometimes Didi and me, to wait in the bedroom while he rummages for an instrument to inflict pain, to release his rage. The mounting dread, the psychological torture of waiting, is a part of the punishment.

When I am forty years old, the sight of certain objects still catch my breath, quicken my heart rate, and propel my feet to flee. A branch of a particular girth. A stack of bamboo sticks piled in a neighbor's yard. Even a telescoping selfie stick, which didn't even exist in the 90s. It's not rational, but these are the type of items Didi and I knew as kids never to bring home. We could imagine their force, imprint, and the swelling on our red-inflamed skin afterward because they inevitably became instruments for Baba's temper.

"Baba beat me with a two-by-four once until it broke," Didi recounts to me when we are grown. "Then he picked up one of the broken halves and kept beating me with it."

I don't remember the two-by-four. The countless nights of punishment blur together. For the most part, I hide for self-preservation. I turn my back on Didi and join my parents in calling him the troublemaker. Bu ting hua. He just doesn't listen.

"You and your brother never do anything fun. All you do is sit at the restaurant," Crystal says. A short and spunky teenager with curly brown hair and a pretty smile, Crystal starts working for my parents when she is sixteen and stays for several years—longer than most. She is kind and nurturing. Over and over, she invites Didi and me to her house. "Come over. We'll have fun!"

Crystal works on my parents for weeks, asking again and again, until they have no choice but to relent. The date is already set when Didi does something to anger Baba. The beating with a broom handle is especially severe. Didi's back is covered with horizontal lines of black bruises from where each blow struck. Some parts are swollen purple and red. I'm not sure why Mama and Baba do not force us to cancel the outing. Perhaps they don't want to lose face since Crystal has asked so many times, or maybe Baba feels guilty about his overreaction.

Baba often expresses a mixed sense of remorse after losing control. He tenderly applies ointment to our bruises and says, "I don't like beating you, so please don't make me angry next time. Don't force me. You think you're hurting, but I promise, it hurts me more than you."

Before we leave for Crystal's house, Mama and Baba warn repeatedly, "Promise you two won't go swimming. She can't see Didi's bruises."

We promise. They say it is the only way they'll let us go. We say okay.

Our excitement level for this simple outing is akin to a trip to Disneyland. Once we arrive at Crystal's family's Phoenician rambler house, Didi runs wild with a water gun, and Crystal curls my hair in her bedroom. Sitting at her vanity, I admire her figure skating photos and medals on the walls. The attention she lavishes on me feels both luxurious and uncomfortable. We see Crystal at the restaurant all the time, and we are so close to her, but being in her space, I feel awkward and nervous. I don't know how to act and what to say to her. Finally, she asks, "Do you guys want to go swimming now?"

"No, it's okay," Didi and I both respond.

"What? But why not?" Crystal insists, not understanding why two kids in Arizona who never get out would refuse a day in the pool.

"We didn't bring bathing suits," I answer. This was on purpose, of course, orchestrated by our parents.

"You can borrow my T-shirts and shorts," she says, without skipping a beat. "Come on!" And she goes rummaging to find something suitable.

"No, thank you, Crystal." I am a terrible liar. Lies lead to punishment, but so does the truth. I am frozen.

After much back and forth, Crystal finally asks, "Are you two afraid of water? You're both afraid of water?" She correctly detects our fear, but of course, it isn't of water.

I decide I should do something to make her not suspect anything weird. I really do want to go swimming, so I take the clothes she offers me and change. It will be okay just to dip my toes in, I think, while Didi is having the time of his life chasing people with the water gun and splashing water. He is careful to keep his shirt on the whole time.

But eventually, I let Crystal pull me all the way into the water. Didi and I both have a wonderful time.

When Crystal drops us off at the restaurant, our parents thank her. As soon as she leaves, Mama and Baba ask, "Did you go swimming?"

"Didi didn't, but Crystal made me," I answer.

Mama and Baba are furious. "Beautiful Jade, how could you? We strictly forbade you." Mama looks so disappointed as she brushes her hair back nervously with her fingers. She looks like she is about to cry. Mama is so pretty despite no longer having regular visits to the beauty salon, like she had in Korea, where she could gossip with the women. Instead, she perms her bangs late at night at home, after the restaurant closes. I help, squirting the smelly chemical onto the pink plastic rolls.

"How could you tempt your brother like this?" Baba's words sting and bring me back to the moment. "Do you know what could have happened if Crystal saw those bruises?"

I hate myself for betraying my family, especially Didi. I cannot detect the fear that lies beneath my parents' anger. I am weak and selfish for risking our family's secret.

In writing this book, I ask Didi what he remembers of this day. The warmth of his smile seeps through my end of the phone.

"All I remember is Crystal took us to McDonald's afterward. I was so happy."

CHAPTER 12: Basketball Dreams

AGES 12 TO 17 — PHOENIX, ARIZONA

In 1993, when the Phoenix Suns play the Chicago Bulls in the NBA Championship finals, everyone in town catches basketball fever. Didi, who is almost ten years old, gets it extra bad. His love of basketball turns into a lifelong passion. He begs my parents for expensive basketball jerseys to wear to school and covers his room floor to ceiling with giant posters of his heroes—Jordan, Shaq, and Barkley. Didi plays basketball every chance he gets.

On report card night, I bring home straight A's as usual, but this doesn't matter. My good grades have become an expectation. My poor brother brings home abysmal grades, much worse than normal. Didi and I wait at home petrified. We're watching *Full House* after school, trying to ignore the impending doom. We don't look at each other. We know that when Baba gets home, it's every man for himself.

Later that night, I sit alone in my bedroom adjacent to Didi's, listening to the crying intensify next door. I don't want to be caught in the crossfire, but I creep out anyway. I stand in the carpeted hallway and look into Didi's room, afraid of what I'll see.

Baba's back is to me. Didi is kneeling in front of him, head bent. The light is turned off, and the room is dark, but I can still see in the evening light. All of the basketball posters from Didi's walls have been ripped into shreds and lay crumpled on the floor. Baba is wielding a large cleaver in his right hand. Didi is moaning. Holding it just above my brother's head, Baba hacks at the basketball. Over and over, until every ounce of air is squeezed out.

We never talk about this night. Not until we're both grown. "When he had the cleaver, I legit thought I was gonna die," Didi says with a shudder. "Do you remember that night?"

Mama rarely intervenes when Baba disciplines us. When he is especially out of control, she sometimes tugs weakly at his arm and says, "Hao la...Hao la . . ." which translates to "Good enough. That's good enough." This momentarily redirects Baba's wrath onto Mama.

"You're at fault too, Woman. You call yourself a mother, yet you never discipline the children. I have to do all of it," he'll shout at Mama before returning to Didi. "You force me to be the bad guy. Look how you've spoiled him rotten."

But Mama isn't home the night Baba hacks the basketball above Didi's head. She is at the restaurant. She is usually at the restaurant during the beatings. She prefers not to see. Her feeble protests rarely work anyway. She is Baba's devoted follower and, in the end, powerless to protect us.

Baba does not act out of malice toward us. He tells us this over and over. He believes he is failing as a father if we don't cower before him. To rule by fear is good parenting so we will fall obediently into line and carry out his will like well-trained mules. "You are a part of me," Baba says. "You are like my arms or my legs." It does not occur to Baba that Didi and I might grow up to have free will.

When Baba loses control, which is often, his anger wipes away all reason. In a country where he feels powerless, in a job that is grueling and endlessly chips at his pride, Didi and I are the subjects he can manipulate, control, and beat without recourse. Didi and I never talk about our treatment by Baba. We are too afraid. We don't trust each other not to tattle in the face of imminent threat. We are both willing to give the other up in hopes of mercy for ourselves.

"Do you remember that time I broke the CD drive on our new computer?" Didi asks me, decades later.

"I don't." Not at first, but the memory conjures itself once he fills me in. There are too many memories like this that trap us in panic.

"I must have been around thirteen years old maybe when I thought I broke the computer?" Didi adds. "I was so afraid to face Dad that I was seriously thinking of ways to kill myself before he got home that night because being dead would be better than what he would do to me."

I am shocked at the revelation that my happy-go-lucky brother had suicidal thoughts. Back then, I was too wrapped up in my own such thoughts to be aware Didi's.

"I'm sorry I was never there for you, Didi. I'm sorry I never took your side. I wish I could have protected you. I wish I was more mature and less selfish back then," I finally put into words the guilt I've carried for never protecting or comforting Didi as I should have as his older sister. I confess the incident in Korea with the camera in the wardrobe, how I allowed Baba to beat him, who was just a baby, in my place. I tell him sorry cannot begin to answer for my wrong, but he stops me.

"Nah, Sis. You don't have to feel bad. I don't remember at all," Didi chuckles. "I blame no one but Dad for what happened to me."

Didi may not remember that day in Korea, but I will never forget.

When Didi continues to struggle academically and my parents who do not read English don't know how to help him, they make me responsible for his grades. When his academic performance does not improve, I receive beatings alongside him every time a report card arrives, no matter that my grades are perfect.

"How can you be so selfish?" Baba yells sitting on the edge of the bed with Didi and me kneeling in front of him. He always makes us kneel before him for punishment. Baba is talking about the grades that I work so hard to earn. "You can't only take care of your own grades and not care about Didi. He's your responsibility too."

The injustice forces me apart from Didi, making it impossible for us to be on the same side. Didi hides his assignments from me, lying about them whenever I ask. There is no other way for me to find out. There are no parent portals or emails with the teacher. My parents cannot control Didi, and neither can I.

As Didi and I get older, we are allowed to stay home after school more often and for longer periods of time. During these times, Didi watches reruns of *The Fresh Prince of Bel-Air* or escapes into the desert air on his bike to meet up with neighborhood kids. He cannot be bothered with schoolwork in these moments of freedom. When we are at the restaurant, he is engrossed in his Gameboy or playing with a deck of cards…anything but studying.

"He won't do a good enough job. You can do it much better and earn him an A+," Baba says one night when we learn of a big project for Didi's history class the night before it is due. Baba's threatening tone gives me no choice. That night, I build Didi a beautiful model of an Egyptian boat out of a cardboard box that used to hold soy sauce packets. I paint it intricately, matching it to the photos in the text book and tie chopsticks onto it for oars. Didi takes no issue with this. He grins ear to ear and cannot wait to take credit for my work.

Balancing Didi's school work on top of my full AP course load, restaurant work, and after-school activities means I am often working late into the night, shaking with resentment. Teaching Didi the lesson that he is not good enough to do his own work, that his parents support cheating, and that he could get away with it all has me boiling.

"But Baba," I plead, "Shouldn't Didi do his own work? What about what he is supposed to learn from these projects?"

"Don't worry about it. Just get it done and don't talk back!"

My father had been an educator in Korea for over a decade, yet he cares more about grades than learning. He cares more about avoiding immediate failure and saving face than anything else.

"If I didn't have you and Didi, I could lead a carefree life," Baba often says, settling down in front of the television after work. He droops his eyes in mock drunkenness and twists his wrists about to accentuate the light-hearted life that could have been.

CHAPTER 13: Mei Ban Fa

AGE 13 TO 17 – PHOENIX, ARIZONA

My mother met the man who becomes Baba during her senior year in college in Taiwan. She chose a partner as dominating and controlling as her father, someone who would fiercely protect his family from everyone but himself.

Softer men pursued her, but she found shelter and familiarity in his dominance and romance in his volatility.

Those four college years were the only ones she was free— unbound from the control of her father in Korea—before she became an obedient wife to Baba. The young woman in photos from those days is one I hardly recognize. So fierce and self-assured, leaving me to wonder— where did she go? What happened to her spirit?

I would give anything to meet her.

What are my mother's true interests and tastes? I pester her with questions, "What music do you like? Do you have a favorite book? Where's the best place you've ever been? How about a favorite dish?"

The answers to all are a disappointing mix of "I don't know" and

"I like what you like."

At mealtimes, she lets the family pick the choicest morsels she prepares and swallows what is left. Again and again, Mama stands up to bring another banchan that she remembers is in the fridge, another leftover dish to reheat and add to the meal. Often, by the time she sits down to begin eating, Baba, Didi, and I are nearly finished.

"Mama, this dish has gone bad," I tell her. The meat in the dish she reheated has a distinctly rancid taste and I spit it out. I stand and move to throw out the dish.

"No, no!" Mama shrieks, panicking. "Wo chi, wo chi." I'll eat it. I'll eat it. "Mei Huai Ya," she says. It's not spoiled.

"Mom!" I groan. "It *is* spoiled. You'll get sick!"

She takes the plate and hoards it toward herself, waving me away.

"It's fine," she cries. This is the only time she puts her foot down.

I shake with frustration. We have an abundance of food, we own a restaurant for goodness sake, but Mama insists on eating spoiled food.

"Throwing food away is a sin," she says.

What were Mama's dreams before she became my Mama? Was it simply to marry and have children as was expected of her? If that was the case, why did she go to Taiwan to pursue a history degree when she could have just as well married and settled down in Korea earlier?

Later, as an adult, when I take her out for meals, even without Baba around to watch her every move, she cannot order for herself. The choice between chicken or fish paralyzes her. The need to make decisions for herself, long absent from her life, causes panic.

"You choose what you like," she closes her menu and adjusts her glasses, eyes downcast.

I have spent enough years in therapy to know I'm mourning a make-believe mother. One who could have taught me to love my own body instead of adding to my insecurities. One who could have fought back against my father, for herself, and for us.

How much can I blame her, though, for standing by like I had during all the beatings Didi endured, that I endured? Can I hold her accountable as a mother for never finding her strength, when she is a victim herself?

Mama extracts joy from what she can and blocks out the rest. She buries her head so often and so deep, her eyes and ears fill with sand. A born nurturer, she devotes everything to her identity as our mother. She envelops us only in gentleness and love. After working all day and night at our family restaurant, she comes home and insists on doing all the household chores. She refuses to use the dryer. I find her hang-drying clothes on the back of railings and dining room chairs at two in the morning.

She waits on my father and brother hand and foot. This becomes a constant source of conflict, the older I get. I am irate when teenage Didi parks himself in front of the big screen TV and mumbles, "Mama, bring me water" without taking his eyes off the basketball game. I see the shadow of Baba—who orders Mama around like this every day—in Didi, which makes me lose my shit. A screaming match ensues.

"Get your own water," I yell. "Mama works all the time. She doesn't need to be serving you."

"Mind your own damn business!" Didi screams.

"This is my business," I retort, and it's an all-out fight.

Mama turns frantic. "Please stop fighting," she pleads with tears in her eyes. This scene replays over and over.

Decades later, I realize Didi is right.

I should have let them be.

Mama derives joy and purpose from waiting on my brother. The traditional tasks of taking care of her family make her feel close to us. No matter how tired she might be, it is how she defines herself, and how she collects self-worth. I am wrong to impose my beliefs on her when she does not want me to advocate for her. It takes me years to learn this lesson, one I had not yet learned as a teenager.

Baba loves telling the story of how he met Mama. "One look and I was smitten…She was a vision. She came to a dinner at my college apartment in Taiwan with some mutual friends. After the meal, we drew straws to see who'd have to wash the dishes. Your mama drew the short straw! Can you believe it?" His laugh shakes the table. "She's been doing my dishes ever since."

Though my parents both still smile wistfully thinking of those charmed college days, now they fight daily—about the messiness of our house and the disorder on the restaurant shelves. Baba shouts about the employees, the blocked plumbing, or the broken ice machine. They clash about customers and how many soy sauce packets should be given out for free. Baba insults Mama's family, saying they are low class. They fight about my weight, my skin. They fight all the time about Didi's misbehavior. He is a kid who talks back, sneaks out at night, plays too much basketball, and never turns in his homework.

"Why do I always have to be the bad guy?" Baba screams. "Why am I always the disciplinarian? Don't you care?"

Baba throws pots and pans at Mama's feet while he yells. The kitchen staff snickers and squirms. They don't want to bear witness, but they don't know what to do.

One day, at the restaurant, Baba looks grim and a little embarrassed. "Go talk to your Mama, Beautiful Jade," he points to the parking lot. "She's in the van."

Mama is crying alone inside the beige Nissan Quest minivan that had replaced our beloved Ford. I slide open the door, sit in the seat beside her, and close the door again.

"What's wrong? What happened?" I am startled at Mama's matted and puffy appearance. She is sobbing harder than I've ever seen.

"You're old enough now, Beautiful Jade. You can comfort me."

Mama struggles to get the words out between gasping, short breaths. "Your Baba wants to buy a bra and panty set as a gift for Hyung-Sook."

"What?" I lean in toward her on the leather seat, stunned.

Hyung-Sook, a Korean divorcée younger than my parents, works at the restaurant as a cashier. She speaks good English, and I have been grateful to her because she takes significant pressure off of me, making the business calls to phone companies and insurance agents. Every call she makes is one I don't have to.

She and Baba flirt, but I had assumed it was harmless because Baba flirts with everyone.

Mama snorts and blows her nose. "Your Baba says it was an innocent idea. He thought it would make a good gift. 'Very unique,' he says."

Blood drains from my face. Suddenly the minivan feels like a coffin. My eyes dart around, and all I see is beige, beige everywhere. Beige seats, beige carpet, beige interior. I can't look at Mama, I want to look anywhere but at her. This is my Baba she is talking about. Despite all his faults, I always put him on a pedestal. That's how you survive a dictatorship. You worship him even as you are abused.

Later, I will learn Baba had asked Mama to confide in me about this. She needed someone to talk to, but he didn't want it to be her sister or best friend from college or even an ajumma in town. He wanted to control the damage. At thirteen years old, I was strategically assigned to absorb this shame.

Baba is willing to sacrifice my image of him to protect his reputation. I cry alongside my mom in that minivan, patting her back—our hearts both broken.

"Who can I talk to about something like this? It's too shameful to discuss with anyone else," Mama says between sobs. "It has to be you. You're our person, Beautiful Jade. Mei ban fa."

Mei ban fa. There is no other solution.

"Divorce!" Baba threatens, red-faced.

"Fine, divorce," Mama echoes weakly, sobbing and unable to keep the tremble out of her voice. Mama, like me, has been conditioned that a man can easily move on after divorce, but a woman will suffer. A man can remarry and build a new life, but what can a discarded woman do? Who will want a used woman with two kids? How will she make a living?

After their fight, Baba comes home late, two or three in the morning, and blasts the television so loudly it wakes Didi and me. We stumble into the living room, rubbing our eyes to see what is wrong.

Baba seems genuinely shocked to see us, as if in his rage, he'd forgotten our existence. "Go back to bed," he orders. The TV volume remains ear-splitting.

No one sleeps that night.

Soon, I get stomachaches. I catch colds easily and recover slowly. I stay up worrying about catching gruesome sexually transmitted diseases, even though I've never had sex, never even held hands with anyone. I worry I will catch diseases from toilet seats. I worry about nothing and everything. Weeks pass, and I'm still too worried and afraid to sleep.

Mama turns to me in frustration after she and Baba fight, eyes bloodshot, and declares, "It's all because of you and Didi. We only fight because of you."

My parents make up eventually. They always do, even though it can feel like an eternity while they're fighting. One Sunday, when things are peaceful again, we have a leisurely family meal at our corner table at the restaurant. We're still open, but when we eat around two or three in the afternoon, there are hardly any customers to interrupt us. Baba makes Mapo tofu and fried calamari, a special treat. It is always a treat when we eat food that's not on the Oriental Express menu. Toward the end of lunch, as our bellies are getting satiated and happy, Baba asks Mama with a teasing smile, "Would you still want to be my wife in your next life?"

Didi and I freeze our chopsticks in midair, afraid to breathe. We await Mama's answer, ready to take cover. Any answer other than an affirmative would surely risk Baba's thunderous rage, which makes her courage all the more surprising.

Mama's voice is shrill and cracked as she speaks words laden with melancholy. "In my next life . . ." She looks up into the vast Arizona skies through the large windows of Oriental Express. "In my next life...I want to be reborn as a bird, so I can fly, fly, fly."

CHAPTER 14: Sanctuary

AGE 13 — PHOENIX, ARIZONA

The strip mall where The Golden Phoenix Oriental Express is nestled is painted flamingo pink with turquoise trim, a southwest sunset color palette. Didi finds escape roaming the stores—Safeway, Walgreens, Blockbuster Video, and other smaller businesses that come and go through the years. Me? My sanctuary is the Juniper Branch of the Phoenix Public Library, which sits angled in the center, kitty-corner from Oriental Express, a sea of parked cars between us. To me, the library looks like a mother who watches over the hustle and bustle in peaceful benevolence.

I didn't have a library in Korea. There wasn't one in the Chinatown where I grew up, not even one at my school. When I first walked into the expansive, air-conditioned library at age ten, not long after my parents bought Oriental Express, I was in disbelief. I held no negative judgment for the thin, worn carpet and popcorn ceilings.

To me, the library is a glorious haven.

The entrance leads to the children's section. Rows and rows of books—from picture books graduating to chapter books—start immediately next to the librarians' desk to my right. The shelves of fiction back into the children's nonfiction, then into the VHS tapes and the CDs. I believe this is the half I am allowed in. This is the half of the library where I learn English, lost in books about witches and magic.

I'm not certain I'm allowed in the other half of the library, which starts with Young Adult books and then transitions into Adult volumes. I am too afraid to ask, but as soon as my English improves, I sneak over to the Young Adult section with my heart beating fast. The whole time, I worry someone will catch me and throw me out.

I am enticed by the steamy covers of romance books with the passionate kisses and embraces, the heaving bosoms in period dresses. Like a thief, I scan these shelves as quickly as possible, looking for books with plain and subtle covers that I can read around my parents without being discovered.

At the front desk, I hold my breath, hoping the librarian won't notice. Hoping she won't stop and humiliate me by saying, "Honey, this book is for adults only." But the librarians never do. When I get home, I try to hide them from my parents. I am also mostly disappointed that subtle covers also mean lukewarm content, despite being from the romance section.

Mostly, though, I am absorbed in literature that's non-controversial for my age. When I enter middle school, I feel at home in the Young Adult aisles. I am obsessed with *Anne of Green Gables* and read everything I can by Lucy Maud Montgomery. What first draws me to the story is the familiarity of the plot and images—I recognize the story of the red-headed heroine. I'd spent summers watching the Japanese anime adaptation of the series on my grandma's grainy television in Korea. Encountering this source material of my once favorite show is my past and present loves fused. The universe makes sense.

Next, I devour *Dragonwings* by Laurence Yep, captivated by Asian American history so removed from my journey. As a new immigrant, I feel a disconnect—at once small and vast—between myself and the Asian Americans born in America. English is still somewhat new on my tongue, and our papers say we are, "permanent aliens." I don't feel the confidence to stake my claim on Gold Mountain.

I can't believe it when *Joy Luck Club* comes out in theaters. I read everything I can by Amy Tan, who leaves me sobbing and afraid and completely immersed in her world. I am frustrated each time I look up the one copy of Maxine Hong Kingston's *The Woman Warrior*, it is checked out and never returned—my holds on the title ignored.

Meanwhile, at home, Baba begins to nag me daily.

"Don't fill your head with this useless trash. It's addictive."

"You'll ruin your eyes."

"Shut off the light and go to sleep!"

Another crisis of his making. Another reason the air around us turns unbreathable.

He calls Second Aunt to talk sense into me, but Second Aunt does not see a problem. "Have you read *Gone with the Wind*?" she asks amicably. "Just make sure to get good grades, Beautiful Jade."

Still, Baba scolds me regularly, "Stop reading these addictive trashy novels. Read science books and nonfiction. Maybe you'll learn something."

My favorite librarian is a short, bespectacled woman in her thirties. Some of the other librarians gave Didi and me the side-eye when we were always there as unsupervised children, but not Lisa. She talks to me every time like I am important.

Lisa is checking out my books when I blurt out, "I got my period."

I am thirteen years old. A few days earlier, I discovered my underwear covered in blood. I ran and told my mother, who panicked, and immediately told my father. Behind the counter, they spoke in hushed tones, both wearing grave faces.

"It's so early," Mama said, even though it isn't.

Mama and Baba, always afraid, worry about what this means.

Lisa tries to mask her surprise over the sound of the beeps as she scans my books. She smiles politely and grasps for something appropriate to say.

I shared too much information.

A few months earlier, Lisa had said to me out of the blue, "Michelle, you are beautiful."

Not *you look beautiful*, which is a temporary state of being. *"You are beautiful."*

Looking back, I wonder if I looked particularly sad in that moment causing her to gift me a positive affirmation. That was a time when I was consistently told to lose weight and to change. When I felt fat and ugly, both at home and in school. The unexpected compliment lifted me up, so much so that I feel its power thirty years later.

I swallow Lisa's words whole and hoard her attention, but she and I don't know each other that well, even though I see her all the time.

After that, we carry on as usual. I will never mention anything too personal again.

Nevertheless, the library is my third parent—the American one, along with television. The library teaches Didi and me things our parents can't or won't teach. The things that, if we asked, would make them recoil and ignore. "Ah-hay! Bu yao lien nah!" You don't want your face! How shameful!

Didi and I search for our own answers. When we're home alone, we watch R-rated movies checked out from the library and on late-night cable television. In a rare conspiratorial operation, Didi and I check out an educational video called *Where Do Babies Come From?*

In goofy animation, sexual intercourse is explained, as a man and a woman grind in bed. Squealing and grossed out, Didi yells in disbelief, "The man pees into the woman?! Ewww!"

CHAPTER 15: Joy

MIDDLE SCHOOL – PHOENIX, ARIZONA

Baba and Mama see themselves as progressive, reasonable parents. After all, they met and dated in college instead of agreeing to an arranged marriage like so many of their peers. They don't think they're strict or unreasonable, but, of course, they are when compared to my non-immigrant friends. I am rarely permitted to socialize with friends outside of school, and I am definitely not allowed to sleep over at anyone's house. Dating is absolutely out of the question until college.

They see themselves as progressive because they don't forbid me from having male friends, and I am grateful for this. The best male friend of my dreams (the one who is supposed to be the Dawson to my Joey and the Gilbert Blythe to my Anne Shirley) shows up my sophomore year in high school.

David moves to town from the East Coast, and we hit it off immediately. Thin and just about my height (5'8") with dark brown curls and a kind smile that extends beyond his face, he has the preppy Jason Biggs in *American Pie* look down pat. A product of my environment and pop culture, I immediately develop a deep crush.

Not only is David in most of my AP classes, he also joins The Paperclips, the creative writing club, even though he isn't a writer. He just wants to hang out. I swoon. We giggle through our classes together, collecting searing looks from teachers who normally adore us model students. We partner on as many projects as we are permitted. On the rare nights I am allowed to get away, we hang out past the 11pm city curfew, talking and laughing until we are both in tears. Everything is better, funnier, and more brilliant when we are together.

At home, things do not change. Didi and I both fear and idolize Baba. There is no other way to survive under a dictatorship. We compete for his good graces and wait on egg shells for his moods to turn bright.

Mama is a workhorse, head down, toiling with all her might. She cooks potato soup, fried rice, and kimbap to make us feel her love. Though Baba's volatility means we never know whether we're standing on quicksand until it's too late, Mama is forever ready with a tender embrace and an adoring gaze.

But if Mama, the frugal homebody, were in charge, our home would contain only the barest of necessities and loads of hoarded empty containers. We would never leave the house.

Baba alone determines our fates. Baba decides whether I am allowed to go on fieldtrips and whether I can see friends. He controls what clothes I can wear. Baba alone holds the keys to our family's joy. To remain in his favor is survival.

If Baba is happy, his joy is contagious. When the restaurant is slow, sometimes we leave Mama to run the place and Baba takes Didi and me on day trips to Sedona or Lake Pleasant. He teaches us to fish, to knead our own bait out of cheap stale white bread, peanut butter, and a bit of water.

Baba buys a home karaoke system from Los Angeles that plays Laserdiscs, large and heavy like weighted silver vinyls, and lets us rent movies from Blockbuster. He procures a fake Christmas tree and sets it up in the middle of the restaurant and orders Didi and me to put up decorations. Every holiday season, Baba and I spend hours painting the windows of Oriental Express with wreaths, ornaments, Santas and reindeer—our annual masterpiece that wraps around the whole restaurant is always a hit with the customers. Though we rarely receive presents, I still love the holidays. Mama gift-wraps objects we already own, like socks, for Didi and me to unwrap.

"The fun is in opening the presents. Doesn't matter what's inside!" Mama exclaims, giggling. "Gifts are wasteful. You have everything you need."

Since Thanksgiving and Christmas are the only days the restaurant is ever closed, we squeeze all the family fun we can into those two days.

One year, when I am thirteen, Baba takes us to Disneyland on Christmas Day. The drive from Phoenix is over six hours; the trip to Los Angeles is grueling, involving overnight driving to make the most of the day. Backaches and leg pains plague Baba chronically, so when we get there, he says he will wait in the van and orders Mama to go into the theme park with us kids.

Mama doesn't want to go on any of the rides. She is easily overwhelmed. "You kids go on. I'll wait for you here at the ride exit," she says, never imagining the snaking lines at Space Mountain would take over three hours.

By the time Didi and I find her, Mama is crying, panting, and in a full panic, believing she lost us in the massive crowds.

We stay all day at Disneyland because we've already paid the entrance fee, but Didi and I get to ride only three rides total. We spend over six hours waiting in line.

When we get back home, our neighbors tell us that Mama, Didi, and I were captured on the news, cutting across the parade barricades in our rush to leave. The coverage was about Disneyland's record-breaking attendance day.

"I want you and Didi to have good childhood memories," Baba repeats. "I didn't have a good childhood. I want you to."

CHAPTER 16:
Intergenerational Education

INCHEON, SOUTH KOREA

When I was three years old, and Mama was very pregnant with Didi, Baba moved us from the noodle factory in the countryside to the city to take over another one of Yeh-Yeah's other business ventures—a bathhouse. We lived on the second floor of the bathhouse for the next four years. I was only allowed in the women's section. Nudity all around me was the norm. The ajummas who worked the exfoliation table took turns holding baby Didi and keeping an eye on me.

I wouldn't live in a home that wasn't also a business until I was seven years old. Baba decided at that time that it would be best for us to leave the bathhouse so he could teach full-time at the Chinese school in Incheon's Chinatown. The apartment unit we moved into was also owned by Yeh-Yeh, like every other place I had called home. Second Uncle had been living there with his family, but when his three kids grew into teenagers, they needed more space and moved to a bigger house. Moving from the bathhouse on a busy street to the quiet apartment complex in Chinatown with trees and grass was like entering a different world, like we had crossed into a green refuge.

I started first grade early, when I was five, because Baba and Mama were busy running the bathhouse and didn't have childcare. My best friend and slightly older second cousin, Ying, was starting school, and I wanted to do whatever she did. She and I had attended the same Korean daycare and preschool in front of her family's hole-in-the-wall jajangmyun restaurant. Ying and her family, along with their little mutt puppy, lived in rooms behind their storefront. She was everything to me.

Baba snuck Ying and me out of school for off-campus lunches with his colleagues, a luxury not afforded to our classmates. The best places to eat, the ones with the most delectable banchan, were hidden, unlicensed, tiny establishments packed with hungry people. The fare was never fancy, but always house-made. The soups exploded with complex flavors: fermented soybean, kimchi, seaweed, or fish. Simultaneously comforting and refreshing, these were the best meals of my life.

At Sun Yat-Sen Elementary School in Incheon's Chinatown, my class of fifty children was taught by Teacher Moon. She was my teacher through first and second grade. My parents talked about her, tsk-tsking their sympathy, because the poor woman was a gua-fu, a widow. That was a word I had never heard before. Baba took me to meet her before my first day. We approached her in the schoolyard, and I was struck by how put together she appeared, more so than the moms I hung around. She was older than Mama but younger than my grandmother. I wasn't good at judging adult ages, but I'd place her in her late forties. She wore make-up, smart black pumps, a pencil skirt, and her hair was in a perfect perm of glossy 1950s curls. Teacher Moon smiled at us—a smile that appeared warm, but was actually steely if you looked closer. She was a well-guarded fortress.

I hid behind Baba's legs, my itchy white stockings feeling itchier by the minute. He pulled me forward, presenting me to Teacher Moon.

"Beat her hard if she doesn't listen," he grinned.

Sticks and sectioned off two-by-fours were distributed by the school administration. This actually might have been Baba's job as the discipline director. All teachers were revered and encouraged to discipline the students, whether in first or twelfth grade. Punishment by public shaming was also encouraged, as was forcing students to hold up their arms or kneel on cement floors in torturous positions for hours. Baba gave Teacher Moon his full blessing not to go easy on me.

If the intention was to make me fear failure, it worked. I had been conditioned to fear adults in positions of power since birth. School discipline was not new, but now, there was the threat of double beatings if something went awry. Thankfully, I was eager to please and a focused student, so school was mostly uneventful in those first years.

What sticks out in my mind, though, were the moments Teacher Moon taught history through personal experience. As a child, she witnessed the atrocities at the end of the Japanese Occupation, which lasted from 1910 to 1945.

She stood with haunted eyes in front of the dimly lit classroom, lined with the windows shaded at all times by a large oak tree, the building on the left side, and a high cement wall immediately to the right. Her words turned acidic as visions of the past pulled her far, far away. "My sister," she said, with a quiver. "The Japanese. They buried her alive."

A hush swept across the second-grade classroom—all of us students were stricken with horror, wide-eyed. Someone cleared their throat in discomfort. It was as if the ghosts of war, all of our ancestors, had captured us, holding us immobilized in our desks. My childish imagination immediately conjured a sandy pit with my teacher's sister in it, bloodied and tied up, as Japanese soldiers stood around callously snickering.

Though four decades had passed, the country, like Teacher Moon, was still in recovery. Television programs—from historical melodramas to comedies—regularly depicted the atrocities suffered by the Korean people at the hands of the Japanese military. I watched historical K-dramas about young women and girls, wearing white hanbok, kidnapped to serve as sex slaves for the troops. I listened to stories from adults around me for as long as I could remember. My parents didn't believe in censoring violence, only kissing and sex. I learned about rape before sex. Girls had something extra to fear. Something unimaginably horrible. The trauma of war was still raw and passed down. "Never trust the Japanese," was a mantra. "Never forget."

By the time Mama and Baba were born in the mid-1950s, the country had been decimated by the Korean War. For generations, my mother's family ran a small noodle shop in the southern city of Daegu. My Lao-Yeh, my maternal grandfather, was the only person I ever knew who smoked a pipe and wore a fedora. He was dark and dashing, appearing far younger than his years. Sitting in the small, shabby dining room of the restaurant he and my Lao-Lao operated, between noisy puffs, he gestured his fingers up toward the sky. "I was just a kid. I was at school when the bombs started dropping from the sky."

History had a way of seeming both real and made up at the same time. As a child, everything seemed to have happened so long ago. I couldn't fully process it at the time, but I never forgot what he told me either. For years, both during the Korean War and after it was frozen in cease fire in 1953, people starved. As a result of having survived those times, Lao-Yeh and Lao-Lao never threw anything away. They saved every jar and empty bottle because they were used to surviving on nothing. They scrimped and saved like no one else. They didn't even buy toilet paper—using thin tissue calendar paper of dates passed instead—they buy nothing beyond what passed as a necessity for them.

Mama inherited this instinct to hoard from her parents who survived the Korean War. She diligently prepares for an unseen apocalypse, so the house is always full of empty shampoo and lotion bottles, waiting for their day where they might come in handy, instead of going into the recycling bin. Empty liquor bottles and heart-shaped candy boxes explode from the cabinets because "they're pretty, and I don't have the heart to throw them out." Mama will never get rid of any piece of clothing that she's owned. Her spacious walk-in closet is an overflowing archive of the decades since we immigrated in 1990.

Once, as a teenager, I offer to clean out her closet for her, inspired by the makeover shows of the times. "Let me clean out the clothes for you that you'll never wear again, Mama," I say with good intention. Mama's eyes widen in fear, and her voice turns shrill. She bends her knees and puts up her palms in a defensive fighter stance in front of her closet door. "No! I don't want you to."

I did not expect my casual offer to set off panic. She acts as if she were being attacked. But it isn't completely out of the ordinary for Mama to suddenly panic. My parents dwell in survival mode, like birds caught in a trap, ready to fight or flee. Mama freezes or flees often, while Baba never stops fighting and screaming. He is a man's man, full of han, a birthright masculine anger.

"Beautiful Jade, answer me!" Teacher Moon shot me out of my six-year-old self's reverie. Maybe I was thinking about the latest episode of my favorite cartoons or just imagining myself floating on a cloud with a magic wand. That was what I coveted most then—a magic wand that could bring to life anything I drew with it. Dashed out of my dreams, I splatted into the reality of my second-grade classroom and felt the hard, splintery wooden desk beneath my hands.

Teacher Moon banged her stick on the table in her. "Answer me!"

I had missed the question entirely and had no words, no answer. I looked down in shame, tilting my face so that my braids would hide my face.

Sharp and tall in front of the chalkboard, my teacher shook her head and tsked. Her eyes glisten with feigned pity. "You are nothing, Beautiful Jade. You are worthless."

Don't tell Baba. Please don't tell Baba, I prayed. How would I face him if he knew?

She didn't tell Baba, not that time, but the fear that she might one day stuck with me.

Baba liked to summon me to his office using the school inter-com system, often for no reason at all. I could saunter into Baba's office whenever I wasn't in class to doodle on scrap paper. This kind of access was unthinkable for other students. I was Teacher Yang's daughter—a reputation both good and bad.

The teacher all students feared the most was Teacher Wong. He taught gym and was later my fourth-grade teacher. Built like a brick house and tightly wound, his gravelly voice from decades of heavy smoking made the hairs on my neck stand. Infamous as the cruelest teacher, he beat students mercilessly with the school-issued two-by-fours. He was also known in our tightly-knit Chinese community for severely beating his wife and kids. Rumor had it that after his wife tried to leave him, he switched to beating her on the head so her hair would obscure the bruises from prying eyes. When his temper exploded, this practice carried over to the classroom. He repeatedly cracked students on their heads.

When I told Mama about this, her eyes clouded with worry, but she said nothing. All of the adults already knew. The classroom was the teacher's domain, and it was to be respected, just as control of the home was the father's domain. Domestic violence was not declared illegal in South Korea until December 31, 1997, long after we immigrated to the U.S. in 1990.

As punishment for failing to memorize daily chapter assignments, which we had to recite in front of the class, Teacher Wong forced students to stand on the platform beneath the flagpole in the school-yard. For me, public shaming would be far worse than an anonymous beating. The idea of me—Teacher Yang's daughter—standing out there was petrifying. What if word traveled to my father? Or worse. If Baba saw me himself? I'd face a far greater fury. So I made sure to study every night. All but one day. One day, I forgot the words. I stumbled over the recitation when it was my turn and almost peed my pants.

The class hushed in surprise. I was not one of the usual characters who was caught not knowing the material. "Back of the class," Teacher

Wong grunted. I joined the row of students already lined up there, their books in hand, furiously trying to retain the words.

The rest of the class took their turns—each standing up to recite and sitting down with satisfied relief if they succeeded, or making the death march to the back of the class if they failed. Teacher Wong glared at the nine of us at the back of the classroom. "Get out of my sight," he snorted in disgust. "And don't come back inside until you've memorized it."

My trembling made it difficult to walk. I lagged as the other students, each with their faces buried in their textbooks, stumbled ahead. As I rounded the building, my heart beating with fear, I gave in to the sudden urge to run. I turned on my heels and scampered in the opposite direction.

I was sure I would be caught, but in the meantime, I hid in the muddy, spidery alley behind the bathrooms. I memorized furiously, repeating the passage over and over until it affixed to my mind in record time. I snuck around the building and back into the quiet hallway.

I entered the classroom as if walking on glass. "I know it now," I said quietly.

"Let's hear it then," replied Teacher Wong. When I finished, he ordered in his usual gruff way, "Sit down."

I never told anyone about that day. After that incident, schoolwork felt like a matter of life and death.

Teacher Wong's gym class was torture. He took joy in our injuries and our pain. Though only a little chubby at this time, I was often called Shao-Pang, or little fatty, by family. Sometimes, Teacher Wong ordered our class of seven-year-olds to run shuttle runs (also known as suicide drills). Once, while my lungs burned, I collided with another girl heading the other direction. Her head hit my nose with full, crushing force. Blood gushed down my white gym uniform.

Our underfunded school did not have a nurse. We had an ancient wooden cupboard with sparse first-aid supplies that students could take to bandage themselves when injured. Teacher Wong assigned a student to walk me to the supplies and left me crying alone in the classroom. Never having seen so much blood, I felt faint. The empty room spun around me. I couldn't make the bleeding stop. No one was there to help. The class continued running death drills outside. Twenty minutes that seemed like an eternity passed, and my nose was no better.

I stumbled back out to the schoolyard, sobbing and hiccupping, not knowing what to do. As soon as I entered Teacher Wong's sight-line, before I could say anything, he roared, "What are you doing here? What do YOU have to do with THIS?" He pointed violently from me to the class.

My classmates froze, and I flinched. I didn't understand what his words meant, but it was clear he didn't want to deal with me. Holding myself up against the wall, I stumbled back into the classroom and slumped back at my desk, now littered with blood-soaked tissues. I honestly wondered if I was going to die.

When class ended, my best friend Ying ran to Baba's office for help. Soon, my father swept me up in the safety of his embrace.

"Teacher Wong is holding a grudge against me, Daughter," Baba told me later with a sheepish grin. "We had too much to drink the other night and I beat him up in an alley. If only he'd shown you the slightest bit of kindness, I would have been grateful . . ."

CHAPTER 17: Country Potatoes

MIDDLE SCHOOL – PHOENIX, ARIZONA

On a rare weekend day when time moves slower and Baba seems calm, I approach him with the question that has been on my mind. We are at our new house. When I graduated elementary school, I wanted to go to the new middle school with all my friends, who all happened to live in a wealthier zip code than ours. Our family had long outgrown the two-bedroom apartment, anyway, and according to Baba, who heard it from a friend, it would soon be illegal for me and Didi to share a bedroom.

The new house—white with pink and green trim and an orange, clay-tiled roof—is located five miles north of our old apartment in a newly developed neighborhood deep in the desert suburbs. Our new four-bedroom house could easily fit three of our old apartment units inside it. Didi and I are ecstatic to get our own rooms. I can't believe all of this space is ours. Mama, Didi, Baba, and I all relish the moments when we are home, where we enjoy peace and privacy. At the restaurant, we are forever in service of our customers in one way or another.

"Baba," I ask while he and I are sitting at our dining table. Didi is watching television in the adjoining living room. "Can you tell me about our family history for my class project?"

I am excited because I already know my story will be different from those of my classmates. Also, I am a nerd who gets excited about school assignments. I'm sure my question will make Baba happy, thinking he will brag like he had in the school atrium about Yeh-Yeh's name on the placard. Instead, his face turns stony with inner conflict.

He stands up slowly and says, "Come with me."

I swallow hard, and blood races to my head. Not knowing what this could be about, I follow Baba to our guest bedroom. He sits down on the mattress. The room has no other furniture, and the walls are bare and white.

"Shut the door," he commands.

Without a word, I obey. I wonder why we had to move away from Didi's earshot. What is he going to tell me that needs to be guarded behind a closed door?

"Yeh-Yeh left China as a penniless teenager because there was not enough food to eat," Baba says. "He was starving, Beautiful Jade. He lived a harsh life. Extreme droughts and famine in northern China were common. Yeh-Yeh ventured out, not wanting to be another mouth to feed for his family. He was homeless and worked any job he could for his passage to Korea. Yeh-Yeh had no formal schooling. He couldn't read or write, but he was smart and could work hard. Yeh-Yeh was creative and entrepreneurial. He could take soybeans and squeeze them into oil, then sell it for a profit at the markets. Just like that, he grew one business into another, each one bigger than the one before."

This is the first time Baba has ever spoken of Yeh-Yeh's suffering and perseverance. I am in awe as I recall the noodle factory with wide-open fields, where eggplants and grapes grew on twisty vines. One of my earliest memories is Baba holding my little hand up to snip a bundle of grapes from the factory grounds and catching them in a small paper cup, the sourness of the grapes making me pucker. All of Yeh-Yeh's sons and their families lived on the premises in red brick buildings, which formed a courtyard. I think of the bathhouse in the city that Mama and Baba managed for four years, where we lived upstairs. Yeh-Yeh worked hard, along with Po-Po, my grandmother, and his seven children.

A day of work at the bathhouse would begin at five o'clock each morning and continue late into the night. There was always trouble in the boiler room, floods and fires causing panic.

Before we moved to the apartment, Baba managed to find time to work a second job as a teacher at the Chinese school while managing the bathhouse with Mama. My mother nursed my newborn brother in the ticketing booth situated between the men's side and the women's while I, at three years old, looked at picture books donated to the school from a book drive in Taiwan.

Though I can't imagine how exhausting the bathhouse years were for my parents, I remember them fondly. I spent all my time with Mama roosting on her lap in the cozy ticket booth, feeling grown up whenever she let me hand change to the customers.

Second Uncle ran the third family business, China Tower, one of the largest restaurants and banquet halls in Incheon. China Tower still stands, multiple stories tall, looking more like a glassy office building than a restaurant. Every Chinese wedding banquet in the community had been held there. Before the invention of karaoke machines, the venue hired keyboardists to accompany guests in song. I loved going to these parties, donning my best dress, dancing and giggling with cousin Ying on stage. My dad, uncles, and aunts were famous for their singing. No one on Baba's side of the family was a wallflower.

"Everything we have, Yeh-Yeh built with his hands," Baba motions around us in our guest room like we are in the center of the universe. "This house, our restaurant, were paid for by Yeh-Yeh's blood, sweat, and tears."

When I was six, my favorite uncle, Mama's baby brother, said to me, "There was no greater man than your Yeh-Yeh in his generation."

I didn't understand what he meant then. My favorite uncle, my fun uncle, lived in Daegu and was visiting us. Standing on the balcony atop the bathhouse, he had paused to take in the Incheon sunset. Pointing to the horizon, he continued, "Your Yeh-Yeh owned all of this land, as far as the eye can see until the government seized most of it because he's Chinese."

Baba was the youngest of seven children, spanning twenty years in their ages. Because it was considered bad luck for pregnant women to be seen at weddings, Po-Po, who was expecting Baba at the time, missed her eldest daughter's big day. Like me, Baba was nicknamed Shao-Pang, little fatty. According to family lore, Baba was born such a large baby that there was a write-up about the birth in the local newspaper. Baba doesn't like to talk about this, so I assume it's true. Eldest Aunt came home to help Po-Po with the newborn baby. When it was time for her to return to her husband, Po-Po—still in recovery from the difficult birth and exhausted from work—sobbed and begged her daughter not to go.

Baba's second eldest sister, Second Aunt, who would petition our immigration, practically raised him. She was pulled out of school in seventh grade to help at home, despite her stellar grades. She would never let her Beautiful Six daughters forget her bitterness about this. Second Aunt commanded her children to zheng kou qi, to fight for breath for her, meaning they must take full advantage of the opportunities she could not access.

When Second Aunt married and moved away, Baba rarely saw her again. This mother figure who raised him disappeared from his life overnight. His remaining siblings were a sister closer to his age, but with whom he was never very close, and three much-older brothers who bullied him viciously into adulthood. One of those brothers, while drunk, chased him with a knife, threatening to kill him. Baba cited this incident and his relationship with his brothers as one of the reasons why he was leaving Korea. "There is not much for us here."

Anytime Baba is reminded of the childhood of neglect and abuse, his face darkens as he tries to forget.

"I don't have any good memories from my childhood," Baba repeats. "I want you and Didi to have good memories."

One slow summer Sunday afternoon at Oriental Express, Mama is working behind the counter. Didi and I are at our usual corner table. My nose is in a library book, and Didi is playing his Gameboy. Baba is sitting at the table next to us, flipping through the ad inserts from the newspaper.

"Wha…Broccoli is on sale at the grocery store down the street, and it is so expensive to order right now," he exclaims as if he has struck gold. Most of the food for the restaurant is purchased from a major supplier, but in a business with such slim margins, Baba also keeps an eye out for local deals. "Kids, in the truck now!"

I slowly put down my book like it is magnetized to my fingers. Didi and I climb reluctantly into our sauna-like Dodge Ram pickup, dreading the hot whoosh that will envelop us when we leave the comfort of air-conditioning. Inside the truck, I move gingerly, careful not to burn my thighs on the scorching upholstery, but it's hard when wearing shorts.

Baba sings at the top of his lungs to an old tape of Chinese pop songs for the entire three-minute drive. It is uncomfortable to move outside when it's over 100 degrees, but Baba, motivated to score bargain broccoli, is light on his feet. The three of us walk into the well-chilled, large chain grocery store. It's not hard to find our bearings. Didi and I run ahead to help Baba find the produce section in the back. We spot the broccoli before Baba does. Full of energy, Didi is jumping around in front of the misters when Baba catches up to us. "Bag up all the broccoli here," he orders in a whisper with sparkling eyes. Didi and I do as he says.

I wish we could have paid and left the store with our cart half-filled with broccoli and Baba's pride intact, but that is not what happens. Wanting more, Baba finds an aproned employee and asks if there's more in the back.

"Oh, let me check," says the produce guy. His eyes bear no emotion. He doesn't care who buys the broccoli. We follow him to the employees-only area and he emerges through the thick strips of plastic and hands Baba a full, waxy cardboard box of green gold.

"Wha…!" Baba is all smiles. He thanks the grocer profusely, and we are on our way to the checkout line.

Before we make it there, a short, portly man in a white shirt blocks our cart. "STOP!"

The aproned employee from the produce section follows closely behind, his face blanched. The manager, by contrast, is red-faced and out of breath. He runs to catch us. "Sir, we cannot sell you this broccoli," he says firmly, looking up at Baba. "This is for a store promotion. You clearly own a restaurant."

Embarrassed, Baba hulks out instantly. His imposing six-foot-three figure has grown wider with age and stockier with hard restaurant labor. He is easily the largest Chinese man many people in Arizona have ever seen. Baba's face is aflame, his arms thrash in wild gestures and he struggles to make his point.

There was no published limit to how much you could purchase.
Nowhere did the ad say you can't buy the broccoli for a restaurant.
None of this comes out.

Didi and I are caught in the line of fire. I don't know what to do. I wish we could all disappear.

"Are you going to hit us?" the manager asks. "Are you going to hit this man?" He points to his employee. "I will call the police," he says loudly.

The store manager looks down Didi's and my wide-eyed, scared faces. "Your children are here. Please calm down. This is over broccoli."

The standoff feels like an eternity, but Baba eventually stops baring his teeth. He swallows the foam at the mouth. His shoulders relax slightly. He shoves the cart aside, and Didi and I totter after our father out of the store.

We never speak of the incident again.

There are two other instances that I'm aware of where the police were called on Baba. One is at an L.A. Fitness, where he lost it when the salespeople would not let him out of the membership contract he signed. Baba misses the bathhouses in Korea, and the hot tub and sauna at gyms are the closest equivalents he can find. "Just sign at the x," the big tan bodybuilder had urged him. "You can quit anytime."

Later, when Baba does want to quit, he finds the bodybuilder singing a different tune.

"What you do mean I can't cancel?" Baba becomes louder and louder. He punches a wall. Several trainers approach, but Baba does not calm down. Baba can't understand any contract in English, let alone this one with pages and pages of corporate fine print.

Baba believes men should stand by their word, and he cannot fathom that the promise of that big man was worth shit. He had been deceived, and he would smash up the entire building if he could.

Thankfully, when the police arrive, Baba is smart enough to calm down. He calls them sirs and is impeccably polite and respectful. There is no arrest.

Another time, the police are dispatched to a car dealership because Baba's aggressive haggling turns threatening. Baba does not know how to take no for an answer. After that incident, Baba brings Didi on impulsive car shopping trips knowing a child might garner some sympathy, and the dealership might stop short of phoning the cops.

As an adult, I reflect on how bodybuilders and thick-skinned car dealers were terrified enough of Baba to call the police, but Didi, Mama, and I spent decades believing we did not have that option. Instead, we faced Baba's wrath a thousand times over behind closed doors.

"I'm just a country potato," Baba says whenever his English fails him.

Baba knows everyone underestimates his education and intelligence. He loves to boast about being yang-ban, Korean for aristocratic and high-class. Baba enjoys what he deems patrician pursuits—calligraphy, classical music, and the like. Exceptionally eloquent in both Mandarin and Korean, he hates stumbling over English words like an ogre. He gives up on the language that never ceases to fight his tongue.

"Country potato" becomes an excuse he uses to avoid parent-teacher conferences, school events, and other functions where I need him, where Didi needs him.

"Why would I go? And feel like a da biao ze?" A big stupid idiot.

But during famines in China, children were lucky to find a potato. Potatoes were the only available sustenance. They kept my ancestors alive.

Potatoes are my favorite food.

When Baba tells me about Yeh-Yeh's destitute journey, I sit straighter and flex my arms instinctively. Despite their flaws, Yeh-Yeh, Baba, and my other ancestors fought hard to provide for our needs. I give Baba a tight hug. No matter how much Baba likes to put on airs, the truth is we come from poor, uneducated farmers. We are the masses. We are no better, no worse than anyone. Though Baba feels shame in our roots, I take extra pride, for we are fighters.

We are survivors.

CHAPTER 18: Daughter

TEENAGE YEARS – PHOENIX, ARIZONA

"I wish you and Didi could switch bodies," Mama says dreamily.

The first time I remember her saying this was years before we immigrated. We were in Daegu at my grandparents' house and restaurant where she grew up. It's a place I associate with long, hot summers and Lunar New Year holidays, with warmth, nurturing, and so much good food.

"If you switched bodies, you would be the boy who is smart and hardworking. It wouldn't matter that you are fat. It doesn't matter if *boys* are fat."

As we get older and move to America, I excel in school and Didi struggles academically, so her reasoning deepens. "If only you could switch. Didi could be the girl. A girl can be skinny and pretty and it wouldn't matter that she doesn't do well in school."

Mama repeats this dream often, wearing her signature dimpled smile at work at our takeout restaurant or at home late at night, while she looks at the two of us with starry eyes.

When I sat on Baba's lap at five years old, he whispered to me, "With your white skin and your tall height, Daughter, you will be so beautiful when you grow up." He grinned, "You'll lose your baby fat and become even prettier than your mother. I know it."

From both Mama and Baba, the message is consistent. Nothing I accomplish matters unless I am beautiful too.

"Don't you care about her?" he shouts at beautiful Mama, like she is withholding secrets from me. "Must I do everything?"

Baba is angry with Mama every day. He yells at Mama for wearing too much makeup, or not enough make-up. She is his verbal punching bag.

Sometimes, Baba will watch the restaurant on Sundays during the lull between lunch and dinner so Mama and I can go shopping at discount stores to score designer clothes. I'm happy to show off my new outfits at school, but when Mama wears hers, she receives Baba's fury.

"Why are you wearing those jeans? They're too tight and make you look like a college student," he scolds and forbids her from ever wearing jeans ever again. All jeans. Mama obeys, as she always does. Her closet slowly withers into matronly pieces of black and brown.

Though Baba finds endless things to yell at Mama about, when he explodes at her about me, I become numb.

After living years under the Arizona sun, my naturally light complexion is no longer white, no longer something for Baba to brag about. The baby fat does not melt off like he promised. Instead, I steadily gain more weight every year. My middle school cafeteria lunches of French bread pizza, fries, and milkshakes add to my bulk. And as I go through puberty, I am intensely awkward with acne threatening to take over my face. Baba is irate.

This is a failure when failure is not an option.

Baba's daughter is supposed to be effortlessly beautiful, like Mama, but I'm far from it. In my preteens and teens, he constantly drags me in front of Mama for the way I look.

"Why aren't you teaching her?" he screams. Mama and I choke

back tears. "You're not teaching her to take care of her skin, to take care of herself!"

But Mama *is* an effortless beauty, born with an hourglass figure. She was regularly mistaken for a model in her twenties. She's never dieted a day in her life. She doesn't have to do anything to be beautiful.

"In college, I couldn't try on clothes when I went shopping with my girlfriends," she says to me when it's just the two of us trying on clothes. Her eyes dance with happy memories. "Everything looked so good and I didn't have the money to buy it all."

Her beauty does not fade with age. She is in her forties when a young male customer hits on her. Didi and I are sitting at the corner of the restaurant. The customer waits his turn in line to get up to the cash register and declares to my mother in a creepy, husky voice, "I want you to be the mother of my children."

"Wah?" Mama and the Korean ajumma who works with her behind the counter cackle like witches. "I have two kids already!" she says in her heavily accented English, pushing up her gold wireframe glasses with one hand and holding up two slender fingers with the other.

No, Mama cannot help me. So, she doesn't say much when Baba rages. Mama never says much during Baba's tantrums, no matter the cause. She's learned it only makes them last longer and makes them worse. We silently bear Baba's storms until they blow over.

"Must I do everything myself?" shouts Baba, his words razor-sharp. To him, my body is an international crisis. Baba calls his sisters in Atlanta, in Taiwan, and goodness knows who else in Korea, Los Angeles, and across the country for advice on how to make me smaller.

When he returns from his latest trip to Los Angeles—the closest place to Asia that is within driving distance—I am summoned to the living room. Baba hands me a round, pink container, smaller than the palm of my hand. He is stern and not really looking at me. He is disgruntled that I've added another problem to his plate.

"Put this on every day," Baba barks. "It's made from genuine crushed pearls and it will lighten your skin."

I twist open the tiny plastic container to find a thick white paste.

It is chalky and streaky and smells sickly sweet of artificial roses. Instinctively, I wrinkle my nose and recoil.

"It's very expensive!" he adds.

When Baba notices that my face has broken out in pimples, he takes it as a personal offense. "Girls must take care of themselves." His face, marred with acne scars, is angry and disgusted. "Your face can't look like mine. You're a girl!"

"Go, now," he says, handing me a twenty-dollar bill from his worn, black leather wallet. "Go to Walgreens and buy a face brush and a new face soap."

Always doing as I am told, I step into the hot desert night and walk from Oriental Express across the parking lot to the drug store. I enter the familiar, bright space and savor the welcoming chill of the cool air conditioning all over my skin. Aisle by aisle in the beauty section, I search. I look all over, but I have no idea what I am looking for at all. I've never heard of a face brush. Finally, I ask for help from a red-vested employee who points me to a small clear plastic cup on a counter holding five small, round brushes.

I show Baba my purchases back at the restaurant. He grunts his satisfaction. "Twice a day, you must scrub your face," he commands.

My complexion does not improve. Frustrated, Baba takes me across town to our doctor, a short, middle-aged Chinese American man from Michigan who speaks poor Mandarin. He is the only Chinese-speaking doctor my dad can find in Phoenix at the time. The doctor doesn't say much when he examines my face. Looking back, my pimples were moderate at worst, barely noticeable in photos. He prescribes a behind-the-counter topical gel that is supposed to help, but I don't honestly know if it makes any difference at all.

"Girls are supposed to love to be beautiful!" Baba is beyond exasperated that he can't change me. He can't make me prioritize my appearance. For me, it isn't an act of rebellion. I simply don't know how to transform myself into the willowy beauty he thinks I should be.

From an early age, my body has been assessed for its aesthetic appeal.

"Beautiful Jade has perfect legs," said a female teacher to Baba at our Chinatown School. I hadn't started school yet and never thought about legs at all. I didn't know they were something that held beauty. They had simply been limbs that allowed me to walk, jump, and climb.

"No one has eyes bigger than you," a small-eyed uncle in Taiwan said to me, and I find myself looking at them in the mirror the next chance I get. *No*, I think. *They're not that big.*

In Korea, my skin was very fair, and that was a good thing according to many grown-ups. *So, so white.* They congratulated my parents as if they achieved some great feat.

My dimples, the right one deeper than the left, also drew compliments.

"If only she weren't fat," they said in unison.

By my early teens, a recurring fixation takes hold in the corners of my mind, spreading inward and downward: an image of taking a knife to my body to trim off the fat. Scarlet blood blooms artfully, soaking through bleached white cloths. I want to pull a Radio-Flyer wagon of fat onto stage like skinny Oprah in 1988. A victory. But I am too afraid to act on it. It is merely a fantasy. I wish I could afford expensive weight loss surgeries, ones that would suck all the fat out of me or cut my stomach down to a size appropriate for an Asian girl.

My parents pay for gym memberships and drive me to aerobics and yoga classes. The beefy trainers are irritated that they have to work with a kid. At night, Baba orders me to do jumping jacks in the living room while the rest of the family watches television, eating cut fruit. A Costco treadmill appears in our home soon after, along with cases of Slim Fast. Baba brings me a printed black-and-white copy of the cabbage soup diet. I don't know where he got it, but it's intended for people preparing for heart surgery. The recipe calls for an assortment of canned vegetables and has a tomato base. I am allowed to eat only the cabbage soup for seven days.

When the cabbage soup fails, there is the caveman diet and sometimes straight starvation. I try it all, each time hoping that this latest diet will bring the transformation that will make me worthy.

As a teenager, desperate for romance and popularity, I want more than anything to be thin and beautiful too. I believe being thin will solve everything. When I become depressed, the worthless feeling saturates every inch of me. I dare not eat. I don't deserve food, not while I am so fat.

Baba eagerly agrees to sign me up for Weight Watchers and later, a predatory local weight loss center. After taking Baba's money, the two consultants there—middle-aged women who lost a bunch of weight themselves—take turns berating me, a high schooler, for things like eating corn. In their small office, they keep a can of Slim-Fast in their drawer. "You don't drink this stuff, do you?" they interrogate. "This stuff is poison! Just poison."

No matter the cost, whatever I suggest for weight loss, Baba is on board. All of us hope each time that this is the one that will take, but it never does. My weight hardly even yo-yo's. Each failure is a grave mark on my character, of my lack of willpower. The guilt from the money my parents spend on me is crushing. Some days, I lie in bed crying and hating myself.

"I know it's hard," Baba says in a soft, soothing voice. "I wish you looked like your mother, but you don't. You take after me. You can't give up, Beautiful Jade. You must keep trying. I believe in you."

I sob harder.

"I'm a man, so I know," he adds. "A woman has to be beautiful to be respected in this society. A woman has to be beautiful to be wanted. There is no other way. It's not fair, but that's the way it is. Don't give up. Jia Yo."

While the tactical methods prove futile, Baba deploys another—shame. We are peacefully watching television on a rare afternoon off work. Suddenly he reaches over and pinches my belly fat.

"Ige moya?" he teases in Korean chuckling hard. What is this?

Tears flood my vision instantly, and I turn away, trying to keep my stomach away from him.

"What? You're crying?" He says this whenever when he notices my tears. "You're too sensitive." He shakes his head in disbelief. "You can't be this sensitive."

When Didi and I were younger, Baba and Mama would check on us while we slept—especially on nights they worked at Second Aunt's or Uncle Johnny's restaurants and left us home alone. I would pretend to be sound asleep most nights, soaking up the love that radiated from the doorway.

My parents still do this from time to time, throughout high school, but Baba gives me a new nickname. "Good night, Snow White," he says lovingly.

I sit up, blushing but suspicious.

"You know why I call you Snow White? You're so big that your bed looks so small," he snorts, closing the door. I hear him laughing all the way down the hall.

CHAPTER 19: Worry Wart

HIGH SCHOOL – PHOENIX, ARIZONA

I don't have the words to describe what's happening to me. By high school, I am too afraid to eat. I skip meals until I am ravaged with hunger, then I eat and eat and eat, trying to fill the black hole inside. Afterward, I hate myself. The cycle continues. I become so depressed that brushing my teeth feels impossible, let alone taking a shower. I procrastinate everything. Even going to the bathroom seems like a summit up Mount Everest. If I do manage to crawl in there, I am stuck on the toilet, immobilized for over an hour. Too nervous to pee. A death grip of indecisiveness cages me at every moment, at every decision I must make throughout the day. Getting dressed in the morning is paralyzing. I imagine a grave significance and symbolism behind each article of clothing. If I pick the red sweater, it means I'm in love. If I wear the blue shirt, it'll mean I'm rejecting everyone. I spin and spin. I am too afraid to choose.

After a long day at the restaurant, Baba, Didi, and I sit down on the floor at a large, low table in front of the television in the messy living room to eat dinner. Mama is still in the kitchen rummaging around when I knock over my glass of water in my haze. It is not the first time. After days without sleep, my movements have been noticeably slow and clumsy.

"Stop this!" Baba yells. "Don't you see what you're doing to me?"

Baba droops his eyes and paints a false, exaggerated frown on his lips. He swings his arms around in limp movements, knocking over his glass in mockery. "How would you feel if I acted like you? Why are you acting this way?"

I can't answer him. I don't know why.

"Why can't you snap out of this?"

I don't know either. I want so badly to escape the sad, sloth-like haze but I cannot. I hate myself for it.

When Baba is in a softer mood, he tries to comfort me. I'm in my dark bedroom, catatonic, when he says, "You are the pillar of this family. You must get back to being yourself."

I wish I could disappear—a falling pillar giving way to the wreckage. I want to die, but thinking of possible ways to take my own life makes me afraid. I hate myself for my weakness, for not having the courage to act.

Weeks pass. My eyes refuse to rest and my mind boils with worry about exams, projects, and restaurant stresses. Conflicts with classmates that exist only in my imagination haunt me. Michelle and I, though still amicable acquaintances, grew apart years ago after we were assigned to different cohorts in a middle school of a thousand students. I made other friends, but high school social structure is cutthroat. I never know where I stand. I fixate on conversations, replaying them a million times in my mind, feeling ashamed about my imagined mistakes.

Meanwhile, Baba loves to go shopping and assigns me countless mail-in rebates to complete. They are for innocuous items like highlighters and pens that Baba doesn't need. If I don't submit them in time and miss the window to recoup what Baba terms "free money" from the sales ploys, the guilt adds weight to my already heavily laden shoulders. The responsibility of saving my parents' hard-earned dollars selling Kung Pao Chicken is on me. I can't manage. I try to stay on top of them, but it feels futile. Each a ticket of my failure. I vow to get on top of them. I buy a thick binder at Walgreens and painstakingly fill out the rebate forms and receipts I photocopy at the public library on coin-operated machines, but it's just too much. I can't keep up with Baba's impulse buys. The binder is bursting, and so am I. The million little failures pierce me awake each night.

"Why can't you sleep, Beautiful Jade?" asks Baba, when I come to my parents' room, tearful and tormented late at night, night after night. "Why can't you relax?"

"Baba, do I have to do those rebates?" I plead, guilty and desperate. "There are so many."

"Take it one by one, Daughter," he coaxes. "Mei Ban Fa. There is no other way. No one else can do this but you."

In a half-conscious nightmare, there are three parrots in our restaurant. Their once brilliant feathers are dull and patchy, their eyes melancholy. They have no voice and cannot fly. They remain on their perch, day after day. I am awake but I am not. I want to wake, but my limbs don't move. I am trapped.

Fall of my junior year, I can't stop smiling. I excel at everything. I am adored. I sign up for drama, creative writing, art club, student ambassadors, and speech and debate. Everything and more. I can do it all on top of my full load of Advanced Placement courses.

I am the happiest girl in the world. I have my driver's license. Out of necessity, more than anything, Baba had a friend teach me to drive when I was fifteen so he wouldn't have to pick me up after my activities at school. Now, I have freedom, and he has one less bother to resent.

I speed down wide-open desert roads with the windows down, blasting Alanis Morrisette in Mama's emerald-green Dodge Intrepid.

My long black hair dances in the warm, citrus breeze. I am immersed in the breathtaking sunset—the orange, violet, crimson, and rose of unimaginable brilliance, I count each as a celestial embrace. The world is mine for the taking. I can't believe how lucky I am.

Lying in bed, I pop up periodically to jot down ideas only to find barely legible gibberish in the morning. I don't know what tips me over to the uncontrollable crashing feeling, like the delirious drop on a rollercoaster.

The exhilaration trickles through every pore like dappled light. I am too blissed out to sleep. My thoughts do not slow down. I karaoke loudly to the Beatles, "I WANT TO HOLD YOUR HAND! I WANT TO HOLD YOUR HAND!"

Didi looks at me in alarm, but he says, "You are like a real pop star."

I feel like one too, like a million-billion dollars. I sing so loud, a neighbor yells over the cinder-block fence to ask what we're doing.

Later in the night, I flip through magazines on my bedroom floor, swimming in dreams. I will be the first Asian American, plus-sized model. I will act in movies, and have hit records, and everyone will know who I am. The world is spinning in my head.

A few more weeks without sleep and I believe that I am holy.

The name "Michelle," derived from Michael, means "one who is like God." *I read that on a mug at a gas station, so it must be true.* The universe is sending me secret messages. It's later than two in the morning and I'm still awake dreaming when the radio DJ says, "And this song goes out to Michelle . . ." I lose my mind. My arm hairs tingle. *I LOVE THIS SONG!*

Every television show and movie contains a secret message for me to decipher. I secretly run the world, or, more accurately, the world works in accordance with my choices and movements. I am Truman in the movie *The Truman Show.* I believe people have been watching and filming me all my life and I am not supposed to find out. Everyone is trying to set me up. Every boy is in love with me.

Mania. I don't know its name or what it is, but I am living it. A parallel universe where nothing is what it seems. I no longer have any control over my brain, my thoughts, or feelings. Everyone I love looks at me with confusion and worry—or worse, anger. Surprise and fear registers on the faces of acquaintances and strangers. When I feel like this, I can grab shards of glass bare-handed. I can jump off bridges and fly. I can dive into waves because I can breathe underwater. I set the world afire because I am god.

Inevitably, my superhuman powers smash into a wreckage of shrapnel and severed limbs. When the test dates or the theater performances approach, the mania pops into despair. I am buried in shame. *How am I supposed to study for all the finals at once? How am I supposed to memorize all these lines? People are counting on me. Why did I think I could do all of this when I am worthless? How could I have been so stupid and arrogant?*

I am a failure. I can't show my face. I wish I could die.

The spiraling, negative thoughts choke me for weeks until report cards come out and the performances come and go. Despite the dead certainty of failure, straight A's somehow greet me like old friends. The disaster of a performance seems like no big deal. I am worried sick that I had messed up, but my friends and their families tell me my performance was amazing. I can't tell if they're lying. I don't *think* they would lie.

I can breathe again. I survive.

No more of this cycle, I tell myself. I won't do this again. I swear to myself that I will be vigilant, that I will catch myself. But as hard as I try, I never see it coming. I am not in control.

CHAPTER 20: Psycho

JUNIOR YEAR IN HIGH SCHOOL – PHOENIX, ARIZONA

"Mama, wo hai pa." Mama, I'm scared.

I am so scared, I can't sleep. It feels like vultures of guilt, worthlessness, and worry are circling me, pecking incessantly. I can't chase them away. No matter how much I try, I can't snap out of it. I stumble to my parents' room in the middle of the night, trying to escape my dark thoughts. Crying, I sneak into their warm bed next to my Mama and whisper, "Wo hai pa."

My mom welcomes me into her warm embrace. When did I start to do this? The earliest I remember is sixth grade. I must have never detached from the safety of co-sleeping. Fear and anxiety driving me back to my mother's side time and again.

I am convinced I am a complete fraud, undeserving of all the good grades and awards. I am the worst person alive, utterly undeserving of love and affection. It is a matter of time before I am found out.

Mama's soothing presence helps a little, but the racing thoughts, worries, and fears never leave me. My nightmares seep into consciousness as hallucinations until I don't know what is real and what is imagined. I have failed all of my exams and am expelled. My parents are arrested and imprisoned. The restaurant is shut down.

Nothing makes sense. My head spins like I'm at a theme park getting on and off of the most thrilling rides as I walk upright down unremarkable hallways.

I am convinced that the school is holding a secret vote. I am the subject of a secret reality TV show or movie. Everyone has been watching me. Now, the producers are looking for a love interest for me for the grand finale.

My friend and crush David is in Spain and out of the running. I am thrilled and anxious for the unveiling so life can get back to normal and I can rest. I can't wait for the torture to end. I don't want to be lonely anymore, to be kept in the dark. I want more than anything to be let in on the secret that has been orchestrated around me for months, for years, perhaps for all of my life. I want the secret stage lights to turn on and dispel my misery. I'm ready for the big reveal of the happiness that was meant to be mine all along. I imagine glittering confetti and balloons raining from the vast blue skies.

I wait and wait. Class after class ends. I become increasingly impatient and agitated. *What are they waiting for? Can't they see I figured this all out already?* The aching hole in my stomach stretches wider and wider. I am hungry for those imagined cheers, for that confetti to fill me back up. I *need* this. I *need* everyone to be happy for me. I want to be wrapped up in hugs. I want to see my teachers' and classmates' faces running with mascara-laden tears of joy, each declaring how much they love me.

But it doesn't happen.

Why isn't it happening? What is taking so long?

Maybe they couldn't figure out who to pair me up with to conclude this movie of my life. Maybe they couldn't agree. Maybe they're waiting for me to overcome my fears and make a grand gesture. Is this another test? The most difficult one yet?

In the middle of AP English, I shout the name of my crush and break down into sobs. He isn't in this class, thank goodness. My shocked English teacher sends for someone to escort me directly to the school counselor's office.

I don't remember the rest of the day. My worst episodes leave gray, fuzzy gaps in my otherwise excellent memory. I don't know what the counselor and I talk about, but I return to see her several more times.

She is a stern woman in her fifties with graying hair cut into a shoulder-length bob that complements her wardrobe of long skirts and patterned scarves worn despite the Arizona heat. She has a snarky sense of humor, betraying her honesty, which I like. Her office is slightly larger than a cubicle, cluttered but not too cluttered. Having a safe adult to confide in is life-changing, at least at first. I am so excited by the potential of what she can be for me. The counselor laughs when I mix up my words from lack of sleep. It feels good just to talk to someone. I keep my appointments with her a secret from my family.

My parents reinforce that we as ethnic-Chinese children are different from other American children. Outsiders wouldn't understand, and we should never reveal how our family works. So, in our sessions, I don't talk much about my family beyond the pressure I feel to get good grades. I talk about boy troubles, feeling lonely, depressed, and not being able to sleep.

I have had three appointments with her and have looked forward to each session. But when I tell her that I confided in two teachers about my struggles because they noticed I was not myself and asked me what was wrong, she reacts unexpectedly.

"You talked to them?" she says to me with her brow furrowed in disappointment, her tone suddenly flippant. "You know what your problem is, Michelle? You're telling too many people about your problems. You need to learn to keep things to yourself."

I am stunned.

Is she right?

I feel so stupid.

I feel betrayed.

Like my parents, it turns out she believes I am bringing my problems onto myself.

I never go back to her again. She believes I'm only embarrassing myself.

Why am I so "dramatic?" Why do I go "crazy" and believe all that nonsense?

Why am I so miserable I can't breathe?

I hate myself. I hate being this way.

I'm so ashamed.

Why can't I just snap out of it like Baba demands a thousand times?

I awake with so much energy and conviction, it is vibrating off of my body. I'd seen "Spirit Day" marked on a printed calendar distributed by the school, and I've been ready for weeks. I dress confidently in a school t-shirt and jeans. I then strut into my bathroom down the soft-carpeted hall and dig around the drawer for my brown eyeliner. I line my eyes into the most dramatic cat-eyes possible. Then, from my brows, I draw lines down both sides on the bridge of my nose. I fill in the triangular tip of my nose, then I add whiskers. I draw a line down between my nostrils, in the natural valley. At the corners of my mouth, I draw curved up lines. I step back and admire my work.

My face has transformed into that of a mountain lion, our school mascot. I can't wait to get to school and show it off. I walk onto our sprawling high school campus. It was newly constructed the year before I enrolled, so everything is sparkling new. As I walk into the crowd of students, I realize no one else is dressed up but me. I scan the crowd for anything unusual, but everyone looks the same as always. Only I stand out. Everyone stares at me, alarmed, and then they snicker and whisper as they pass me. I wait for the announcement of an assembly or other festivities that does not come. Spirit Day was moved unbeknownst to me, or I have the date wrong, but I am sure it is today. It has to be. My dramatic makeup continues to startle people, but I am so pleased and confident, it never occurs to me to wash it off.

"Psycho," a boy barks at me as he passes in the hall. The ugly word is loud enough to hang in the air above all the gossip, chatter, and the shuffling of a hundred pairs of feet.

The name burns.

I fear the truth of it, the destructive wildfire the label contains. Is it my fate?

"Baba, I think I need to see a mental doctor," I interrupt my father who is in the living room, watching a Chinese drama with Mama. I have to ask before this courage that I've worked months to muster dissipates.

I can barely hold my eyes open. Every part of my body feels so heavy, but I can't sleep. I haven't slept in weeks. I don't know what to do. I'm so ashamed that something is so deeply wrong with me.

Baba's expression darkens. He turns off the television. I brace for an explosion, but he, too, is quietly desperate. The fear in his response mirrors my own uncertainty. His reaction is more chilling than anger.

"We can't, Daughter," he shakes his head and cradles my face with his big, warm hands. "If you see a mental doctor, it will be on your permanent record. What college will accept you then, no matter how good your grades are? If word gets out, who will marry you? Your life will be over."

I am shocked. Is this true? Would seeking help spell my doom?

I am only sixteen years old. My parents tell me my future is riding on keeping my condition a secret, so I believe them. I inherit the worries of my parents, their distrust of "the system." They teach me to fear the world. A mental illness is the ultimate, unforgivable shame. It is better to not acknowledge it.

Let's hope it goes away by itself.

You'll grow out of it.

Months pass, and my condition does not improve. My parents, despite their denial, are worried. I am still clumsy and sloth-like in my reaction to everything around me. Other times, jumpy and fragile. My confidence is shot. I panic at making the simplest decision. I am immobilized in any situation with any stress or tension. I can't feel anything. I can't process anything. I stop smiling and laughing. I mope, trying to remain hidden. The most pitiful sound that escapes me is the one I make to mimic laughter, to seem normal, when nothing is funny anymore.

Baba simply can't understand why I can't snap out of my haze. He wants his happy, capable daughter back. Baba wants to make me smile again.

One night, I'm in my room when I hear the garage door open. There is kerfuffle and shuffling.

"Don't come out yet, Beautiful Jade!" I hear Baba call out. A moment later, he adds, "Okay, Daughter. Come out and see."

I walk into the living room disheveled and groggy. There is a huge white Styrofoam cooler between the couch and the television, so long it reminds me of a coffin.

"Open it," Baba says, eyes gleaming. I am afraid of what could be in there. Baba's expectation already weighs heavily. I don't want to disappoint.

My weighty, slow arms lift the lid. I nearly scream.

Inside scuffle about a dozen turtles of different kinds, mostly red-eared, all the size of a horseshoe or larger. Startled, I drop the lid. Blood drain from my face. More numbness fills me—*I can't handle this. I can't handle them.*

"Pet turtles, Beautiful Jade," Baba beams, proud of his idea to bring me happiness. "Your favorite animal."

The pit in my stomach expands. The weight in my chest drags me down even deeper. *I need fewer responsibilities, not more.* I shrink, shrink, shrink. I can't handle this. I can't handle twelve more lives when I don't even want my own.

I can't take care of those turtles. They join Chocolate in the growing tally of innocent lives that suffer after crossing our threshold. They merge into the massive cloud of self-hatred hovering over my bed, spiraling out of control in my conscience along with my exams, college applications, work, my parents' insurance, mutual funds, phone bills, and taxes. I can never rest. I am never at peace.

When I don't get better, when I still mope around and stumble through my days like a zombie, Baba tries something different. After school, Baba tells me to get in his truck, a large silver Dodge Ram.

I climb in, not knowing where we are going. I am nervous and excited at the same time. Baba drives solemnly for eight hours across the familiar desert highway to Los Angeles. When the roads are empty, the drive feels soothing, but when we get into the metropolis, Baba's sudden lane changes and furious speed make me afraid.

"I found a doctor for you to talk to. He's the younger brother of an old classmate of mine from Korea," Baba reveals. "We can trust him. He will keep it off the record."

I am desperate for someone to tell me what is wrong with me. I want to be fixed. *After years of suffering, could this be the answer?* I tingle with fear and anticipation.

The next day, I accompany Baba on errands in the sprawling city. At close to five o'clock, we pull up to a single-story, red-brick office building in a nearly empty parking lot. Baba and I wait in the unremarkable lobby until the clinic closes so we can guarantee our appointment is "off the record."

In Phoenix, I am often the only Asian person in class. My parents enrolled Didi and me at Sunday Chinese school not only for language learning but so we could have Asian peers. I am grateful to my parents for doing this. I form important friendships with Jennifer, Sam, Joan— all of us with both Americanized names and Mandarin ones we use in class. Nevertheless, it has been a long time since I've seen a young Asian man as handsome as this doctor in person. He can't have been long out of medical school. His complexion is smooth and with his shiny, full hair and white coat, he looks like a doctor in a K-drama. It feels like time slows, and I can almost hear a lovey-dovey soundtrack.

Inside the clean and neat exam room, Baba and the doctor intro-duce themselves in our Shandong Mandarin, and then I am introduced. I shake the doctor's hand, which feels silky soft. Baba then leaves the room.

"It's okay. You can talk to me. Tell me what's been happening. Tell me what's going on," he says in American English with a kind smile as soon as the door closes, like he has all the time in the world for me.

Is it my destiny to be alone with him now? I wrap my arms around myself. The cute doctor's undivided attention is disorientating. The excitement of the trip and change in environment speeds up my thinking. I had been in a haze just hours ago when Baba had me get in the truck. Now, I feel very alive and alert. I smile, feeling like I can't stop. My head swims.

"I can't sleep. I have been depressed for a long time. I go so long without sleep that I've believed movie plots are about my life," I admit, embarrassed-laughing to mask my discomfort. "It doesn't make sense at all, but if a movie has the name 'Michelle' in it, I'll think it's about me. I'll listen to the radio at night and think the DJ is talking directly to me. I scare myself."

We talk for a long time.

"Do you use drugs?" he asks.

"No," I laugh. The idea is ridiculous. I have never even touched alcohol or a cigarette.

"Anything else I should know?" He repeats this question a few times until he is satisfied with my response.

I hold my breath when we finish talking. I am under the doctor's swoony spell and ready to learn what is wrong with me, but he guides me out the door and ushers in Baba in Mandarin.

I wait alone in the dim, deserted hallway for my verdict, ready to accept the worst news. When Baba reappears, he does not meet my eyes. He frowns mutely in thought as we walk out of the building and climb back into the truck.

When we are back on the road to Phoenix, I can't wait anymore. I ask, "So? What did the doctor say? What's wrong with me?"

"NOTHING is wrong with you," Baba roars, turning to focus his eyes on the horizon far away. "You have an overactive imagination.

You just need to get some sleep."

Just get some sleep.

Something I have been trying and failing to do for years.

If I could just do that, we wouldn't be here.

I want to hurl myself out of the truck.

If there is nothing medically wrong with me, then I am the one failing.

How am I going to survive being this failure, when failure has never been an option?

CHAPTER 21: Anytown, U.S.A.

AGE 16 — PRESCOTT, ARIZONA

"I'm such a coward." My cries choke into sobs.

"What's going on? You can tell me," says Jackie, my blonde, curly-haired camp counselor at Anytown, USA.

We are standing in front of the grainy mirror in a rustic bathroom located in the Prescott pine forest.

"I want to kill myself." I utter the words aloud for the first time in my life. "But I'm too afraid to even try it. I'm such a coward."

I often fantasize about ending my life, but each method I imagine sounds too painful, frightening, and out of reach. I am too weak to follow through, and I hate myself for it.

"Listen to me," says Jackie, bracing my face in her hands to make sure we are eye to eye. "Look at me. You are not a coward. It takes courage not to kill yourself. You are brave."

I don't believe her, not for an instant. What she says does not make sense to me. I continue sobbing, hating myself, and wishing for the courage to end it all.

Anytown is a leadership camp I attend somewhat by accident. I find out about it from my high school's morning announcements. My ears perk at every mention of the word "scholarship." I apply for every one for which I am remotely qualified, ever since that eighth-grade promise to myself to do everything I can to earn my way through college without being reliant on Baba.

I have never been allowed at a sleepover, let alone a sleepaway camp, and I am not exactly clear about what Anytown is going to be like. Honestly, it doesn't matter to me. It would beat working at the restaurant or sitting at home. And it is a scholarship, it would look good on my college applications, so Baba can't say no.

Anytown's organizational mission is to "educate, liberate, and empower youth participants to become community leaders." The emphasis is on opening up young minds and educating against "racism, sexism, homophobia, classism, and other injustices" that affect our lives.

I apply for the program and am awarded the scholarship. Then, I all but forget about it for months in the busyness of life until summer, when it is time to attend. I remind Baba when we're sitting at the restaurant, at our usual corner table.

"You'll be away from home for a week?" Baba also has forgotten and is unhappy. "How do I know what you'll be doing? Why must you spend nights away?"

"Baba, you already said yes," I insist. "We've already committed. It's a scholarship from school."

His frown does not disappear. "How do I know what you will be doing? What is the point of this?"

"It's a leadership program that will help me get into college and get more scholarships," I say. He does not like this idea one bit, but as I suspected, he does not have good enough reasons to stop me from going.

I'm depressed when I prepare for the trip. The "I can't taste anything, nothing is funny, I can't focus, I'm worthless" kind of depressed. I go through the motions and pack a bag, hoping for the best. I hope everyone won't hate me at Anytown. I hope I won't embarrass myself.

Baba makes his displeasure known with every curt word and movement, but he still drives me to the meeting point. I step onto the school bus that transports us about two hours north. The dry desert scenery slowly changes as we climb in elevation and arrive into the cooler woods, away from my sheltered existence.

At Anytown, teens from all over the greater-Phoenix area are thrown together. I meet youth from South Phoenix, which is a new experience. There are more Black Americans than I'd ever seen in one place because even in Atlanta, we had lived in a predominantly white neighborhood. About half of our group is Black. After we settle in, we are asked to sit in a circle in the woods. The counselors lead ice-breaker games and cheesy camp songs that are completely new to me.

The all-girls cabin I sleep in is just as diverse. One girl is very pregnant and asks to leave early once she realizes she can't climb the hill to the cabin very easily nor would she be able to sleep well in the shabby bunk bed.

Anytown kicks off the week with promises that the camp is a safe space. Everything shared in the group is considered confidential. As the walls come down, I share some experiences with racism of my own, like when a young boy called our house and threatened, "I am going to bomb your house like Hiroshima. I know where you live!" before proceeding to read our address aloud, presumably from the White Pages.

"Why are you doing this?" I asked him. He hung up without answering.

Each time I answer these semi-regular calls—each time I face the "ching-chong" chants and "open your eyes" taunts at school, or when a customer treats us as if we are less than human, making dog meat jokes to our faces—each time is a sucker punch in the gut.

The hate knocks all of the air out of me, no matter how much I want to believe that it doesn't matter, that I should shake it off. Just as I am lulled into a sense of belonging, a racist act shocks me out of feeling at home and puts me in my place. Revealing these experiences at Anytown leaves me raw and open to sharing even more than I ever had before.

Group discussions, big and small, on all sorts of deep and uncomfortable topics dealing with race, gender, identity, and prejudice, take place throughout each day. There are many emotional outpourings ending in group hugs. We are physically and emotionally depleted after most days.

I do not sleep much. I rarely sleep well in new environments. A cabin full of strangers, on an unfamiliar bunk bed, after days full of emotional dialogues is not the most conducive to rest.

Cassandra, a Black girl from our cabin, is the first to break down. "There is a Taiwanese girl at my school. Her parents own a convenience store," she mumbles. "My friends and I jumped her. We hurt her so bad, we put her in the hospital with broken ribs." Cassandra taps her right fist into her left palm in quick succession as she speaks. It is as if she is reliving that horrible scene in her mind, unable to unsee or take back what happened.

The other girls pat her back. Cassandra can hardly speak between heaving sobs, "And I see Joan here… And she reminds me so much of the girl from school…And Joan is the sweetest person…" She breaks down into inconsolable, remorseful sobs.

Joan is indeed sweet and also very petite and Taiwanese. Joan and I have been going to Chinese school together on Sundays for years. She is one of only two people I know coming into camp.

I fight to keep the shock and horror from my face. Everyone hugs Cassandra, trying to comfort her. I do too. She and Joan embrace the longest, but I don't understand why she and her friends attacked the Taiwanese girl at their school. I don't understand why Joan being sweet is an eye-opening experience for Cassandra. It hasn't sunk in that Anytown might have provided the first opportunity for Cassandra to get to know someone like Joan, someone like me, and vice versa.

There are still so many moments when I feel like I don't understand at all. There is so much left unspoken.

I reflect on the violence in Los Angeles in 1992, when my grandparents in Korea called us, their voices trembling with worry as they watched images of Koreatown being burned down. "Are you safe?" they asked. "Make sure people know you're Chinese, not Korean," they advised naively, as if Americans could make a distinction between the two.

"Everything is fine," my parents answered. Los Angeles is far away. The riots do not concern us when Mama and Baba are dealing with running the restaurant in all their waking hours.

"Don't be afraid of me. I won't bite," Pookie says with a wide, friendly smile outside the Anytown cafeteria. "You don't need to run from me."

Pookie is perhaps the most muscular teenager I have ever met. His basketball jerseys reveal bulging arms covered entirely in tattoos. And, in the last days of the camp, he calls me out on the bias I don't know I am carrying.

I laugh, embarrassed. "I wasn't running," I say, but he did just catch me as I was trying to side-step him, I realize.

I smile sheepishly as he wraps me in a warm, kind bear hug. My eyes are opened. I had no idea I'd been avoiding him all week. After that day, I hug Pookie at every natural opportunity, of which there are many.

One evening midweek, a counselor asks me to follow him. He walks me toward the cafeteria and says, "Michelle, your dad's here and he wants to see you."

"What? What do you mean my dad's here?" There are still several camp days left. Baba is supposed to pick me up at the drop-off location in Phoenix at the end of the week. He isn't even supposed to know where this camp is located. Why is he here?

While the rest of the campers watch the talent show, I find my father on the cement top by the cafeteria entrance in his worn, nylon jacket with a worried expression.

"Are you okay?" he asks.

"Of course, I'm okay, Baba," I say. "Why are you here?"

He is silent for a beat.

"Come home with me now," Baba pleads.

How has he found this random spot in the woods? Baba has dragged Didi here too, who is kicking around the edge of the forest. He is far enough away that we can see him in the twilight, but he can't hear us.

"Come home," he repeats.

"What are you doing here?" I am exhausted, depleted, and depressed, but I do not want to go back yet. I want to finish.

"I was worried about you. I don't know what you are doing here. I had to see for myself," Baba has spiraled into paranoia again. There is so much he fears about American culture, so much he doesn't understand. I wonder if he imagined that my high school had sent me on a scholarship to a drugged-out orgy in the woods, and I'd come back knocked up, not knowing who impregnated me.

"No, I am not leaving, Baba," I stand my ground.

Baba can't drag me away. Not in front of the watchful eyes of all these counselors. A few of the more imposing ones appear against the wall of the building, standing straight and shoulder to shoulder. They look at Baba with stony eyes, but the same eyes are melted caramel when they turn to me.

"I wanted to make sure you're okay," Baba says. Reluctantly, he leaves, but the red flag he raised signals all of the staff. The counselors glimpse what my dad is like. I can't imagine what hell Baba had raised to gain access to this camp. If I wasn't before, now I am marked as at-risk. The staff is on alert.

All of the emotions, rawness, and lack of sleep culminate that night in the bathroom, when I confess to my counselor Jackie about wanting to end my life.

After crying for a long time with her standing with me, I allow four more shameful, tiny words to escape, "My dad hits us," and then sob even harder, the secret I've been holding finally released.

I am terrified that what Baba says will come true: that the police will be notified immediately, he and Mama will be taken to jail, and I'll lose everything. What would I do then?

"Michelle," says Jackie, who is very athletic, while making a fist. "That is not okay. It makes me so angry. And there is so much I would do, but I also know it's cultural…It's cultural, so I'm trying to understand that it's different."

My big confession, after building up for so many years, brings little relief. Jackie is saying the same thing Baba said, only in different words.

"We're Chinese. We're different. This is the way Chinese children are raised. For us, it is the way. It is not wrong for Chinese children to be beaten."

I don't know what I wanted to happen. I don't know what I needed Jackie to say, but I remain in a state of misery, confusion, and helplessness. I don't want Baba to go to jail, but I don't want to hurt anymore. Without Baba, I believe our family would not be able to survive, but at the same time, I live in constant fear around him, and it makes me want to die. I fear what state I'll find Baba in when I come home.

Despite the philosophy of the late nineties that allows rampant abuse to be overlooked systemically due to "cultural sensitivity," sharing my suicidal feelings and the pressures in my family with an unbiased adult helps me in a way that I don't fully appreciate at the time. I've let someone in. Something changes in my mind because someone else knows. I am no longer alone. The disobedience has begun.

On the last day of camp, several counselors reveal themselves to be police officers. It is a hidden lesson about how police officers are human beings who should not be feared. Jackie is one of them. I shiver and cannot look her in the eye. The fear seeps into my bones that police may come knocking on our door at some random night to arrest the monster that I love. One more worry added to the cyclone that keeps me up at night…but no one ever comes.

CHAPTER 22: *Unfilial*

AGE 17 – PHOENIX, ARIZONA

"Dofu nao, fan tong!" Baba is screaming at Mama after a long day at the restaurant. Tofu brains, useless rice pot. "Your entire family is classless trash." He is sitting on the living room floor, legs crossed, leaning his back against the couch. Baba points at Mama while insulting her, his face is red. Who even knows why he is angry. Why he is yelling at her. It's what he does.

Mama is in the adjoining kitchen with only the island serving as a barrier against Baba's terror raining on her. She cries silently while washing the dishes.

Normally, when Baba is yelling at Mama, Didi and I try to fade into the background or retreat to our corners far away whenever possible. But after Anytown, I feel different.

A fire is lit. I'm terrified, but the fire forces me to act.

"Don't speak to Mama like that!" I stare down Baba with all the gravity I can muster. "You should not be insulting her, especially in front of me and Didi."

A chilling silence befalls the room. I wonder if this will be the end of me. The end of all of us.

Didi and Mama do not move a muscle as their eyes dart between me and Baba.

"And don't insult her family," I charge like a bull with my words. "Her family is my family and Didi's too."

None of us ever challenge Baba like this. In Arizona, there is no one to tell him when he is wrong. He doesn't expect this from his darling daughter, whom he loves best and who loves him best.

After a moment to recover, he utters a guttural, "Are you happy now?" toward Mama.

"Your daughter is protecting you," he adds.

Then, to my surprise, he stops yelling. Grumbling, he quiets down. Our evening ends, and soon, everyone is in their beds.

For the first time, I realize I have power over Baba. He cares about what I think of him.

Nevertheless, I receive over a month of silent treatment for my battle cry. Starting the next morning, Baba pouts and stomps around, slamming doors. He yells at everyone but me. He huffs and puffs with tortured expressions. He makes eye contact to show his disgust and then quickly turns away—countless times a day—all psychological warfare, intended to convey my unworthiness and his wordless condemnation.

The quiet is refreshing, almost freeing, for a while, but the sensation does not last. Baba is determined to force me to suffer his power.

Mama is conscripted to plead with me. "You should not have spoken to Baba that way, Daughter," she speaks with a voice warm as sugared pear, tucking a strand of my hair behind my ear. "You know how he loves you best."

The irony is that the strength to stand up against my dad was not only born of Anytown, of being a product of my adopted American culture and education of independence. That power is stoked by Baba himself. I idolize his intelligence, energy, and confidence. While my mother has no interests to share, my father's insatiable passions include everything from music to motorcycles, art, and traveling.

I face the undeniability of who I am. When I'm depressed and anxious, I feel worthless. Like Mama, I cannot make decisions. I, too, cannot decide between chicken or fish. I panic and shriek at the slightest disturbance. I hide.

When I am manic, I feel like a superhero. Like Baba, I am all-powerful and all-knowing. I can do anything and everything. I'm proud beyond measure of all that I've achieved on my own. Anyone who challenges me is a fool.

Unchecked, I am Mama and I am Baba, but I don't want to be.

I would rather be Michelle and live in peace, in the balance in-between.

CHAPTER 23: Brother and Sister

AGE 17 – PHOENIX, ARIZONA

"Just don't make me angry and we won't have a problem," Baba rages back when Didi and I gently suggest anger management, after we learn of the concept on television.

Mama, Didi, and I are all miserable. So is our father. I feel trapped.

"If you tell anyone, they will call the police, and Mama and I will go to jail. Do you want that?" he screams.

"You'll be taken to live with strangers, and Mama and I would have to pay them for it," he spits. "Do you want that?"

I think about calling the police myself many times, when just thinking about it is an unspeakable betrayal. I come close to picking up a phone once. *How could anything be worse?*

Baba has me kneeling in front of him as he faces me sitting cross-legged. We are positioned strangely close to the television in the living room. I don't know why we are here, and I don't know remember what I had done to anger him.

"You need to show me more respect," Baba demands after a long tirade.

"Baba," I am tired and desperate to get through to him. "I already show you so much respect, but you never respect me."

Baba tosses his head back, roaring. His loud laugh, echoing off the high ceilings, startles me. "Me? Respect you?" he scoffs, as if I said the most ridiculous thing in the world. "You are the child and I am the father. This is not a two-way street. I'm not supposed to respect you."

He shakes his jeering face. "Me respect you…?"

Didi and I fight constantly. Mama blames us for Baba's tantrums. With the stress of school and restaurant work, and Baba's anger getting worse, life is becoming unbearable.

I shove open the door to Didi's room during an argument with such force that the door handle busts a hole in the thin drywall. Our suburban house is one of a million built quickly by developers in Phoenix. Things tend to fall apart easily, but this is a mistake I will pay for. Baba will not be lenient.

Just then, the garage door opens. I know I'm dead. As soon as Baba enters, Didi screams for him to come look at what I had done. I'm crying, making futile pleads of "I'm sorry," and "It was an accident." Baba does not hear me. His eyes flash into that of a beast's. He grabs hold of my head and rams it into the wall just above the hole, over and over.

"This is how you respect the house Yeh-Yeh bought us!"

I am genuinely sorry. I beg and beg.

Could foster care be worse than this?

In the midst of another one of Baba's rages, I walk out of the front door—a monumental act of defiance. Up until this point, neither Didi nor I (or Mama) ever try running away. I'm not sure why. We were too afraid to run, I guess.

Tears streaming down my face, I don't know where to go. I run as fast as I can, the rows of identical suburban houses and red rock landscaping blur past my peripheral vision.

Should I run to my friend's house to borrow their phone? Am I ready to expose our shame to the world? Am I ready to commit the ultimate betrayal to the parents who raised and love me? Am I ready to be alone?

I don't make it far. A few blocks away, I crumble onto the smooth sidewalk, heated by fierce rays of the Phoenix sun. I lie down flat, allowing the hot cement to soothe my skin from head to toe. It feels like a hug.

I cannot do it.

They are all I have.

Before long, Didi rides up on his bike and sits next to me. Didi, darker than ever, is no longer the skinny little boy with chicken legs. In middle school, he put on weight and muscle and sprung up in height. He is tall now, just a few inches behind my own five-foot-eight frame, but he still has his baby face.

Without words or movements, we silently acknowledge each other's pain. We are alone in this world, the only two people who can ever know what our life is.

The sun sets, gloriously orange as ever, as we walk home together, burying our secrets yet another time.

On my wedding day, over a decade later, Didi is dashing in his dark suit, lighting a sparkle in the eyes of my admiring friends. He is a strapping six feet in height; it has been years since Baba could dominate Didi physically.

When the love of my life makes a plan to propose, he calls Didi about it, not my parents. It is Didi, not Mama or Baba, who tears up when he first sees me in my wedding dress. It is Didi who tells me I look so beautiful.

"I looked up to my sister so much as a kid. She basically raised me," my not-so-little-anymore brother declares in a toast before our guests.

Hearing this, I am undone. There is no way I was even a decent sister, let alone a remotely qualified parent. A child myself, I had not been ready to parent. Three years older and flailing in my own issues, I never paid enough attention to Didi.

I was unaware of how much he was watching me, how much he needed me, or how much I needed him.

CHAPTER 24: Afloat

AGE 17 – PHOENIX, ARIZONA

"I missed you," I say to David as we give each other bear hugs.

"I missed you too," he says, grinning. There are sparkles in his deep, dark eyes with the longest lashes I've ever seen on anyone—so long they bother him when he wears sunglasses.

I grin back and nearly choke on his strong cologne.

I had been so excited to spend this evening with David, and it is better than I imagined. He has just returned from his semester abroad in Spain. He is taller, tanned, and his dark wavy hair is long, curlier.

We nibble on tater tots and sip cherry limeades from the Sonic Drive-Thru in the car while he shows off a thick stack of beautiful photographs from his adventure. Our months apart were spent exchanging delicious handwritten letters, but I'm so glad to have him back. He shows me countless snapshots of Spanish architecture, new friends, and a girl he made out with once. "We rolled around on the grass," he says, proud of himself.

I roll my eyes and laugh, incredulously. David is one of those people who mentions romantic encounters in other cities, but never with someone anyone at our school or in our circles could ever know.

After hours of catching up, David is driving me home when I spot something out of the corner of my eye.

"Look, there!" I point into the starry desert night at a quiet intersection on Pinnacle Peak Road. There is no one around. Nothing but cactus and the vast midnight sky. "See that street sign that's fallen? We should steal it!"

David is shaking with laughter, slouching over the steering wheel. He is scrawny despite his attempts to bulk up. "No way, *I'm* not getting it." His grin is pasted over his entire face. He looks like a teenage Paul Rudd to my enamored eyes.

I swing open the car door, sprint, and hop over the roadside barrier. Bending down to retrieve the yellow and black square caution sign, I'm surprised to find how heavy and bulky it is. I'm undeterred. My heartbeat is pounding in my ears. I seldom break rules, let alone laws. I don't know what has come over me that makes me want to do this, but when I'm with David, I am often emboldened. With him by my side, I feel I can do anything.

I pick up the sign and shuffle awkwardly toward the car. It feels much farther now, and I sidestep like a crab. David suddenly stops laughing long enough to scream, "POLICE!"

I see him sitting in the car. He has been shaking with laughter this entire time, but now he is beside himself, gasping for breath.

"Shut up!" I yell. "Quit joking around!"

"I'm serious!" David calls back, voice cracking from glee. "POLICE!" He points backward to the lit intersection.

Sure enough, there is a City of Phoenix police car stopped mere feet away.

What are the chances? This desert road in the Phoenix suburbs is dark and devoid of cars—except this patrol car that suddenly appeared as if by magic?

To return the sign, I would have to retrace my steps back to the barrier. I am closer to the car, so I make a run for it. Dropping the sign in the backseat, I jump in the passenger seat.

"Go, Go!" I chant.

David manages to drive his getaway Jetta at a tortoise speed. We're both laughing hysterically until we're both crying. The police either never notice us or decide to look the other way. I am grateful.

After his time in Spain, David also trades his relaxed t-shirts and cargo shorts for fitted button-ups and tight jeans, a decidedly euro-metropolitan aesthetic. In the Phoenix suburbs of the 1990s and early 2000s, when the preppie or grunge style rules the masses, David now very much stands out, but the smiles in his eyes and the ginger-tea warmth in his voice remains the same.

David and I do typical couple things together, like going to the movies and sharing fries. I can't believe it is real. He also insists on paying for everything when we go out. Because it is the 1990s, and I'm just a kid who doesn't know better, I hope that his insistence on paying means that he harbors romantic feelings for me. But to him, we are just friends. In dark movie theaters, my hand lingers next to his, wishing for him to move his hand a few inches to wrap mine in his. Almost as often, I attempt to conjure the courage to reach over, but I'm too afraid. I wonder before each movie starts if this will be the time he'll casually drape his arm over my shoulder, *Saved by the Bell* style. But no matter how many times we hang out just the two of us, it never happens. Instead, I try to be happy with the hyper-awareness of how close he is to me in moments like this, to absorb the gentle heat of his arm touching mine as we share an armrest.

During slow weekend shifts at the restaurant, David comes to keep me company. I supply him with unlimited free food. Like Michelle DeAngelo, chicken fried rice and sesame chicken are his favorites. With him there, working at the restaurant is so much fun, and I feel like the luckiest girl in the world.

At my house, David and I sing hours of karaoke together—duetting to "Save the Best for Last" sends my heart aflutter. Crooning "I Can't Help Falling in Love with You," he turns his head, looks into my eyes, and holds out his hand for me. I die.

I speculate and dissect everything that happens between David and me with my girlfriends for hours. What did that look mean? Why is he always just his normal, happy-go-lucky self the next day? Is it nothing more than friendship? My friends don't have any answers.

"Do you want to go to prom together...as friends?" David breaks into his usual charming smile.

"Oh? Wasn't there someone else you wanted to ask?" I respond as if I haven't been hoping for him to ask me for months, probably years.

"No...I wanted to ask you."

I don't believe him. He likes someone else. Still, I melt, relieved that he is merciful and shields me from the truth that there is any other.

Getting Baba's permission to let me go to prom will be the next mountain to climb. I take deep breaths, preparing myself to poke the bear. It will need to be a long campaign that has to begin immediately.

"We're just friends. It's not a big deal. Everyone goes," I plead. "It's not dangerous. It's a school event. I'm going with David and a big group of friends."

I had long gotten the sense that my parents like David, though they try their hardest not to emote around him. They don't know how to handle their teenage daughter spending so much time with a boy, but he's a sweet guy, and there's nothing not to like.

"What is prom? Why is it such a big deal?" Baba grunts his disapproval at my request. He resents me for putting another decision on his plate. He calls every friend and relative he can think of who'd raised a teenager in America to weigh in. "Should I let her go?"

Several excruciating days later, Baba answers, "Fine, you can go. But no spending the night anywhere. I want you home by midnight."

I can't believe my luck. I screech and embrace Baba, overjoyed to partake in this American rite of passage. I'm so thrilled to be normal for once. Baba looks mournful, as if he already regrets it.

Mama and I go to the mall on a Sunday, convincing Baba to cover the restaurant. I try on dresses at Macy's, but as a generous size 14, most Junior dresses don't fit me. In the Women's section, we decide on a flapper-inspired, long black dress with rows of fringe. My hair is done at a no-frills salon near our restaurant. I suspect it's the white stylist's first time working with Asian hair because she is as surprised as Mama and I are when all the curls she painstakingly irons fall right out into a messy mop as soon as she tries to coax them into an updo. My hair does not look good, but I'm too excited to complain. I don't usually wear makeup, but I apply some subtle eyeliner and lipstick.

David pulls up to my street in an old limo packed with three other couples. We split the cost to rent the car for the special night. This is the first dance I am attending with a date. I am too excited to think straight. I don't know what to expect, so I run into the street, up to the limo. But David walks me back to my house. I'm ashamed for him to see the inside of it, which is messy. I was not expecting anyone to come inside.

In the empty entranceway, David opens the clear plastic box— nestled within is a delicate white rose corsage accented with little pearl beads. I didn't know to expect this, that was how clueless I am about prom culture—what only happens in the movies and what happens in real life.

David ties the corsage on my wrist. I beam. This is the first time anyone has given me flowers. "Thank you so much. It's beautiful!"

When we come back to the limo, the other couples begin to get out of the car.

"Why are you getting out? Aren't we leaving?"

"Don't your parents want pictures?" one of the guys responds.

"Oh," I say. "My parents aren't home. They're at work."

The other couples shrug and get back in the limo.

They had lined up and posed at each of the houses before mine. I'm sure they don't mind having to skip it this time, but I'm still a little embarrassed that my parents aren't here to make a big fuss. No one is home to document this milestone. I am lucky to be allowed to go at all. My parents are rarely around to celebrate anything, let alone a school dance.

After the event, I try hard to pay David back for those junior prom tickets, my part of dinner, and the limo. We play fight, shoving bills at each other while waiting in the school auditorium. A classmate watches, rolling her eyes. Try as I might, he won't take my money.

When our formal prom photos themed "A Night to Remember" are ready, I can't wait to show them to Baba and Mama.

Mama looks with mild interest at David and me standing in front of the photo backdrop of a night sky with Disney-like stars, but Baba snaps his head the other way. "I don't like this," he says. "It looks like you two are getting married."

He doesn't look at me or the photos and instead glares at the Chinese soap opera on the satellite television. "It isn't right. You're only in high school."

I don't know then how afraid Baba is all the time. What he demonstrates as anger is fear. Baba is afraid of losing me, Mama, Didi, and everything else.

So I look at the photos that Mama and Baba refuse to and the cheesy souvenirs still fill me with joy as I relive the night. Even though there hadn't been a kiss, I hope this means my relationship with David is more than platonic. This hope, this feeling like a normal teenager with no other problems but worrying about whether my crush returns my affections, is an escape and keeps me afloat through dark times.

CHAPTER 25: Privileged

AGES 17 AND 18 – PHOENIX, ARIZONA

Ever since I was escorted to the counselor's office from the AP English class sobbing, the other students have given me a wide berth, but not Angela. She finds me afterward to check on me.

"What happened? Who hurt you, Mica?" she demands, using her nickname for me. "I'll beat their ass." She smashes her right fist into her left hand, face scrunched adorably. Angela is wearing her usual worn, oversized sweatshirt and jeans and ill-fitting thick glasses. She self-identifies as Blasian—Black and Asian—and took to me right away when we first met freshman year.

She has a tough girl reputation and is my only girlfriend who gets into fistfights on occasion. I would never want to be on the receiving end of her fury, and I am beyond moved by her protectiveness. I didn't know she would literally fight for me. I don't feel deserving of her protection, her outrage, or her affection.

Embarrassed, I say, "Oh, it was nothing. I was being stupid, but thank you."

"Okay, Mica, but if you need me, you let me know," she assures me. Angela is tough as nails on the outside, but she is tender and fragile underneath. She respects my space and doesn't push the matter further.

Angela's dad was serving in the military in the Philippines when he met and married her mom, though they are now long divorced. When I go to the mall with Angela, the gaze of strangers pricks my skin by extension. It is a challenge to be any person of color in the suburbs of Phoenix, but harder if you're Black, I learn. I am so flattered that Angela treats me like kin, as one of her own.

Angela, David, and I are in Speech and Debate together, but Angela is the star. She's been in it the longest and wins the most awards. Both Angela and David dream of becoming lawyers, and I think maybe I can be one too, especially since it is one of the two career choices available to me according to Baba. I default to lawyer because of my squeamishness around blood and organs. Already spread too thin across multiple extracurricular activities and too intimidated for debate competitions, I only dabble in a few speech tournaments. After a lifetime of being trained never to talk back, I clam up during most arguments, formal or otherwise.

Angela is the opposite. She shines in competition—whip-smart and sharp-tongued, she dominates round after round. Later, Angela is voted 'Most Likely to be President' by our senior class of over five hundred students, an endorsement of her power and tenacity. I am voted 'Most Likely to be the Next Bill Gates.' As a non-technical person, I take this as a great insult, that my classmates think of me as the nerdiest, least attractive kid in class. I have no doubt Angela can become president one day, if she chooses.

She and I talk on the phone and hang out at each other's homes. Our houses don't look immaculate like so many of our white class-mates' homes. There is clutter, there is neglect. Imperfection is every-where in our most intimate spaces. In each other's imperfect homes, we can be ourselves. When I tell Angela about my stresses, my depres-sion, my crushes, she cannot relate.

"Oh Mica, I wish I had your problems," she sighs with a faraway look in her eyes.

I am disappointed. Angela minimizes my struggles, saying hers are far bigger by comparison, but she won't tell me what hers are, so I can't understand.

My mind flashes back to the time in World History class when our sweet and conservative, recently immigrated Albanian classmate made a joking comment, "Because I am pure, okay?"

"What do you mean you're pure?" Angela became so angry, I thought she might hit the girl. "What do you mean you're pure?" she demanded again and again until the classmate was trying to hide her tears, not sure how she offended Angela so much. I, too, am taken aback by the pain that is brimming just beneath my dear friend's tough exterior at all times. She is barely holding it together.

The true traumas Angela battles, like mine, are not spoken in high school. Hinted at and glossed over, speculated but not confessed or admitted—we imprison ourselves in our secrecy, our shame, our family loyalty. Barely staying afloat ourselves, we aren't mature enough to comprehend or take on each other's problems, but still, looking back, I wish I had done better.

For a while, her future looks bright. She enrolls at an in-state university on scholarship. On a visit home freshman year in college, she tells me, "Mica, I'm doing so well, but no one cares. No one sees me."

"What do you mean no one sees you?" I try to find the answer in her sad eyes but cannot possibly see. "Why does it matter if anyone else sees you doing well, if you succeed? Isn't it enough that you're doing well? I see you!"

I don't understand. On the surface, my friend *is* doing so well. And I never realized before how gorgeous she is. In college, Angela is transformed. She buys clothes that fit her instead of the hand-me-downs she was forced to wear in high school. She trades her old, unflattering glasses for contacts. Her hair is straightened and smooth. She is wearing makeup. She's lost weight. She looks like a model. She's getting good grades. Why is she miserable?

The stifling control Baba holds over me looks too different from the neglect of my friend's upbringing.

Soon after that, I lose my beautiful Angela. She begins acting out, self-destructing, heavily self-medicating. When I work up the courage to tell her I'm worried about her, Angela becomes defensive and verbally attacks me and my family. Through all the drama, I am never truly angry with her. I care about her too much and recognize that she is in pain.

I can't convince David that Angela's issues are serious. He recognizes she is using a lot but so are many of our peers in college.

Not long after my confrontation with her, Angela invites David over to her small apartment for drinks. They do shots. She puts on a sparkly two-piece stripper costume and attempts to seduce him.

"Nothing happened," David tells me. He is laughing. "I was in shock."

I don't think it is funny at all. Angela has known for years about my deep, unrequited love for David. She is willing to sleep with him to get back at me. What I feel at that moment isn't jealousy or betrayal. Instead, seeing the lengths to which my friend would go to hurt me breaks my heart. Do I mean that much to her? She once would have fought our whole high school to defend me, and now, she is willing to sleep with someone she has no romantic feelings for to hurt me.

Years later, Angela and I reconnect online, letting bygones be bygones, knowing our problems were never really with one another. But she again falls into a place where I cannot reach her. She will never climb out of the pain caused by those who robbed her of her childhood, caused by everyone who let her down. Still, I think of her often.

I am privileged to have had parents who were always there for me, who were overly invested in a strict definition of my success. No matter how much Baba terrorized us, he was also my safety net. My parents' love for Didi and me was never and has never been in question for us—this made all the difference.

Chapter 26: Cream of the Crop

AGE 17 – PHOENIX, ARIZONA

The first time I learn about the Flinn scholarship, my heartrate quickens and sweat gathers in my palms. *This is it,* I think. *This is the opportunity I've been waiting for.*

A spokeswoman talks to us about the highly competitive, prestigious program: an all-inclusive, in-state scholarship with a study abroad stipend. I've been waiting for this chance at my dream. The scholarship accepts two percent of its applicants, who need to meet the minimum requirement of a near-perfect grade point average, rank in the top two percent of the graduating class, and have a 1370 or better SAT score to apply.

Unlike some other kids at my school, my parents do not pay for me to attend SAT prep classes. They do not take me on any college tours, in-state or out. Navigating college applications is something I have to figure out on my own, something I am quite overwhelmed by. My family nickels and dimes every purchase, however trivial and necessary, so I balk at all of the application fees. *How many orders of*

Kung Pao Chicken will we have to sell to pay for six applications? When I learn that a classmate's parents fill out all the college applications for him, so he needs only to focus on writing the essays, my jealousy bleeds over to anger.

As much as I want to, I cannot imagine going to a college far away and cannot make such an important life decision based on brochures and hypotheticals. I don't know how I will pay for it, where I will live—I cannot envision my life far away and alone after being so closely controlled by Baba. In-state is easier. In-state will be less shocking.

The Flinn scholarship offers the prestige, the comfort, and a way to travel abroad. It is a chance to change my fate—my most viable ticket out—if only I can leap high enough to reach it.

"This scholarship is for the cream of the crop," the representative says. She is a short, older woman with a slight build and a pixie cut. "Cream of the crop" is not a phrase I've heard before, but I begin to hear it over and over in Flinn circles.

I pour everything into essay questions. One eloquently worded question is about my thumbprint and what it means to me. I write about Yeh-Yeh and how my grandfather's struggles make me who I am today. My family is not religious, and I'm not one to pray, but I wish so hard as I drop off my application in the mail, kissing the manila envelope carrying all of my hopes and dreams.

Opening the letter that announces me as a finalist puts me on the rooftop of a skyscraper. I am so happy and nervous. My whole life, everything I've worked for, comes down to this. With one leap, I can soar to unknown heights or crash to a messy, unsightly end.

In an ill-fitting charcoal blazer from Ross Dress for Less, I face the first interview panel of my life. It is a blur. I smile through it, blasting as much charm as I can muster. My years of customer service training at my parents' restaurant come to my aid.

Each day, in all of these years since we immigrated, my parents have been buckling under the weight of running the restaurant in a new country. Unaccustomed to manual labor, Baba's right ankle swells from standing all day and managing multiple woks at once.

Baba diagnoses himself with a serious coronary issue by consulting his Chinese medicine texts, though he has no medical training at the time. His diagnosis pushes him into the blackest of moods.

Once, behind the glass of the small sliding window into the kitchen, I see an explosion of flames reaching the top of the hood fans.

"In the kitchen, you have to be quick. The idiot cook who caused the fire jumped back, stunned," Baba laments angrily. "I threw in a wet rag to smother the flames, but hot grease splashed onto my hand."

Baba unwraps his bandages to show Didi and me the melting flesh, shiny from a thick coat of clear ointment.

"Do you see what's happened to my hand? And my swollen ankle? Do you see how hard I'm working for you two?" Baba trembles with rage, resentment, and bitterness. His hand is bound for weeks as it heals. When the bandages come off, it is no longer soft like a teacher's but calloused, leathery, and scarred. "You must not let my suffering be in vain. You must zheng kou qi for me and Mama. Become an admirable person. A doctor or a lawyer. Someone we can be proud of."

The literal translation of zheng kou qi is to fight for a mouthful of air. The air of vindication. We cannot fail him.

I am home watching TV in my pajamas when the phone rings.

"Hi Michelle," says a warm voice on the phone. "This is Helen Rosen from the Flinn Foundation."

This is it. I hold my breath.

"Congratulations!" says Helen. "You've been selected as a Flinn Scholar Class of 1999!"

"Ahhh!" I run around the house screaming with joy. Didi comes out to the living room to see what the racket is about. It is the happiest moment of my life.

Dazzling white marble floors and sparkling chandeliers greet me at the scholarship banquet hosted at the Arizona Biltmore. I have never been anywhere nearly as fancy before, and I feel like Cinderella. I fought my way to the ball in my dark blue button-up shirt from the mall and a black pencil skirt.

I stand tall, literally and figuratively, in my too-high platform heels (another Ross Dress for Less find), believing I've finally made my parents proud. Baba raves about the halibut with cream sauce and the tender filet mignon plated dinner. A white waiter spoons cream sauce on every piece of fish from guest to guest. Treating my parents to a high-end meal for the first time because of my own hard work, I am proud of myself. I feel it in my bones. We have finally arrived.

The Flinn Foundation generously allows each scholar to invite one educator who has changed our lives. I invite my favorite English teacher, Mrs. Yip, who taught me both freshman and senior year. She is seated at my table, grinning ear to ear, with her young son as her guest. The evening is a dream. I love meeting all of the other nineteen scholars, and I can't wait to befriend them.

At home later that night, I am still floating on a cloud when I encounter Baba, slouched over in his room, scowling in front of the television.

"What's wrong, Baba?" I swoop in for a hug. Though it may be surprising to others, we are a family that hugs often.

He dodges me and barks, "Don't touch me! Get away!"

I flinch.

"What happened, Baba? I thought you were happy."

"The other parents at that banquet were doctors and engineers. Me and your mama, we're nothing but country potatoes," he hisses, turning his back. "You frustrate me. It's too much, Beautiful Jade. You've accomplished too much. Leave me alone."

Baba's reaction stings, but I won't let him rob me of my joy.

I won a major victory toward my independence—perhaps Baba knows this too.

PART

II

CHAPTER 26: Orientation

AGE 18 - TUCSON, ARIZONA

Orientation week at the University of Arizona is thrilling. I don't even mind standing in long lines for paperwork. I try to appear cool and relaxed while attempting to calm the nerves in my stomach. I am ready to leave the old me behind. The one who is "crazy." The one they call "psycho." The one who can't control her thoughts. I hate that girl. No one wants to date her, to love her.

The Flinn Foundation gives me an opportunity to reinvent myself, to shed that old-me skin. I will become the extraordinary person they think I am, worthy of fancy banquets, professional photo shoots, private lectures with world-renowned artists, thought leaders, and Supreme Court justices. This is a new beginning. I am determined this time will be different.

The magic of college is too much to hold in. I feel like there are kernels of corn popping inside my brain, dyeing everything with bright fuchsia fireworks. There is a whole new world, a new life to begin in this charming college city two hours south of my old epicenter.

In one snaking line full of freshmen, under glaring, no doubt unflattering, fluorescent lights, a guy in a ripped t-shirt several people ahead of me turns and smiles a toothy, crooked grin. I look behind me to see who he is smiling at. No one else is paying attention. He has to be smiling at me. When I smile back, he picks up his longboard off the ground, adjusts his baggy jeans and backward cap, and saunters toward me.

Oh my god. He's coming over. Oh my god. Who is this guy?

"Hello!" he says, all smiles. "How's it going?"

"Good." I reply. "How are you doing?" I nod along, as if small talking with random guys is something I do all the time.

A few more words are exchanged, and I piece together that this is not a random guy. Ben and I met before at the Arizona Biltmore at the Flinn Scholarship Banquet. I had not recognized him without his navy prep school sportscoat trimmed with gold buttons. I am flattered he remembers me and goes out of his way to say hello.

The validation and recognition that comes with being a Flinn scholar is incredible. Everywhere I go, department chairs, professors, and university administrators praise us as "crème de la crème," but the built-in social circle is my favorite part. Greek life is big on campus, but I have never even heard of sororities and fraternities before coming to Tucson. The system is completely foreign to me, and I don't think I'd fit in anyway. However, the community that the Flinn Scholarship offers is a very exclusive and nerdy club.

The 1999 class of Flinn Scholars consists mostly of males. This means I make half a dozen new male best friends, who are brilliant, kind, and interesting—I love it.

My feelings for my high school friend, David, remain, but he attends a different school in a separate city, and though he also stays single, he is busy with his own college life. For the first time, I have a real social life. I can go out as much as I want, whenever I want. I don't have to worry about the restaurant, Didi, or my parents all the time. I thrive, almost convincing myself that I belong with my new clique and in my new home.

Other times, I continue battling my imposter syndrome. The negative thoughts resurface, convincing me that I don't deserve the scholarship and that it was a mistake that they chose me. I believe every other Flinn scholar is *naturally* gifted and intelligent, but I have to work myself to the bone just to keep up. I convince myself that I somehow slipped through into this superhuman league and doubt my qualifications incessantly.

Though I desperately want to, I never date. I never kiss anyone. I'm always sober at parties full of drunken hook-ups. I will nurse a bottle of beer for hours to put people around me at ease, but hold the drink as a prop.

I'm sitting on an old brown couch in a dark room full of people. Loud music is playing—it's "Smooth" by Santana with Rob Thomas. Ben appears and pulls me up to dance. That song plays all the time and somehow it's become our song. We have a great time dancing, we always do, but it's nothing more than another platonic friendship. For as long as I know him, he has a beautiful girlfriend. To all girlfriends of my male best friends—even the long-distance ones—I'm never a threat. I'm just a good friend.

When the song ends, Ben, the life of the party, is pulled away somewhere. I sit back down on the couch, pick up the same half-empty bottle of beer. Suddenly, I remember being seven years old. Didi was four. The phone rang loudly in the middle of the night in our small apartment in Incheon. Mama shook us from sleep to slip into the cold night to pick up Baba at the bar, who was drunk.

When we arrived at the bar, Baba and his friend were outside. My dad could barely stand.

"I can drive," Baba slurred and wobbled, keys in hand.

"No, let's take a cab," Mama urged. She doesn't know how to drive.

"I said I'm fine to drive!" Baba insisted. Tormented but obedient, Mama buckled Didi and me, both scared silent, in the back seat and got in the passenger side.

Baba immediately drove us over the barricade into lanes of busy oncoming traffic. I felt helpless as we violently lurched over the curb. *We are all going to die here.*

Loud honks. Screeching tires. Dizzying lights. Then there was a jerky thud as the car rolled back to its previous parked position. For a moment, the silence held us captive.

Baba relented and we caught a taxi home. That's when I knew— Mama can never stand up to my father, even when it's life and death, even when it means we could all die.

In Korea, where guns are illegal, there is no gun ownership culture, but Baba loves guns anyway and purchased an air rifle that he used to shoot tiny house sparrows for sport.

Our family treated Baba's BB rifle with the same regard as if it was a real firearm. When Baba came home drunk in the night to retrieve his rifle, Mama's attempted to stop him in vain. She was no match for his strength and size.

Awakened by the commotion of Baba's inebriated yells and Mama's desperate hushed pleading, I crept out of the bedroom all four of us shared. Bleary-eyed and frightened, I watched as Baba left our apartment with the BB rifle strapped around his sturdy chest— the door slamming behind him. Mama paced the small living room in her nightgown, frowning, not able to go after him and leave Didi and me home alone.

Soon, the police station called.

Baba was spotted scaling the large entrance gate at our apartment complex. They arrested him. Mama shook us from sleep again and rushed us to the police station to retrieve our father. Baba was seated and handcuffed with his hands behind the back of the chair, his head lolling in and out of consciousness. On K-dramas, I had seen police dump buckets of cold water on drunk bad guys, to sober them up for answers. When we arrived, Baba was drenched.

Years later, Didi tells me that this night is his earliest memory.

A piece inside me breaks to learn that my baby brother's first recollection of life on earth is seeing our father out of control and detained. Before Didi ever remembers sun beams warming his face, or licking an ice cream cone, or splashing in a rain puddle, he remembers the terror of that night.

Therapy, years later, uncovers many other memories I had repressed involving Baba and his drinking in Korea. I am crying in a ring of onlookers as he brawls with a neighbor in front of our bathhouse at night. I call out to Baba again and again, sobbing, but I am never heard. Grown-ups yell all around me, trying to pull Baba and the other guy apart—everyone else mere mortals to my father's hulk-like stature.

I will recall my mother's frazzled, high-pitched panic when she can't find my father on the night of my long-awaited kindergarten Christmas dance recital. I am all dressed up in my costume—a pleated red skirt and fitted white top that Baba had spent weeks shopping for. He'd watched me practice for months. Tonight's the big night, and Baba goes missing.

On stage, I dance under the spotlights to winter carols with a fake smile plastered on my face, and afterward, Mama drags me and Didi through the crowded audience to continue her search for Baba, who never shows up. When we eventually find him, he is in his familiar blackout state. He will never be held responsible for what he cannot remember.

But all that is mostly behind us here in America. Baba never loses control quite like that here. He is too afraid. He could never get into much trouble drinking alone at home. In America, where he is friendless, he mostly drinks a few beers or some cheap red wine in front of the Asian satellite television programs until he falls asleep snoring.

The isolation in our new home country is both a gift and a curse. Though we are no longer buoyed by social support, Baba is untethered from daily temptations.

I'm jolted out of my past when an exuberant couple bumps into me while dancing. I laugh, and the guy next to me, an older Flinn scholar I don't know very well starts talking with me, but it is so hard to hear him above the music.

My memories associated with drinking leave an indelible mark—

heavy drinking never appeals to me. I am never going to take the risk. I always play it safe.

Without liquid courage to foster reckless behavior, I continue to harbor long, unrequited crushes on people like David who are unavailable. I allow flirty boys to confuse me with their sweet words and gestures, fully knowing they are devoted to their girlfriends, their faith, whoever, or whatever, knowing I am not special to them. Not enough, anyway.

The longer this goes on, the lonelier and more unlovable I feel.

The possibility that being surrounded by some of the brightest, most dynamic people on campus at all times may have deterred actual romantic prospects from finding me never crosses my mind. When the idea is suggested by sympathetic girlfriends, I dismiss it right away.

"If someone was genuinely interested in me, they would find me," I say, without recognizing the irony. Due to my lack of self-confidence, I am oblivious to signals from people who might have been showing interest in me. I do not believe any decent person would find me and my fat awkwardness attractive. I don't feel lovable, so I don't recognize or trust love when I experience it. I am closed to possibilities.

CHAPTER 27: Flight

AGES 18 TO 20 – TUCSON, ARIZONA

My first night at Yuma Hall honors dormitory at the University of Arizona, excitement courses through my veins. I cannot lie still in my new bed with its crisp, extra-long sheets. Classes haven't yet started. My roommate hasn't arrived. Cool-to-the touch, stark, white walls box me in my own space, hours away from my family, my past. It feels so luxurious. I am drunk with freedom.

Ever since we emigrated, Baba's singular focus has been to have a doctor in the family. Didi's bad grades dims my father's hopes for him over the years, but the pressure on me doubles.

"You have the brains, you have the ability, so why not become a doctor? You must. It doesn't make sense not to. It would make us so proud. There is nothing better."

My protests are ignored, even as I declare an international studies major and an art minor I keep secret from my parents.

The ritual of Baba and Mama sitting me down to convince me to change my career track repeats with mind-numbing regularity, but

Baba is never able to change my mind. Left without another choice, Baba resolves to get a doctor in the family by becoming one himself. He applies for a Chinese medicine and acupuncture doctorate program based in Los Angeles taught in Mandarin and Korean. For years, Baba commutes from Phoenix to LA for his classes—adding further strain on the family and restaurant work dynamic.

But, here at college in Tucson, I don't have to worry about Baba. I am giddy. With nothing to do with my nervous energy in the wee hours, I step out into the glaring fluorescent-lit hallway and begin feverishly decorating the door with origami, paper flowers, and photos. I imagine my brilliant handiwork will dazzle passersby in the morning, initiating conversations that will lead to lifelong friendships.

"Whoa. Looks like a kindergarten classroom," an RA observes and keeps walking. That's the only reaction I get from anyone, including my pretty, new roommate.

I can't wait to meet Val, who moves to Tucson from across the country. She has long, beautiful, curly hair and a self-assurance I lack. Though she keeps her distance at first, we eventually grow to become close friends. I make other new friendships that last a lifetime—Leslie, a fifth-generation Chinese American who also lives in the same dorm and Teresa, a sassy, brilliant pre-law student in my English class. Though the three of us are very different, we bond over our shared identity of being Chinese American women.

But before freshman year gets going too far, after two days in a wired state, I call the campus health center and schedule an appointment. I am nervous to go in and almost cancel at the last minute. The building is made of red bricks, and the interior is clean with many collegiate posters on the walls. It is a maze as I try to find the right waiting room in the right department. I check in and grab an empty seat. Many students are waiting. We all look nervous and avoid eye contact, afraid to be recognized in the behavioral health center.

The counselor who sees me has long, straight brown hair that is brushed back. She has smooth, tanned skin and wise, piercing eyes. She does not smile, not once. She is all business.

"I can't sleep," I tell her. "I've had trouble sleeping for a long time."

I'm telling her a fraction of my struggles. I'm holding so much back. I don't tell her about losing my mind, about thinking people are filming me, about believing there was a vote at my high school about me. I am terrified of sharing any of it.

What if Baba is right? What if they will take away my scholarship and kick me out of school if they learn how crazy I am? I am trying to gauge her reaction.

"I'm excited about college but also so nervous. There are so many expectations to live up to, even more than before because of the Flinn scholarship."

She furrows her broad brow. "You're a Flinn scholar?"

I nod with trepidation, eyes on the floor. Not sure if this is safe to say.

"Oh, well, we get all the Flinn scholars in here," she sighs as if she's just figured me out. "There's so much pressure."

I am prescribed Valium, as needed, for sleep. There are no more questions or attempts to diagnose a condition. I am dismissed as a stressed-out overachiever.

I overextend myself as a way of life. I can't seem to help myself. I take twenty-one credits at a time because there are too many courses I'm interested in. There are too many causes I'm passionate about too. I establish a mentoring program for children adopted from China that organizes cultural events and matches them with student mentors from Asian American clubs on campus. I become an officer in too many student organizations. Force of habit? I don't know. I don't know why I do it. I'm a speeding locomotive that can't stop.

I crash into depression during midterms and finals. Each time the workload becomes too much, I berate myself for being so stupid as to believe I could do it all, just as I had in high school. I hate myself for never learning my lesson and never being able to escape this self-destructive cycle.

My anxiety chases away sleep. The Valium does not help. I am afraid to increase my dosage or take it too frequently. I read about the medication online and learn it can lead to addiction. I also don't go back to the health center because I regret sharing I'm a Flinn scholar. I am an imposter, paranoid about giving myself away, afraid of losing everything.

Each time I walk out of an exam, I am convinced I have failed... but this is never the case. All the nervous hours studying pay off, even though, often, none of the material makes sense to me. I worry because I don't retain anything, but no one notices. I am a Flinn scholar and, by definition, I should be extraordinarily fine.

The summer after my freshman year of college, the Flinn Foundation whisks all twenty of us off on a three-week seminar in Hungary and Romania to study economic development post-Communism. I am ecstatic for this sure-to-be life-changing adventure.

"I don't want you to go," Baba says, pouting. "Why did Flinn choose these poor European countries? Why not France or England?" No one in my family has ever been to Europe.

I know he's worried, but I'm frustrated he's not happy for me. Back home for the summer, preparing my trip, I roll my eyes as I pack my enormous backpack from REI. About half of us from the Flinn Class also plan to backpack through France, Italy, Germany, and the Netherlands together after the seminar ends.

"Don't go," Baba grunts again. My bags are packed, and I hold my boarding pass in my hands. He and Mama had driven me to the airport, grumbling the entire way. I look around the waiting area, and none of the other Flinn parents act this way. No one else is trying to stop their college kid from taking an all-expenses paid, prestigious, educational trip to Europe. No other parents look angry. Everyone else is happy for their child to take flight. My parents are afraid, but what are they afraid of? I have achieved everything Baba wanted and he is still unhappy.

"I'll call" is the best I can offer. I turn my back, determined.

"Call us every day," Baba shouts after me. "Every day."

Budapest is a marvel to behold. I am swept away by the architecture and the history as we glide down the Danube on a river cruise and private parliament tour. This is nothing like the breathtaking temples in Asia, which are bright and ornate in Taiwan and striking in their clean, balanced design in Korea. I am awestruck seeing this other part of the Old World, completely new to me. There is so much to life, so much world for me to discover.

Back in Arizona, my family rarely eats out. When we do for special occasions, Baba treats us to feasts at Cantonese-style or Korean restaurants. On rarer occasions, we go to Denny's 24-Hour Diner after our restaurant closes to have steak. With Denny's as the height of luxury outside of Asian food, the meals from my European adventure are mind-blowing.

Our program guide introduces us to a bustling falafel spot in Budapest that serves up perfectly crunchy and steaming spheres of spiced salty flavor bombs with all the fresh toppings you can imagine. We discover on our own street-vendor gyros made of warm, pillowy pita bread bursting with slow-roasted, hand-carved meat, sweet, crunchy onions, and out-of-this-world creamy and tart tzatziki sauce. The best part is that they are stuffed with french fries so hot that they burn the roof of my mouth. Experiencing these textures and flavors while huddled in the streets on breezy summer nights with some of my best friends becomes part of my core food memories.

When the Flinn-sponsored portion of the trip ends, a group of us, including Ben, heads to France on the Eurail pass. Everything in Paris, especially after Hungary and Romania, seems impossibly expensive. My friends and I stuff our backpacks with the free, hostel-provided, day-old breakfast baguettes at breakfast so that we can eat them for lunch too.

At a small silver cart within view of the Eiffel Tower, I savor my first crepe. The eggy, silky thin pancake with sliced strawberries and Nutella melting in my mouth is also my inaugural introduction to the hazelnut chocolate spread. *Where has this been all my life?*

The world stops when I taste my first spoonful of gelato on the cobblestone streets of Verona, outside of our rundown hostel. The chocolate hazelnut gelato I devour in Italy ruins me for all future frozen desserts. With our travel budgets thinning by the day, we skip lunch, opting for a generous gelato cone instead.

After freshman year living in the same dorm with many of my travel companions, we were already close, but the long flights, bus rides, and wandering together in foreign cities cement our friendships further. This is particularly true of the time we spend on our own, after the organized seminar ends. Ben is as goofy and playful as ever, picking me a wildflower in Romania, which I press in the pages of my thick travel guide. He and the guys dutifully pick out postcards to send to their girlfriends along our stops. I mail some to David, who is always good about sending them to me from his travels too. I call my parents whenever I can.

My classmates are more confident, and I follow where they lead us. They figure out which train to take and how to choose a hostel, all without the assistance of the internet. I still feel like a kid who needs to be told what to do. I am inspired by the young adults around me. By their example, I become empowered to find my own way too. Toward the end of our backpacking trip, I venture off on my own to visit friends in Cologne and Dusseldorf in Germany while the rest of the group stay in Berlin. I'm a nervous wreck, but I find my legs.

When I reunite with the group a few days later, I am so anxious about the solo train ride that I buy a can of Radler, a beer and Sprite mix, to "take the edge off." Afterward, Ben, who knows I'm not a drinker, finds my choice of beverage hilarious and teases me. I don't know what's so funny.

The trip is everything I dreamed of and more. I'm sad for it to end, but also, I need it to be over. Too many sleepless nights in unfamiliar, noisy hostels, traveling from city to city. Too much excitement. I feel my spirit enter and leave my body. It is not safe.

But soon, I touch the earth in Phoenix. Engulfed by the fiery summer heat, I am at home. I sleep. I eat Mama's potato soup, kimchi, and moo goo gai pan from Oriental Express. I feel myself again. Soon, it is time to go back to Tucson to start my sophomore year.

Val and I decide to both live in Yuma Hall again. We enjoy nights painting our nails and eating entirely too much pizza in our tiny room. She loves the rice I cook in my little rice cooker, which we top with cold cuts, shredded cheese, and kimchi from our mini-fridge. In return, she shares the loaf of homemade banana bread and an assortment of cookies that her grandmother sends her back with after church each Sunday.

The summer after my sophomore year, I accept an internship in Washington, DC, at a nonprofit called OCA-Asian Pacific American Advocates. The organization works to advance the social, political, and economic well-being of Asian Americans and Pacific Islanders, and I am eager to join the mission and to explore our nation's capital. Baba doesn't want me to go and makes my housing situation far more complicated than it needs to be. But I get to go and that's all that matters.

The summer is transformative. In Arizona, in part because I participated in Anytown and because I am an international studies major, I often find myself to be the most politically aware Asian American person in my networks. During my internship, my previous level of political activism is put to shame, but I am inspired by it. I learn so much from my new social-justice-minded friends, especially those from bigger cities with bigger AAPI populations.

Summer in DC is electrifying. Almost every day, I run into someone I know at the metro stops or cafes. The city pulses with power. When I look up into the skyline and see the Capitol Building presiding over the city like a glowing beacon, I get chills.

Having access to walk into government hearings and talk to leaders and organizers is like being folded into the political machine. The civil rights organizations are unified. I attend meetings with OCA at NAACP and the National Council of La Raza to advocate for change, leveraging our power with one another. I further embrace my identity as an Asian American, separate from my identity as an Asian immigrant, and join my voice with those of other people of color.

This whirlwind summer of 2001 includes an OCA convention in Seattle. From there, I take the Amtrak to Portland for another

Chinese American conference to accept a scholarship before flying back to Phoenix to pack for my junior year semester study abroad. I select a scholarship-sponsored advanced Mandarin language study abroad program at Peking University, which some silly people call the "Harvard of China." Baba is eager for me to go this time, unlike the Europe trip. He is already bragging to friends and family about his Beautiful Jade and the places she'll go.

We have no idea what's to come.

CHAPTER 28: 911

AGE 20 - BEIJING, CHINA

I arrive in Beijing in late August. The massive city is hard to wrap my head around. The students in my program are transported by a small bus from the airport to the international student dorm. To my surprise, my home for the next several months is more like a dual-occupancy hotel room with daily cleaning service than the actual dorms where local students stay, packed seven to a room.

My new classmates are mostly from Stanford, Vanderbilt, and other fancy private liberal arts schools. Only a few are from giant public universities like mine—a nice, freckled Hapa boy from University of New Mexico and a spunky girl from University of Washington. No one cares what a Flinn scholar is, and I don't mention it, of course, so most of my new peers assume I'm an unremarkable "State School" student.

Because my Mandarin is good enough to pass for a native speaker in Beijing, whenever I ask for directions, no matter how polite or deferential my manners, I am always met with open hostility instead of the kind patience offered my white or even Korean-American classmates. Like stereotypical New Yorkers, Beijing locals have no moment to spare for me. I look and sound Chinese enough—I should know how to figure out my own way instead of interrupting their day.

Mere weeks after our arrival, local students trample through our international dorm hallways late at night, pounding on each door. "Turn on your TVs!" they shout, echoing down the hall.

I am startled by the interruption of what had been a quiet night. "What's going on?" I ask. We all ask the same question. Somehow, I wander into a classmate's dorm room where several students are gathered around a small television. We huddle together on the edge of the two beds and watch in shock as replays of planes crashing into the Twin Towers is displayed on the screen. *Is this real?*

In the coming days, we're told that the home we'd left behind will never be the same again. America will never be the same. *What does this mean? How can such a big change happen while I am away? What will it be like to go back home?*

The hostility from locals, the cold shoulder from many of the program-mates, and the stress wears me down. Homesickness for Arizona sinks in, too. I miss having people I can relax around. I struggle to close the distance with other students in the program, and I don't know why. *Are people spreading rumors about me? They all hate me, don't they?*

I become hypervigilant.

Luckily, David is studying abroad in Thailand this same semester. He sends me dozens of sweet handwritten letters, which help me feel less alone. I respond to each one on delicate stationery I scour for in street markets and crowded shops. In his neat script, he writes of his hilarious mispronunciations that land him in hot water, making me laugh out loud. David tells me of the vibrant countries he visits and the hospitality of the people he encounters. His postcards of floating markets, ornate temples, and lush scenery fill me with longing as well as nostalgia for the creosote-infused breezes of home. Pinning each of his letters above my bed, I dream of being by David's side, exploring the world together. Each envelope glows, spinning yarns of yearning, tugging at me. Other girls in my program comment with envy that even their boyfriends do not write as often.

"Are you sure he's just a friend?" one asks.

I blush, beaming inside. Even on the other side of the world, David's friendship is a life raft.

For our semester-end final writing assignment, students can choose any topic they want, but it requires approval from the program director. Fascinated by portraits of Chairman Mao which hang inside taxis and restaurants in place of a Buddha or a Christian cross, for protection and prosperity, I decide to research the deification of the political leader.

I am proud to have thought of such a clever topic. I can't wait to interview people about it and get started, but I'm surprised when our normally kind and sweet program director asks to meet with me in her small office.

"You can't write about this," she says with an ashen face and darkened eyes.

"Why, Director Hwang? It could be so interesting. I can't wait to talk to people about their beliefs." Her eyes begin to water. The lines of fatigue, frustration, and age on her face, which I hadn't noticed before, emerge. "The people are not ready," she says. She does not want to fight any longer.

I feel ashamed, and I don't know why. The rejection burns. My American privilege, the naïve assumption that I can pursue any intellectual curiosity, is one I have long taken for granted. My privilege and foreignness are on full display, and I have never felt more American.

I procrastinate on selecting another topic as long as I can. When I can't put it off anymore, I choose what I think is a safe, easy, and crowd-pleasing topic—Yeh-Yeh.

I write the paper on my family history, about how Yeh-Yeh is a self-made man who left Northern China penniless and illiterate to start anew in Korea. This tale of his entrepreneurial spirit and perseverance, of how he worked tirelessly to build a small empire, never failed to garner positive reactions in the US. I had won the Flinn scholarship in part thanks to a similar essay in English.

When my designated Chinese language partner—a local Ph.D. student in political science at the university who, until then, I believe to be my friend—reviews my work, she grimaces. "Your Yeh-Yeh," she spits with a sneer. "He was a landlord!"

Landlords are a class of people who were systematically executed during the Communist Revolution.

She laughs to show me how unimpressed she is with my Yeh-Yeh. In her eyes, Yeh-Yeh was a traitor, a deserter.

Blindsided, I recoil. I failed again, even after a drastic change in subject, trying to write something uncontroversial. I'm colliding headfirst into a China that does not celebrate my thinking, does not understand or embrace me. No more than I could celebrate, understand, or embrace it without reservations. The rejection from my ancestral land ruptures my already murky identity—not Korean, not quite Taiwanese, not *this* kind of Chinese.

As an ethnic Chinese person who had always lived outside the country, I had hoped to reclaim a piece of my heritage here. Instead, I lose my tenuous grasp, more alienated than ever. My indelible Asian American identity reinforces itself. I ache for my adopted home country of immigrants.

As the winter turns more bitter, I venture outside less and less. My sleep wanes and my mood darkens. The negative spiraling vultures that haunt my nights are back, returning to feed on my brain, convincing me that everyone hates me. Many students in the program are homesick, on top of the usual college drama of fights among roommates, hook-ups and breakups, and idle gossip. I imagine conversations halting when I enter rooms and hushed whispers as I walk down hallways. *How am I going survive until the end of the program?*

Skipping meals, I live off the Costco box of Hershey's chocolate bars I brought to give out as gifts. Save for the cleaning ladies, I have no one to give them to. I haven't made any local friends like I thought I would. Our program is very isolated from the rest of the campus.

I fall into the familiar, dreaded state again, too nervous to sleep. I don't deserve food. My thoughts race. *Too much work…not a minute to spare…I must study, study, study.* But I sit, useless, reading the same passage over and over, retaining nothing. My mind refuses to be tamed into focus. *Stupid, stupid, stupid. Why am I so worthless? I am a fraud.* Maybe this time, I will be found out.

Days slip past and my final project and exam dates near. Night after night, I fight for sleep that never comes. Paranoid thoughts race in furious circles through my brain. *I am accused of being a spy. Am I a spy?* Exhausted but unable to stop the racing dark thoughts, I am certain everyone loathes me and is plotting against me to expose me.

When the phone rings, it jolts me from a zombie-like state. "Beautiful Jade," Baba's urgent voice meets my hesitant greeting into the receiver.

A semester of my life needs to be packed up for transport back home, but I haven't organized anything. I am grossly inadequate for the simplest of tasks. I feel like a trampled worm—body flattened, trying to lift my head or tail, not knowing which end is which. Writhing.

Baba is still working on his Chinese medicine degree and is trying to become more expert at acupuncture. He learns of a university in Shandong Province that produces instructional DVDs on acupuncture techniques. Baba is determined to get his hands on those and asks me to travel to the other province by train to buy them for him.

"Baba…I can't," my feeble voice quakes like tiny, coarse grains straining through a sieve. Turning my neck to peer outside necessitates Herculean effort. Grey and black slush covers the sidewalks—my skin constricts at the thought of the biting cold. *How am I supposed to do what Baba asks when the program ends in a week? How am I to fit it in with my exams, final projects, and packing?*

"You must. Ni Yi Ding Yao," Baba booms on the telephone. His outrage at my hesitance multiplies each mile it crosses from Arizona. "Go to Shandong and buy me those DVDs. You must do this. You must!"

His determination to have a doctor in the family, no matter the cost, obliterates any reason. I am already unfilial for rejecting his first command to become a doctor, I cannot reject this simple request too.

"Yi Ding Yao," Baba doubles down, commanding again, in his toughest, scariest voice. He breaks through my fog. "No one else can do this. It must be you." My father's authoritarian roar, a constant in my twenty years of existence, possesses unmatched power over me. His bellowing mauls me like a grizzly bear.

My hairs stand on ends in salute.

"I must."

Pushing, willing myself, I rock for hours, back and forth, trying to work up the courage. *I may be worthless, but this task I must do, even if it kills me. My life is worthless anyway. The end will be here soon.*

Putting on my coat and shoes, I stuff all of my emergency cash in my small shoulder bag and run into the darkness at two in the morning. I sprint into the icy mid-December night, severing my remaining ties to reality.

CHAPTER 29: *Invincible*

AGE 20 - BEIJING, CHINA

Run, run, run. I run until I see a taxi and ask the driver to take me to the train station. I purchase a round-trip ticket to Shandong and board the night train. I am even more disorientated by the time I arrive at dawn about seven hours later. Outside the station, a car stops in front of me. I ignore the fact that this is an illegitimate taxi, bearing the ghost imprint of its former branding. In that mental state, I believe everything is destiny. The unmarked car is an offering from the universe that I should not refuse.

I get in. *Everything will be fine.* The driver peers at me in the rearview mirror during the ride, unable to figure me out. A twenty-year-old woman hailing a cab on her own in the early morning is not normal. At drop-off, he warns me, pointing to the roof of his car, "Make sure you look for a taxi with a light on top next time."

I nod, smiling, overpaying him intentionally. *I was right to believe in him.*

I saunter aimlessly around a market, waiting for the university to open. All around me, harried people yell and rush past me. A sea of weathered beige shades, aprons, and gloves churn around me, but I don't recall anything being sold there. The air smells neutral, like the market's colors, devoid of the usual aromas of a bustling city. *What is everyone yelling about? Wasn't this supposed to be a paper market?* There is no stationary or painted craft papers, only hordes of people yelling in the cold.

When the morning sun glows brighter and streets fill with commuters, I leave the market and meander to Shandong University. I see a big white building on campus just past the entrance. Somehow, I locate the office Baba wants me to find. I don't know how I do it. My memory is very fuzzy during severe episodes. The office I arrive at is empty. Large bookshelves line the walls filled with paperback textbooks. I sit in a chair facing the window and wait for what seems like hours for the right person to show up.

A thin, tall man in his late forties wearing a white lab coat finally shows up. My presence startles him, and he adjusts his wire-rimmed glasses.

"I'm here to buy the acupuncture DVDs. I need the entire set," I say proudly, ready to complete my mission.

"The acupuncture DVDs? All of them?" The man looks truly baffled. The entire set is at least fifty DVDs. He wears an expression of shock as if this is the first time he's ever received such a request.

"Yes, I have the money to pay for it." My parents had insisted I take emergency cash with me to China for the semester. I haven't touched it until this mission.

"I can't give it to you now. It will take at least two days to copy the full set. I will call you when they're ready to pick up."

"I have to come back?" I gasp. My memory becomes even hazier after that. My train does not depart for Beijing until the afternoon. What do I do to fill the time? Do I eat or drink anything?

I do have a vivid, almost out-of-body memory of running around a red, rickety, metal platform and stairs that encircle a courtyard at the train station. Up the stairs, then down the stairs, across the grated platform again and again.

Up and down, up and down. Around and around.

My shoulder bag, containing all of my cash, falls on the floor. Nearly one thousand dollars in emergency funds are inside. Baba and Mama don't trust credit cards, especially don't expect them to work abroad.

I stare at the bag for an eternity; the room spins around me. *Don't touch it. Don't touch it.* It isn't a voice I hear in my head. It is more like a holy mandate I can feel in my bones. I just know. *Leave the bag.* Someone else is meant to discover the bag. They will complete another relay of a holy mission with it.

I touch the sharp edges of the return train ticket in the pocket of my brown peacoat. I haven't rested in at least twenty-four hours and haven't slept in god knows how long. When I arrive back at the colossal Beijing train station, it is already dark outside. People stomp in all directions. Taxis, cars, and buses battle one another for curbside real estate. But I am on another plane altogether, buzzing on a high that assures me only I can now see Truth. Swaying slowly, I am an otter floating carefree, unaware of the sharks swarming beneath me. Soon, my fingers grow icy. I wonder how I am going to get back to the dorm. All my money was in that bag. Still, I grin, positive everything is going to work out.

The universe will provide a solution. *I am invincible.* Stepping outside into the freezing air, I dig my hands deep into my coat pockets for warmth. From the right pocket, I pull a single, crisp, folded one hundred yuan note. *Where did this come from?* I marvel with gratitude, giggling. The bill is enough to cover cab fare back to campus.

"This is Michelle! Bring me a burrrrrrrito!" I call a random friend on the dorm phone.

"What? Are you okay?" He is thoroughly weirded out.

Hanging up abruptly, I call someone else, cackling. "This is Michelle! Bring me some teeeaa!"

In asking my friends to bring me odd items, I am prompting them for offerings because I am a holy being. I am convinced I am doing them a favor because they will be blessed in return. I don't need these items. I am acting on a spiritual mandate.

"Are you on drugs?" someone asks. *Why do people keep asking me that?*

"Noooo." I chortle into the receiver. *I'm not. Of course, I'm not.*

I draw myself a steaming bath and descend into the hot water while singing at the top of my lungs. For some reason, water flows milky white and slippery from the faucet. I assume it is part of the ceremony of my ascension. I am finally meeting my destiny. I must prepare for my spiritual coronation—accept my true identity as a holy being who witnessed the ultimate Truth. All souls are connected, and I can see the red lines connecting soulmates the world over in the starry abyss. The splendor of the master plan, those glorious lines of fate, moves me to shaking tears. I reach nirvana.

Once out of the bathtub, I blast music at full volume, not caring what time it is. The beauty of each dramatic track, especially power ballads like songs by Mariah Carey, stimulates every atom of my existence.

Someone notifies the program director that I am not well. In China, no one cares about my stellar student reputation. They don't have curtains woven from my past achievements to block their view of my illness or to dilute its severity. Model Minority Myth does not exist there. In the land of my ancestors, my illness fully manifests. In the land of my ancestors, my illness is finally seen.

The kind program assistant is deployed to watch over me that night. Her eyes round with fear when she appears at my door.

Baba receives a call with a simple message from the director, "Your daughter is sick. Hurry. Come quickly."

Two days later, my father arrives at my dorm.

He collapses into me without a word, quaking as he weeps, holding me so tight I can't breathe.

Oblivious and confused about all the fuss, I ask, "Baba, what's wrong? Why are you crying?"

CHAPTER 30: Purge

AGE 20 - PHOENIX, ARIZONA

Piercing screams machete their way out of my subconscious like demons purging from my throat. Mama, Baba, and Didi dash from their troubled slumber to my bedside only to find me unconscious and twisting in nightmares.

"Do you remember screaming again last night, Beautiful Jade?" Mama asks concerned in the morning.

I shake my head.

"Do you remember what you were dreaming about?"

I don't recall anything. I feel barely alive. Only a sharp pain lingers in my esophagus.

Other nights, I awake tearing off clothes. I need to escape my skin. I howl at invisible monsters. I offer myself to the other world, to the gods. I have to be naked for gods and spirits to see me and accept me. My parents wrestle down my shirt as I thrash to pull it off, shrieking and sobbing.

My brain continues to wage a ferocious war on itself after I return from Beijing. The battle scorches on night after night. I am confused and angry at why I have not ascended. Why am I still stuck here?

Two weeks of continuous night terrors later, Baba, Mama, and Didi kneel around me in the darkness as if in prayer on the floor of my parents' bedroom. They massage my tense shoulders, arms, and legs, praying and wishing me to fall asleep, to find peace.

"It's okay. Relax. Don't think about anything," Baba soothes, kneading healing litanies into my flesh. "Clear your mind."

I want to let go. To let go means abandoning the life I've lived up until this moment. I am sure I will be freed now. My pain will end for this lifetime. In an out-of-body experience, my spirit departs as my eyelids grow heavy. I breathe deep from my molten core, severing all ties—mental, spiritual, and emotional—from earth. The hot air lifts me up to unmatched heights. I relax, for the first time in what seems like months, maybe years, dying willingly.

I will not wake from this slumber. I have done my duty. I have given all I can.

Now, I will be allowed to soar.

The next day, the unforgiving Arizona sun glares, even in January, taunting me with brightness.

No, No, No. Why didn't god, the spirits, or my ancestors allow me to join them? It was my time—I was sure of it. Why didn't it work? I didn't want this earthly life. How was I supposed to go on?

My memories of my final days in China are foggy, hacked apart, and Frankensteined. Before Baba arrived, a stranger whose name I would never learn appears at my school. The stranger, who was in his thirties, wore a long wool camel coat and a scarf. He handed me his flip phone and I listened to my favorite uncle in Korea, Jojo, tell me in a faraway tinny voice, "It's okay. This is my good friend who lives in Beijing. I sent him to check on you."

Jojo's friend was not thrilled to be there but was begrudgingly doing this unusual favor. When coaxing failed, he dragged me out of my room. I grabbed onto the hand of Matt, the Hapa kid from New Mexico, who lived in the dorm room next to mine as we walk by him in the hall and refused to let go. By this point, the stranger was losing patience. I was not his problem.

Where is he taking me? I was afraid to get in his car. Matt was watching us wide-eyed.

"It's okay," Matt said to me and the stranger. "I'll come with you."

This calmed me down for some reason. I didn't even know Matt very well. I entwined my fingers in his and refused to let go. I was too out of my mind to thank him then, but I never forget the buffer and support he offered so generously and without hesitation.

"Have you eaten?" the stranger asked.

I shook my head no. I hadn't eaten a meal in days. I wonder if this was obvious.

Our first stop was a small but busy beef noodle soup shop. The stranger bought us steaming bowls of noodles. We ate in awkward silence at the rectangular wooden table, each avoiding eye contact. Jojo would owe his friend big for this one.

After I ate, I felt the life return to my body a bit. I felt weak, but my mind was still far away. Next stop turned out to be a Chinese psychiatric hospital with a shabby, overcrowded lobby. The moment I saw it, I wanted to run. In my mixed-up mental condition, I refused to speak in Mandarin. I refused the intake forms, which were all in Chinese. I did not trust the place. The staff had no patience for me. The nurses all looked at me with angry expressions.

The stranger was frustrated, but instead of giving up, he drove Matt and me to an international hospital. This one looked like a modern corporate office with larger than necessary shiny glass walls. Was I more cooperative in this Western environment? Did Matt help me with the forms? There is a gap in my memory.

I do remember a lot of waiting. I eventually met with a Scandinavian expat doctor, who wore a white lab coat over his blue collared shirt. He was clean-cut and no-nonsense when he spoke. I remember all of us sitting on a couch set for some reason, the doctor on one side, me glued to Matt, the stranger on the other. What an odd bunch we were.

The doctor asked me questions. I don't remember what I answered, but eventually, he said, "I can't diagnose her while she is like this."

He prescribed me antipsychotic medications. This doctor seemed angry also, like I'd failed him somehow. He wanted me to get out of his sight—I could feel it. Maybe he, and the other angry doctors I would encounter, were tired of facing mental illness every day in what seems like a losing battle.

Back in Phoenix, my father's eyes age ten years. They are haunted by ghosts of perished dreams he'd long pinned on his prized daughter. In place of the bright dreams are dark visions of my dead-end life—a daughter locked away, no job, no marriage, no grandchildren, no future. Suddenly, in place of the boastful pride he had long associated with my accomplishments, there is a curse of devastating shame. We all now face the intense stigma of shen jing bing, mental illness. Me, the one with the bing, and my family, by extension. When choosing death over shame is honorable by culture, the stakes are as high as it gets.

Over a month. That's how long my family and I hang in a torturous limbo while we wait for an available appointment with a psychiatrist in Phoenix after my return from China. I had been the one in the family to navigate the medical system and with me out of commission, there is nothing to do but wait, especially when there are so few people my parents trust to know about my condition. For over a month, none of us know if there is any hope that I will come out of psychosis.

One of my parents stays with me at all times during this month. This is difficult to do while running a restaurant. Though they prefer to keep me at home, sometimes, I am brought to the restaurant when there is no other choice. We are at the restaurant on a quiet afternoon, sitting at the orange tables. Baba looks at me with such a sad look in his eyes.

"What's wrong, Baba?" I am oblivious because I'm still in my psychotic state.

"Nothing daughter," he sighs.

"Everything is okay," I present a child-like smile, still believing I am a holy being who is waiting to ascend to another dimension at any moment.

Baba turns his head and covers his surging sobs.

CHAPTER 31: The Label

AGE 20 - PHOENIX, ARIZONA

"—Major depressive disorder, but we will have to observe you longer to confirm."

Dr. R is the psychiatrist we waited a month to see. His curly hair, peppered with gray, tops a mustached and bespectacled friendly face. A lifelong jogger, he has a stringy, beef-jerky body to show for it. Everything is monochromatic brown in his office: his dark wooden desk, the chairs, books, and even the art.

I explain everything I've been through this time, holding nothing back.

After a while, the antipsychotics from the Scandinavian doctor in China make me less manic, but I am not feeling myself yet. I am not sane. I don't feel as if I belong in this world.

Dr. R instructs me to stop the antipsychotics and prescribes an antidepressant instead.

As soon as we leave Dr. R's office, Baba announces he is taking me on a road trip to Los Angeles to san san xin—to disperse the heart, to relieve pressure. He believes a change of scenery will serve me well. A trip to Los Angeles, the closest approximation to returning to Korea or Taiwan available, is Baba's solution for so many of life's problems in America.

Hypnotic yellow traffic stripes dividing dark freeway lanes rush under Baba's truck while my mind spins into the stars. By the time we reach the Pacific coast, I can't stop smiling and giggling. Once again, I am in sync with the universe. Baba drives us to the beach. It is glorious!

I dance along the waves in the sand, imagining the water seducing me, reaching further and further up my legs, licking my thighs. Push and pull, I indulge in a naughty game of chicken with the ocean. Baba watches from a distance, any semblance of optimism for my quick recovery evaporating with the sea spray.

Changing medications and trying to heal from psychosis necessitates structure and a comfortable, familiar sleeping environment. Despite Baba's good intentions, being on the move and sleeping in odd places does not prove conducive to me getting the rest I need. I sleep very little. My tenuous grasp on reality is lost completely.

Baba cuts the trip short.

A very grim Dr. R recognizes my active and severe psychosis. He asks if an intern could observe while he questions me. I agree, pleased and proud, not really knowing what is going on. The wide-eyed intern stands beside Dr. R's leather chair, clutching his notebook, pen poised.

"Would you hurt anyone?" Dr. R questions me gravely, his tone both louder and harsher than his usual warm one. That anger and frustration, like the doctor in China, pricks every word. Is it hopelessness? Fear?

"No." I laugh at the ridiculous question. "I wouldn't hurt a fly!" My chuckles meet a stony silence in that brown office, and even I can tell my laugh sounds crazy.

Both men glower at me as if I am possessed. Dr. R is disappointed in me. The intern scribbles notes, breaking the spell.

"I hoped this was major depressive disorder, but seeing as Michelle is experiencing mania after the antidepressants," says Dr. R, his voice dropping an octave. He is looking to Baba, who is also in the room. He is always looking to Baba, whether or not Baba is there. "I must amend the diagnosis to bipolar disorder."

Wait, was the antidepressant a test? Did Dr. R prescribe me that to see if it would make me manic? Is this how things are done? My brain weathered the change in chemicals like a rowboat caught in tidal waves. Is trial and error the only thing we can do?

I am taken off the antidepressant and prescribed Depakote, a mood stabilizer.

Drowsy from my new medication, my mind is still aflame. The feverish battle against the wildfire in my brain will take some time to burn out, to sizzle into calm embers. Baba and Mama are desperate to bring me back down to earth, but there is nothing to do but wait. I am out of reach.

In my manic state before the Depakote starts working, I set up an elaborate shrine on an end table at our house—at the center is a framed photo of Yeh-Yeh with Po-Po and an ornate, brass incense holder Baba uses daily. It also holds my favorite turtle figurines, heart-shaped mementos, and a Buddhist wooden fish for chanting. Each offering is symbolic, to help me communicate with the spirit world.

My parents are terrified.

The next day, everything on that table disappears, even the incense holder.

For days, I mostly sleep. Even upright and awake, I am a zombie. The medication also activates an animal hunger deep within me that no amount of food can satiate. I stuff myself, not tasting anything, while tears leak from my eyes. Baba and Mama pry food from my hands while I fight to shove another bite in my mouth as quickly as possible. Sometimes, I eat so much I vomit. I gain more than thirty pounds in the first months after I am home from China.

"Call me if she ever tries to hurt herself or others," orders Dr. R, who always seems more compassionate toward my parents than me.

My parents think it best to isolate me while I ride out my storm.

They don't want people to find out about my condition. They want this ugly business to be a blip they can cover up later, but after being gone for a semester in China, I want to connect with my friends.

"You shouldn't be on the computer or the phone right now," Baba declares. Every day, he orders Didi to hide the computer wires and phones from me. They move the PC out to the dusty formal dining room table that we never use so they can see who is using it.

Didi is a shoddy babysitter, though, when Mama and Baba aren't home.

I contact my friends with cryptic, nonsensical messages. "I was part of the CIA, but I'm back now."

Another friend asks if I am on drugs. Some of those friendships never recover, but the few who understand and stick by me become stronger than ever.

When I am in public, I am convinced I am being watched again. Because my sleep is inconsistent, I wake up before any of my family members. Some mornings, I go out into the front yard in my pajamas to revel in the beauty of the pebbles, bushes, cacti, and sky. They are so overwhelmingly beautiful. I feel euphoric. I eye the parked cars on my quiet, suburban street suspiciously. The drivers are on a stakeout, observing me, secretly taking pictures of me, and writing reports.

I don't recall the cause of my rage as I cry out, slamming my bedroom door shut and locking it. I flip my twin mattress onto the door to block Baba and Mama from entering, to block out the world.

"Open the door, Beautiful Jade!" Baba pounds on the door. "Open it right now!"

I have to end this.

I have to end this right now.

It has dragged on long enough.

I don't want this life.

I need a fresh start. I need to try again.

I look around my room to see what I can use.

Red nail polish.

Somehow it makes perfect sense.

I know what I am supposed to do.

The intoxicating fume fills the room.

I begin picturing myself slashing my wrists.

With the tiny brush, I paint a deliberate vertical line along my vein all the way up my left arm. Then I slowly move up my right. The cool paint chills my skin, giving me goosebumps.

I am almost done when Baba finds a key and charges through the door, toppling the mattress barricade.

The only thought that runs through my numb mind is simply, "I didn't know there was a key."

I am dumbfounded that Baba could reach me.

Mama is crying. Baba is disturbed by the red lines on my arms and calls Dr. R. who recommends that my parents check me into a psychiatric hospital. "The stay will be for you and your wife as much as it is for Michelle," he says. "You two need respite."

CHAPTER 32: Checked-In

AGE 20 - PHOENIX, ARIZONA

"Take this," I press a small strip of paper into the palm of Red Guy. He is the latest patient who has been checked into the sterile psych facility.

"You know what to do," I whisper with urgency.

Red Guy's eyes widen, grappling with the significance of the task at hand. Rudely awoken from an uneasy sleep, he is now caught in my spy conspiracy. His eyes show me he understands the magnitude of our circumstances as he nods ever so slightly from his hospital bed.

Red Guy is also in his early twenties. He is wearing an oversized red hoodie with red, baggy Dickies skater shorts missing their wallet chain. Perhaps the hospital took that away.

"Hey, what are you doing there?" a nurse shouts at me. She wears a 'fuck my life' expression of exasperation. Red Guy had been sleeping off his high in the middle of the common area where the staff can keep a better eye on him. It is after lights out. I had sneaked out to him to pass on my message.

"Why did you wake him up? He needs rest." She is permanently disgruntled and exhausted.

I do not answer her. She would not understand. This is life and death. The future of humanity could depend on this mission. Red Guy and I embrace tightly, like a brother and sister saying a final farewell before departing for opposite ends of the world. I sneak back to my room. I lose track of Red Guy forever.

In a group session the next day, the energy I hosted the previous night has dissipated. Instead, an inescapable dread descends and traps me until nightfall when the kinetic energy returns.

The facilitator hands out journaling prompts for goal setting. "If I had time, I would _____." The patients, who vary in age from years to decades, are asked to write on our papers and share.

"If I had time, I would be beautiful," my voice quavers. I am unable to meet anyone's eyes. I am not wearing a bra under my thin white University of Arizona t-shirt, which fits snuggly across my chest. My senses are heightened, and I can't stand a scratchy bra on my bare skin.

I feel so fat and ugly. My eyes are puffy from crying and inconsistent sleep. I feel like a crater where a bomb had just been detonated. I can't face what I've done to my life, my reputation over the past few weeks. Me—a Flinn scholar with all the potential—now locked in a mental institution.

A weather-worn, gray-haired man walks up to me after group. "You are so beautiful," he says. "If only I was younger—"

I look down and slowly scoot away, scared.

Guitar Boy exudes cool. He is a shy kid who I am certain is popular in the real world. With his hip ringer t-shirt and nice jeans, he looks like he could still be in high school, though he must have been over eighteen to be in the adult ward. *What kind of problems could he have? With that face and in those clothes?* Then I see them, the tiny cuts on his arms along the shirt sleeves—rows and rows of them. They are so neat and symmetrical, like a woven design on intricate tapestry. He keeps the other patients and me at arm's distance, hiding behind the guitar he is allowed to play while supervised.

When his equally handsome brother and parents visit, I greet them warmly as if I am a new friend, but they meet me with uncomfortable, sideways smiles. They scoot away. They're not here to see me. They act as if my condition is contagious, like they don't want to talk to a loony person. But I saw the cuts. Guitar Boy is one of us.

After just two days at the psych ward, Baba and Mama arrive unexpectedly to collect me. I am pulled from our very structured hospital day to go to the front desk, where I see Mama and Baba standing. They look out of place and afraid.

"What are you doing here already?" I ask.

"We were worried about you." Their eyes do look lined with worry. I don't know how much respite they got while I was here, but Baba could not accept me going to Anytown, he struggled with me traveling to Europe, he didn't want me going to my D.C. internship—the psych ward is no different.

I sigh.

My life is not mine.

I allow my parents to check me out of the ward, and I leave with them prematurely.

Still, the brief hospitalization saves my life.

In my mania, I had been a balloon inflated beyond capacity, stretched painfully taut, dangerously untethered until I popped. Then, a wild, downward spiral of jerky, out-of-control turns took over until all that remained was a pathetic, deflated piece of garbage.

The hospital psychiatrist prescribes a combination of medications that induce sleep heavy enough to squelch my mania and psychosis. The new meds bring me way down. Instead of flying high with celestial beings, I am writhing with the worms again.

Depression is awful, but it is infinitely safer for me there, farther from death and closer to living.

I am hitched again to earth.

Grounded.

CHAPTER 33: Break

AGE 20 - PHOENIX, ARIZONA

"Will I need to be on medication for the rest of my life?" I am afraid to look at Dr. R, afraid of what I might hear. I sink into the brown chair, back in his brown office. It is days after my hospitalization. I'm in shock, just peeping out from the wreckage that is my psychosis, my manic episodes. I can't believe that I had been so disconnected from reality, that I lost complete control.

"At your age," he replies with a soft, dismissive chuckle and a shrug, "there are no broad assumptions for the rest of your life. We don't know how medicine will advance and how you will do."

I meet his eyes in surprise and tug at the sleeves of my light sweater. Winter in Phoenix is pleasantly cool, and the cozy, not entirely necessary, winter wear is comforting nonetheless. Asking my initial question, I brace for a death sentence, a confirmation of my worst fear. But this answer, honest but vague, is not what I expected. Needing psych medication is a new concept that I am struggling to accept, and the idea that I might need medication forever scares the shit out of me. For the first time, I reckon with the fact that I might be damaged for life. That I will always be "crazy," a "psycho."

Dr. R's dodgy answer offers me (and my internalized stigma) a glimmer of hope.

After the hospitalization, I sleep away the hours until my body becomes accustomed to the over 1000mg of the new mood stabilizer medication I put into it daily. No one tells you that a crisis psychiatric hospital stay is like having surgery. Weeks or months may be required afterward for a full recovery. Slowly, the medication works, my body adjusts, and the mental fog dissipates.

"Will I ever be able to return to college?" I pose another fear-filled question to Dr. R like a plea for mercy at that same appointment just after my hospitalization. My Beijing semester ended in December. I have been at home recuperating, but the spring semester will start soon. Too soon. Shell-shocked and drowning in shame, even the thought of starting school sucks all of the air out of me. *Will I feel this way forever?*

I am nearly in tears when I ask Dr. R this question. I want to return to school but also know I can't. Pushing myself to return would break me, but I also am not ready to give up on my education forever.

"You can take a semester off," Dr. R offers, the skinny Santa Claus smile never leaving his face.

"I can do that? And still go back?" Having spent my entire life on the fast track, the idea of taking a break has never before occurred to me. In my family, everything is all or nothing.

"Sure, you can," Dr. R gestures his hands upward for emphasis. "People do it all the time."

I breathe a deep sigh of relief. Another semester, a few more months to recover myself from this rubble of my making, would save me.

I make an appointment with the new scholarship director at the Flinn Foundation office, a shiny new building in downtown Phoenix. I wish I wasn't dealing with someone new, but I have no choice. The last director had retired. The new director is kind and energetic with short red hair and a new-age vibe.

Is there a way to tell the Flinn Foundation that I am too weak to continue my studies right now without making them think they'd been wrong to choose me? How can I make this request without seeming ungrateful and unworthy?

I have no choice but to try.

"Can you tell me what happened?" she asks with care.

I look at the floor, avoiding the answer. I owe the Foundation some sort of answer. They had believed in me and invested in me.

"I had a…breakdown…after my study abroad semester in China." My head is still bowed in shame, and my cheeks burn. I brace for more questions, for anger, for disappointment from her—everything I had felt after my episode.

"Ah, yes. Well, that's okay. People have breakdowns," she smiles reassuringly. "It's more common than you think."

"Really?" I look up, meeting her eyes in surprise.

"Yes, people experience breakdowns during travel often," she says. "Everything will be okay. This is no problem. You just focus on feeling better, Michelle."

And she doesn't pry any further. I never dreamt a prestigious organization chasing excellence like the Flinn Foundation could be so understanding of my condition. I weep from gratitude and relief.

Next, buoyed by Flinn's supportive response, I drive nearly three hours down to Tucson. Baba accompanies me, but I go to the meeting by myself. I am less anxious this time. When I inform the dean who administers the scholarship for my tuition waiver that I will be taking a leave, her answer is altogether different than the Flinn director's.

"If you don't come back to finish your education, you will have to pay back the scholarship money you've used so far," she says sternly.

"What? I've never heard that before." I am entirely taken aback. This university dean works closely with the Flinn Foundation. Some of my friends are very close with her. I'd seen her regularly at various campus functions, but her bristly demeanor is new.

"It's true," she snaps.

I hadn't provided any context. Unlike the Flinn scholarship director, she hadn't asked. "Well, I am going to come back and finish my education, so that doesn't matter." I straighten my back and attempt to be as firm and persuasive as possible—to convince myself most of all.

I am terrified of my future, of what it may no longer hold. Will a semester off turn into two, and snowball into years, once the momentum is lost? Will I lose my scholarship? Will everything I've worked so hard for unravel? Is the potential people saw for my future gone with my diagnosis? My future hangs in the balance. Is being a cashier at Oriental Express and a burden to my parents, all I can ever strive to be?

I don't know anyone else with a mental illness, let alone bipolar disorder. What does life look like after a breakdown, a psych ward stay, and psych meds?

"Are there people who live normal lives with bipolar disorder?" I continue to beg Dr. R for breadcrumbs of hope. He is the only person I can talk to about living with my condition, the only one I can trust to advise on what my future might look like.

"Sure," he shrugs his shoulders gesturing upward with his hands again. "Lots of people."

"Who? Can you give me examples of real, everyday people who are doing well? Because it's hard for me to imagine. Like asking a person to trust that the world is round when they've never even seen the ocean."

"Lots of people," is all he can offer.

Something about his face and the dodgy way he says this makes me not trust it.

"Who? Can you give me examples?"

"My patients," he says, but he can't speak any more to ease my worries.

"Will I still be able to have a job? Live on my own or be in a relationship?"

"Sure," Dr. R smiles with reassurance that begins to transform into a grimace. We are both hitting our heads against a wall.

Even if what he says is true, who would want to marry someone with bipolar disorder? Who would choose to love me? What Baba said to me years ago rings in my memory. I swallow this question whole, like my big bitter pills, shoving it as far down as it can go, trying not to gag. I dare not ask this question aloud. The prospect of spending my life alone or as a burden makes me shudder.

Though the mentally ill label is new to me, the stigma against "crazy" is not. From early childhood, I'd heard my family gossip about people with *supposed* depression.

"She's faking it. Just being lazy and dramatic. Did you see how her eyes light up at the mahjong table? Depressed, my ass!" Baba had spoken about his friend with vehement disgust.

Images of the wife locked away in the attic in *Jane Eyre*, Jack Nicholson in *One Flew Over the Cuckoo's Nest*, news stories of mentally ill mothers drowning their babies flood my mind. I don't want to be one of them, but maybe I already am. Maybe I should hate myself like everyone will.

I turn to the library—my American parent—for answers. I must find someone, anyone, who has written a book about living well with bipolar disorder. A real person to talk to is not possible. Dr. R does not refer me to any support groups or group therapy, so I don't know anything of the sort exists. I am not thinking entirely logically yet, the internet is still relatively new, and is not the go-to resource for information that it will become. A book is what I need.

My ability to focus has been severely compromised because of my episode and is only just beginning to return. My mind races so much, even while I am recovering, I cannot read anything. Getting through even a paragraph is a struggle. Dr. R suggests starting with magazines. My issue with concentration means clinical texts on the subject are out of reach. I am not interested and do not want to feel like a subject to be studied. I feel like enough of a freak already.

Lizzie Simon's memoir, *Detour: My Bipolar Road Trip in 4-D*, becomes a life raft. It weaves together testimonials from real people with lived experiences. Though I'm disappointed that most people Lizzie interviews are still struggling, including Lizzie herself, I take comfort in our shared journeys and common experiences. The book helps me feel less alone.

Still, I wonder if a serious mental illness diagnosis is a life sentence. Saddled with an unpredictable, chronic illness with no known cure and countless fatalities, I can't find many testimonies of survival and hope. The mental illness narrative was, and still is, overwhelmingly that of tragedy. Holding onto faith that I'll be okay feels like having to swim upstream against all odds.

I have no choice but to move forward—put one foot in front of the other. I have no choice but to believe Dr. R that there are "many people," though faceless and anonymous, living well with bipolar disorder. The alternative is to give up, and I am not ready for my life to end before it begins. I want to get better. Failure is not an option.

CHAPTER 34: Hatchling

AGE 20 - ARIZONA AND SEOUL, SOUTH KOREA

Each day, I recover a little more of my former self—a version of me without the extreme and urgent bouts of energy, a version of me that doesn't feel like my insides have been scooped out. The medication and regular therapy provide me with the stability and the ability to sleep peacefully—something I've longed for since my preteens.

Reborn from the ashes of my last episode, but taking a break in the spring semester junior year of college, I feel strong enough to apply for an internship at the Phoenix office of a U.S. senator. This is a second chance, a fresh start. The unpaid role is not very demanding, but it offers structure and prestige vital to the recovery of my sense of self.

Each morning, I dress in business clothes to commute into the city from my parents' house in the suburbs. At work, I am needed and worthy. I make new friends. The unpaid internship pulls me out of my demise and later, provides a solid excuse for why I am not at school during the five months of the spring semester.

By the following term, I am ready to resume my life. Most of my peers, professors, and friends are unaware of what I have been through, but I confide in Val, my roommate. We plan to find an apartment together for the year. At first, she seems supportive. "You must have a mild version," she says. "When I volunteered at a hospital, I met a girl who had bipolar and it was really bad."

I do not know how to respond, though it will not be the last time someone tries to tell me I have a "mild version" of bipolar, not knowing my full story. What can I say? It usually just shuts me up.

Val and I tour several housing options—a quirky guest house in someone's backyard with questionable insulation, your standard corporate apartments, and more. But she doesn't seem to like any of it. There seems to be something she wants to say but is not telling me, but I'm still blindsided when I receive an email from her that says something like:

"I'm sorry, Michelle, but I can't be your roommate next year. I prayed to God, and he told me it wasn't the right decision."

I am gutted. And livid. My friend is abandoning me just before the fall semester, and worst of all, she is hiding behind her Christianity instead of telling me the truth. After two years of friendship, she is writing me off via email. I am convinced my mental illness is the real reason for her change of heart. Val never speaks to me again, and I don't reach out to her either.

Through contacts in the Flinn community, I quickly find alternate housing before my senior year begins. I take the fourth bedroom in an apartment with three guys I don't know well but who are in my social network. Though a little trepidatious about the situation at first, it turns out to be a wonderful, peaceful living situation. I also love that so many of my Flinn friends live in the same small apartment complex, including Ben and three other close friends who are rooming together in the apartment below.

When school starts, I worry there will be gossip about my mental health crisis because I called some friends while psychotic when I first got back from China. I worry about being socially shunned, but it never happens. People are too absorbed in their own lives to remember the strange voice messages or the bizarre phone conversation from months ago, or notice I had been absent a semester unexpectedly. To my great relief, no one pries with too many questions.

Months pass uneventfully. It is as if the life-shattering event that caused me to end up in a psychiatric hospital never happened. I am busy with classes and extracurricular activities, including Asian American clubs, honorary societies, and more.

I am shocked to be named a semi-finalist for homecoming royalty that year but do not think much of it. There are still twenty-five semi-finalist women to be narrowed down to five. I am nervous getting ready for the semifinalist reception, which is our opportunity to charm the judges. Arguably, I am looking my worst ever, still carrying thirty extra pounds on my already fat frame from the new medications. At size 16/18, I am too big for the standard dress sizes and not curvaceous enough to fill out the plus sizes. All clothes look awful on me. In the busyness of the semester, I don't have time to go shopping. I pick a black two-piece from my closet—a loose pencil skirt with a cheap gauzy netting overlayer with a matching long-sleeved top. I look like something between a witch and a nun.

The reception is held in the large common area of a Greek house—the atmosphere is moody and a little dark, though the room is full of chatter. There are couches and chairs and bookshelves around us. I am the only one who doesn't look like a skinny model. All the women are beautifully made-up and vying for attention from the selection committee members who are other graduating seniors. Right away, I notice one woman's low-cut wrap shirt is caught below her bra, exposing her undergarment. She is talking in a circle of women, yet no one calls out her wardrobe malfunction to her. On instinct, I step in front of the fellow finalist I'd never before met, shielding her from the view of others.

"Oops!" I whisper to her, letting her know to fix her shirt, which she does in one swift second.

"Thank you," she says genuinely with a golden smile.

"No problem," I reply and turn around to realize one of the judges is behind me. He has been there the whole time.

A couple of weeks later, at one of the many honor society meetings, the homecoming selection committee marches into the classroom. Some of the members are holding red roses. A hush of anticipation falls over the meeting.

One by one, a selection committee member in a blue blazer and red sweater vest calls out the names of the ten finalists who will make up the Homecoming Royalty of 2002. I can't believe my ears when my name is called, and I feel the envy of the other semifinalists burning me when I stumble up to receive my rose. I am the only non-sorority girl among the women on the homecoming court. It feels surreal.

The following weeks leading up to Homecoming Weekend are a whirlwind of excitement. There are so many events: silly games on the lawn, more receptions, a parade, and more. Donning the white satin sash over our committee-issued University of Arizona Homecoming Royalty polo shirts, I am thrilled. Never before have I come even close to feeling like a beauty queen. I try to expel the negative thoughts of not belonging, of the imposter syndrome, so I can enjoy everything, but I can't stop myself from imagining the order forms for the polo shirts of the women on the court: sizes two extra-smalls, two smalls, and an extra-large.

The whole thing is unreal. So unreal that my father's mood darkens when I ecstatically share the news of my nomination. "Baba, you should come see me in the parade!" I exclaim to my parents before the final two big events. "It's a big deal."

My parents do not understand the concept of school homecoming festivities. Instead, they worry over my mental state, their minds flashing back to my high school episodes, which sometimes involved public votes and crowns.

Baba and Mama drive down to Tucson. They stay just long enough to verify that what I am telling them is true, not something I'd hallucinated in another bout of mania.

Baba slams the door to his truck, taking his leave abruptly. "I was worried about you," he grunts, pulling away.

My parents are too traumatized by my illness to celebrate with me.

They do not see me wave and grin like a fool from a red-mustang convertible down University Avenue. They do not want to be a spectator to the roaring bonfire lit near the school fountain in celebration.

The royalty court members stand on the steps of Old Main for the crowning of the king and queen. When my name isn't called, I am only disappointed for a little bit before feeling genuinely happy. Ben and his lovely girlfriend are crowned the king and queen. Despite sometimes feeling like an imposter who ended up on the court by accident, I feel accepted for the first time. I feel lucky and grateful for my friends, for my life.

The rest of senior year flies by, though I decide to postpone my graduation date due to my semester off. I am not done learning. I want to take more classes. My episode in my junior year had hurt like a grenade exploding, but soon, it seems like a distant, minor blip. After the incident with Val, I only tell people about my bipolar diagnosis on a need-to-know basis. I keep my mental health struggles from nearly everyone, even my closest friends. The only people who know are the ones who had seen me during my episode, to whom I owed an explanation for my odd behavior.

When I am offered a summer consular internship at the U.S. Embassy in Seoul through the Department of State, I can't wait to travel abroad again. A career in the Foreign Service, of applying my Mandarin, Korean, and English language skills in service for my country, would be a dream come true.

"Doesn't the American flag look more beautiful today?" Baba had asked proudly after he and Mama passed the citizenship test when I was sixteen years old. He smiled with his teeth, like an American, as he swore allegiance to the Star-Spangled Banner for the first time as a citizen.

Despite the racism and prejudice we would continue to encounter at the restaurant and in life, I too had stars and stripes in my eyes when I became a naturalized American citizen, by being the child of two naturalized citizens.

Before we immigrated, I was considered Chinese to Koreans and Korean to the Taiwanese and Chinese. China had been inaccessible, its borders closed by its government until 1990. By law, I had never truly belonged to one place. After becoming a U.S. citizen, I revel in the idea that, for the first time, I officially belong. America is my country. After nine years in immigration petition and seven years of permanent residency, she has accepted me. America gives me citizenship and the right to vote in less than two decades what Korea denied my family for three generations. I never take my country or my rights for granted.

The U.S. Department of State internship is a very tangible step toward reaching my dream. Unlike China, which had been a mystery before my arrival, Korea was my childhood home. I longed for the salty air of Incheon harbor to welcome me back.

The world does not spin away from beneath my feet this time. The awareness of my condition, what I should avoid, and my medication keep me well. I thrive, loving the work of investigating visa fraud and interviewing American citizens in jail to ensure no human rights are being violated. I relish the time with my extended family, especially with my favorite uncle, his kind and stylish wife, and their adorable two boys just starting school. My grumpy but lovable Lao-Yeh, my maternal grandfather, also lived with my favorite uncle's family while getting his knee replacement surgery.

All summer, I purchase loads of Spam and oxtail with my discount at the commissary in Seoul and lug it in OCA-issued canvas bags by crowded metro trains over an hour to my uncle's apartment in Incheon Chinatown. The Spam is for the boys, who fight over it during mealtimes. The oxtail, slow simmered into premium bone broth for Lao-Yeh, is a local delicacy far too expensive for my family to buy regularly in Korea. Lao-Yeh eats oxtail soup to his heart's content that summer.

I, too, recharge myself with the flavors of my childhood, the comforting meals that I've long craved—all the soups and stews, the nangmyun, and the street food. My favorite uncle and his wife also introduce me to delectable food trends of the time, like dakgalbi, a spicy chicken barbeque finished with ramen noodles mixed in as the finale in fiery, sweet gochujang. Seeing the love and pride in the eyes of my extended family heals me as well. There is no rejection, no shame. No one, not even my favorite uncle who had deployed his friend to take care of me in Beijing, mention anything about what had happened in China the previous year. They are all just happy I am better.

PART

三

CHAPTER 35: Favorite Uncle

JUNIOR YEAR OF COLLEGE - SOUTH KOREA

When Didi was born, my parents dropped me off in Daegu so Mama could care for a newborn without three-year-old me to look after too. I soaked up the attention from my maternal grandparents and my two young uncles who all lived together in the jajangmyun noodle restaurant the family has run for generations. My Lao-Yeh and Lao-Lao's residence had no professional plumbing. Everything was crafted and rigged by my grandfather and uncles with duct tape and home-mixed cement. An old-fashioned pump for icy water stood in the middle of the small courtyard in the back of the restaurant, near a stinky outhouse with no toilet paper. I was trained to use the tissue-thin calendar paper of days past to wipe myself, but I never noticed these differences in living conditions. I was so well taken care of at Lao-Yeh and Lao-Lao's house, I remember it as a wonderland of adoration, joy, and the most delectable foods.

Lao-Yeh was a skilled botanist who nurtured an impressive, secret rooftop garden in the busy, polluted city. Every corner was cluttered with life—plants flourishing in pots big and small, rubber buckets harboring colorful koi tucked in corners here and there. A black cat caught mice and the occasional tiny bird. Up there, in such an unlikely place, Lao-Yeh coaxed to life two pomegranate trees that bore miracle jewel fruits. He preserved these treasures in his brown, wrinkled, calloused hands to share on our long-awaited visits.

Soon, I learned to listen for the sizzle of frying meat for tangsuyuk. Quick as I could, I'd dash to the kitchen on slippered feet and hold out my palms to whichever uncle was cooking, waiting for a salty, steaming, delicious morsel. The uncles would chuckle, impressed with my speed and my hearing.

I loved watching my uncles expertly hand crank out noodles, prepared fresh for each bowl. And though I adored both my uncles in Daegu, the younger one was my favorite. He was just fourteen years older than me. He was the most fun person, the only adult who truly knew how to play. My early memories of visiting my mom's family in Daegu are filled with Favorite Uncle's antics, often full of silly potty talk and goofy physical comedy. He would do anything to make me laugh.

Favorite Uncle took me on his deliveries by scooter, balancing a tin carrier full of noodle bowls and side dishes of yellow daikon and chopped onions covered in plastic wrap in one arm, steering with the other. I squeezed in tight in the space in front of him. He had unlimited time and patience. In later years, Favorite Uncle taught Didi and me to swim. He built us our first snowman and taught us to throw snowballs. He made me feel like I matter, not just for what I could accomplish, but like my happiness for its own sake mattered. He joined Didi and me on our level, never expecting us to conform to the preferences of adults.

At my grandparents' place, I spent nights cuddling with my beloved Lao-Lao on the coal-heated floors. I've never found sweeter slumber since. One time, I stole an egg from the pantry shed and stashed it under the warm fold blankets in the room with coal-heated floors, hoping to hatch a chick. When Lao-Lao discovered the egg, everyone roared with laughter, while I hid under the covers, blushing and disappointed that my plan didn't work.

When Favorite Uncle was in his early twenties, he moved to Incheon to be near us, but not long after, we announced our plans for immigration.

When I, at age 21, see Favorite Uncle now, who is a 35-year-old father of two boys, it feels as if no time has passed. Jojo is as silly as ever. We laugh when his wife points out how handsome an actor is on TV, and I joke that my uncle, tanned and goofy, is better looking. Even in teasing, I always have his back, and he has mine.

For the first time, Jojo tells me how he was heartbroken by our departure. He tells me how alone he felt in the big, new city of Incheon. As a child, caught up in the chaos of immigration, I had no idea.

Favorite Uncle is the only Asian man I know who sees me, who never teases or bullies me for being fat, and who shelters me from a cruel world. His love and protection is without conditions.

When one of his sons, about six years old, slips and falls in the bathroom, Favorite Uncle cradles him and strokes his hair. "Baba's so sorry it hurts, baby. I wish I could make it go away."

And, just like that, I witness for the first time, a Chinese father apologizing to his child for something that wasn't even his fault. This trip to Korea affords me a view into the kind of father Favorite Uncle has become. I cannot compute the shock. All my life, my own Baba taught me that Chinese adults do not apologize to children because respect flows in one direction only. Yet, before me, my favorite uncle, who still lives in Incheon Chinatown in Korea—arguably more Chinese than any of us—apologizes to his son.

I get chills.

My cousin curls tight into his dad, slowly calming down—the apology is not a shock to him like it is to me. He is used to hearing his parents say dui bu chi. It is normal for him.

"I never hit the kids," Favorite Uncle shudders, shaking away traumatic memories. "Your Lao-Yeh was very harsh. He believed in the 'kill the chicken to teach the monkeys' philosophy. Have you heard of it?"

I shake my head no.

Lao-Yeh is nothing but loving and kind to me and Didi, but I know he had been hard on his children.

"He'd kick your Uncle Johnny, the oldest boy, on the ground until he bled, so the rest of us would fall in line." Kill the chicken to teach the monkeys. Uncle Johnny was the chicken slaughtered as example. "It was brutal."

Uncle Johnny ran away to America as soon as he could, to get as far away as possible. Long gone by the time of my birth, Uncle Johnny was not around in the Korea I remember.

Both Uncle Johnny and Favorite Uncle broke the cycle and built non-violent homes for their families. I'm relieved for my cousins, whom I adore, but I mourn for Didi and myself, who aren't as fortunate.

CHAPTER 36: Fighting

SENIOR YEAR OF COLLEGE - ARIZONA

Sometimes I hate visiting my parents in Phoenix. I stay in Tucson for longer and longer stretches without visiting, savoring my freedom and independence, but I do miss my parents. They call me every day, and usually, I don't mind. When I go home, they ply me with my favorite foods and so much affection that I can feel the warmth of their loving gaze on my face. Every so often, though, Baba gets on my case.

This time, it's because he sees me take my nightly pills.

"Ai-ya!" exclaims Baba from his usual place in front of the loud television in the living room, "Are you still taking that medication?"

"Yes, of course," I snap from the kitchen. "I'm not supposed to stop."

"You don't need them anymore, Daughter. You're better. I've looked it up. My books all say that women grow out of these kinds of things when they're older and stable. Once you marry and have kids, you won't have your struggles anymore. Listen to Baba, stop taking your medications. What if you get addicted?"

I scoff at Baba's wishful thinking, non-scientific bullshit.

"What if I get sick again? I need my medication to keep me well."
I shake my head in disbelief.

"Listen to me, you're better now. You're not someone who needs
drugs. You're not crazy."

There is nothing for me to do but sigh. Thank goodness I have
my own health insurance and can fill and pay for my prescriptions
on my own.

Baba and Mama persist in sitting me down for multiple heart-
to-hearts in attempts to stop me from treatment. My mother is going
along with Baba's wishes. She sits quietly next to Baba with a worried
expression, taking a sigh of affirmation from time to time.

When their attempts at convincing me fails, Baba enlists help.
I am reading in bed when Baba barges into the room and shoves a
phone in my face. "Here, Beautiful Jade, talk to your Little Auntie."

"Who?"

"My sister in Taiwan who is a nursing professor. Talk to her, she
has a Ph.D."

"Wei? Hello, Little Auntie."

"Beautiful Jade, your father told me everything. You should listen.
You don't need your medication anymore. Listen to me. I told him
about some herbs that he can give you. Stop taking the medicine from
the hospital, okay, good girl?"

Great. Another puppet for Baba is just what I need. As if Mama
wasn't enough.

Baba picks up the baton as soon as I get off the phone. "See,
Daughter? Your aunt also says you don't need your medication. She
knows what she's talking about. Listen to us. Stop taking them."

Frustration is far too inadequate a word to express the festering
in my gut. I want to scream at the ignorance, the denial, the injustice.
How unfair that I have to fight my own parents to keep myself well.
How unfair that they refuse to listen to my actual doctors or me.

I want to get out and never to return.

This ridiculous fight restages itself monthly. My parents have seen
me when I am psychotic, multiple times. They'd checked me into the

psychiatric hospital. Baba has spoken with Dr. R many times and yet, they refuse to accept the seriousness of my condition. Mama is forever Baba's faithful soldier. She rarely expresses opinions of her own. This initiative to stop my medication is all Baba. Failure is not an option for my father. Mental illness is a failure, shameful and unacceptable. It does not fit into the story of his life that he fought for so desperately. Baba not only wants to bury the ugliness of my condition and cover its tracks, he needs to deny its existence.

But no way am I going to risk mania or depression again. Not if I can prevent it. I seem to be the only one who recognizes that the treatment means life or death for me.

At the same time Baba is campaigning for me to stop my meds, he is still strategizing ways to mold my future. My father is stuck on the idea of making a doctor out of me, even after everything we've been through.

"What if I become a diplomat?" I remember pleading as a high school senior. Even after I earned the Flinn Scholarship, I have to convince Baba. "I can use my Mandarin and Korean language skills and experiences abroad to my advantage."

This is the only argument that worked, at least temporarily. The potential prestige of having a diplomat for a daughter makes Baba waver just enough, to back off his relentless push for medicine or law.

I would have loved to study theater or art, but I know better than to push my luck. My plan hatched in eighth grade has worked somewhat. His leverage is limited, though not gone.

But here we are again, years and a psychotic break and hospitalization later, and Baba is droning on about the same thing. When I come home from Tucson to visit, Baba and Mama tell me to come sit in front of them in the living room, and I know I'm in for another serious talk.

"Why not become a doctor, Daughter?" Baba says. Mama sits there in quiet agreement, nodding. I'm so disappointed in both of them.

"Why are we having this conversation again?" I close my eyes and cradle my head. I have never felt less seen. I don't even feel like I exists. *Do Mama and Baba care about me at all?*

"My friend's son just got into Stanford medical school," Baba adds, foaming with a radioactive envy. "You're smart enough too. Why don't you do it? Other people only dream of becoming a doctor but can't because they don't have the ability. You do, so why not go for it? It's the best career. You'll get the most respect. It's all I've ever wanted. It's why we came to this country."

It's as if Baba forgot that mere months ago, he pushed me so hard that I ended up in the psych ward. How can Baba and Mama not remember and sit here before me so sternly, especially when there is only a year left of college? How can they continue to blindly push me like this, like they're ramming a log to breach a fortress?

I wonder if I could be having a stroke at my age. I think I might combust. "Baba, I am not interested in medicine. Also, I'm a senior. Even if I wanted to, I can't suddenly change my major now."

I hate the position I am relegated to each time I come home. I want to run away and never turn back.

"Did you forget already?" I am exasperated. "Did you forget how I was hospitalized? Why are you doing this again?"

Baba and Mama's expressions are neutral and firm, unflinching. I can't break through their stiff postures. "That's in the past now," Baba says. "We believe in you. We know you can do it, so we are not giving up on you."

I start to see Baba more for who he is around this time in my young adulthood. The more I see the less I understand.

"When you interned at the embassy in Seoul, I bragged to everyone I knew that you were an ambassador," Baba says with a smug smirk on a random quiet Sunday. It's a sneak attack. I think everything is going well and I am having a nice visit when Baba drops this absurd bomb.

"What?" Appalled, I put down my chopsticks. "Why would you say that?"

"Why not? I could belittle my friends and their kids' accomplishments that way," he replies without an ounce of remorse, looking like a cat taunting a trapped mouse.

"That's terrible." I am disgusted. I feel dirty for being the subject of his lie.

"Why are you getting mad? I thought it'd make you happy." Baba looks genuinely baffled.

"Happy? Why would it make me happy that you're lying about me?" I gasp, barely able to breathe. "When you lie like that, for one, it makes me feel as if my real accomplishments aren't good enough to make you proud so you make up lies."

"Don't worry about it. You're too honest, Beautiful Jade. It makes me happy. That's all that matters." Baba chuckles and I have been dismissed. He has no intention of stopping his lies.

In December of 2003, I graduate with a Bachelor of Arts degree in International Studies with a minor in Chinese. Managing a near-perfect GPA, summa cum laude with honors, I am awarded Senior of the Year by the political science department. Though selected as a finalist for the Truman Scholarship for graduate studies, I biff the interview and am not selected.

My anxiety about what to do post-college is significantly reduced when I accept a graduate internship at the Arizona State Senate, which buys me a few more months of indecision.

Despite my secret diagnosis, my future continues to burn brightly. Nevertheless, I am unable to shake the feeling that I am an imposter. I live in fear of the possibility that the fire inside my head could catch again, burning all accolades and accomplishments to embers. All of my triumphs are built upon the shroud of feathers covering my bipolar disorder.

CHAPTER 37: Taking Flight

ARIZONA

After graduating college, many of my peers are jumping into graduate school, but I am hesitant. Graduate school would not only cost a fortune, but it would require every ounce of dedication and focus I can muster. I imagine triple the amount of dense, academic reading that is required in undergraduate school, and that alone induces panic. I love reading, but I can only focus on material that interests me. Otherwise, I completely zone out. I'm not sure if this is my nature or a symptom of bipolar disorder.

In high school, I could stay up all night absorbed in my history textbook, but in college, I struggled with my non-humanities assigned reading. If I am going to work myself to the bone and go into debt, I want to know without a doubt that the graduate program is what I want and that my education would be a sound investment.

I ask myself what I was most passionate about from my college experience. The answer comes easily—it is undoubtedly the mentoring program I founded for adoptees from Asia. After building the program throughout my four plus years in college, I handed the reins of the program over to an Asian American sorority. The initiative I started will continue to make a positive impact after I am gone.

Now, I wonder if I can work in nonprofit international adoption. It seems like a perfect fit. My ultimate goal continues to be to work in the U.S. Foreign Service, so I reason that my internship experiences at the federal and state levels of government, combined with a job in the nongovernmental organizations sector, will best prepare me to become a well-rounded representative of the U.S. As a bonus, I may be able to utilize my language skills. The idea that I might be able to travel to orphanages abroad and meet with embassies to advocate for children in need excites me the most.

After inquiring with adoptive parent contacts from the mentoring program about the agencies they've worked with, I am soon hired as an adoption consultant at a Tucson-based international adoption agency. I immerse myself in work, launching a waiting children program for children with special needs, applying for adoption grants, and organizing donation drives to an orphanage near the border in Mexico.

Because of my dedication and initiative, I am quickly promoted. With my full-time job in Tucson, seeing Dr. R in Phoenix for regular visits is no longer viable. Since he has been my one and only psychiatrist, I don't know that most psychiatrists do not also do talk therapy as part of their practice. This means that I have to find not only a new psychiatrist for my medications but also a new therapist.

Finding good mental health care is difficult. I hadn't realized how much I'd lucked out with Dr. R. My new therapist in Tucson, Dee, is grandmotherly and compassionate, but my new psychiatrist has startlingly cold bedside manners. He rushes through our twenty-minute appointments and suggests a change in medication at every chance without really listening to me. When I try to talk about my feelings or struggles, or ask him about a solution other than changing medications, he abrasively shuts me down.

"I'm not your therapist," he snaps. "I'm not like Dee."

I don't know why he hates me so much. I don't know what I did for him to act like he never wants to see me. It is as if he is only going through the motions so he can get through his workday. But finding doctors covered by my new work insurance with appointments available near my work is challenging and overwhelming, so I continue seeing the bad-mannered psychiatrist for over a year.

Dr. R generously takes my calls on rare occasions when I struggle with anxiety or depression to a point of near crisis and need additional guidance. But, in general, because of my medication routine and structured lifestyle, I no longer suffer from the unbearable extremes that threaten to destroy me.

Leslie and Teresa, the Chinese American friends from college, are still two of my best friends. After buying matching ceramic pigs together on a beach road trip to Rocky Point, Mexico, we dub ourselves "The Three Piggies."

We explore quaint nearby towns together, like day trips to Bisbee, Arizona. We sample new restaurants, go dancing, and generally savor the young professional's lifestyle. Leslie is an artistic architect-in-training in a long-term relationship, while Teresa is a fun and loyal law student to whom dating seems to come easily. But at age twenty-three, I still have never kissed or dated anyone. Others my age seem to find love so naturally and easily, yet romance evades me again and again. Men never approach me like they do Leslie, Teresa, or other women I know. It makes me feel awful and like something is wrong with me. I continued to live with many insecurities, not the least of which is my secret bipolar disorder that I don't even tell Leslie and Teresa about.

In a world full of people who were thinner, more beautiful, and less damaged, why would anyone choose me?

In the absence of any other romantic prospects, David returns to the space he has always held in my heart. We hang out when I go to Phoenix on weekends. Sometimes, he visits me in Tucson.

One unforgettable moment, David and I are sitting in front of a colorful abstract painting I painted hanging at my parents' restaurant when David says with a sweet, bemused smile, "I don't want to get married until I'm in my thirties, but when I do, I think I want a wife who paints."

I blush, feeling tingles on my skin. I smile and look away shyly.

I'm so close to David, yet he is still a mystery. Like me, he has never dated anyone in all the years we've been friends. At least not in the States. He has never shown romantic interest in anyone around us, but whenever he travels abroad, he returns with stories of steamy affairs and photos of sexy girls—a free-spirited classmate in Spain or a flight attendant in Thailand—as proof.

None of that ever matters to me, though. When he looks at my painting and dreams of his future, I melt. This has to be a sign, his way of hinting at things to come.

When the lease expires at my apartment in Tucson, the rent is increased by an exorbitant amount. Grappling to find a new place quickly, I experience severe anxiety, lose sleep, and am paralyzed by the big decisions before me.

"My aunt owns a condo in Tucson she never uses," David immediately offers a solution. "Why don't you stay there? The rent would only be $250 a month. If anyone asks, though, you have to pretend to be my fiancée. The condo owners' association does not allow renters."

His extended family will have to be complicit in this arrangement. I allow myself to dream that this is further evidence that one day, when David is ready, we'll be together. Being a rule-follower, I am uneasy about the arrangement, but I go for it, believing it will further entwine David and me toward our future together.

In the spring of 2005, when I am just shy of 24 years old, David accompanies me on a trip to Washington D.C. I am there to take the Foreign Service exam, but the trip coincides with the Sakura Festival and David's birthday, so he tags along. We play tourists under perfect blue skies and at the impressive museums and monuments. We goof around while posing for cheesy photos in front of clouds of soft pink blossoms. At night, in our motel room, I surprise David with a package of candlelit Hostess Snoballs, only slightly smashed up pink coconut and marshmallow-covered chocolate cakes, and sing him happy birthday.

The whole trip, I hold my breath. *Will this be the trip our friendship turns romantic? Will a hug linger? An innocent moment turn intimate in the privacy of our own four walls?*

Nothing of the sort happens.

But when David asks me to go to Costa Rica as his plus one for his friend's wedding, my stomach fills with butterflies again. This has to be it. What all my teenage angst culminates to—it has to be the payoff.

My parents, who had misgivings about my friendship with David when we were in high school, have come around. As soon as I graduate from college, they begin asking me if I have a boyfriend, even though they've forbidden me to date all this time.

My answer is always a no. They make assumptions about David and me, and they begin to embrace him. After all, he has been in my life for nearly a decade. He is dependable, kind, and attended graduate school immediately after college, so he'd already earned a Master's degree from a good school.

When I pack for Costa Rica, there is no begging me not to go this time. As the sun sets on Thanksgiving day, I walk out their front door to David's waiting car on our way to the airport.

"Relax and have a great time! Don't worry about anything," Baba says wistfully.

Mama smiles with glistening eyes as if they know something I don't, as if they're letting me go forever.

"Thanksgiving dinner together on a plane?" I giggle as the flight attendant hands us trays with globs of airplane food. "Yes, please!"

"This will be hard to forget." David grins at me, and I melt.

CHAPTER 38: Clueless

COSTA RICA AND TUCSON, ARIZONA

A man in a suit at the counter behind the Holiday Inn hotel in San Jose greets us jovially at check-in as we walk in. The place is much nicer than the franchises of the same chain in the U.S. There is a live orchid on the counter and the floors are gleaming, possibly even marble. "Welcome, Mr. and Mrs. David!"

"Oh, we're not…" David and I both blush and clear our throats. I hide a smile.

The room is standard, and its lone window looks out to a Hooters restaurant in an expansive parking lot. David and I laugh in hysterical fits at every little thing, just hanging out, as we do whenever we're together.

Being international wedding guests, we're invited to the rehearsal dinner the night before the wedding. The small Chinese restaurant is already packed with wedding guests when we arrive. With its red and gold wooden décor and bustling atmosphere, I feel instantly at home. The couple had met in David's graduate program. The bride, though ethnic Chinese, was born and raised in Costa Rica. The Chinese banquet-style rehearsal dinner full of Chinese people is an absolute treat and not at all what I expected when I agreed to come to the wedding. I could have been at a banquet at China Tower in Incheon or The Great Wall in Phoenix. The resilience of my fellow immigrants in the Chinese diaspora, the spirit of survival, and ability to make a better life almost anywhere in the world fills me with pride. I fit right in.

"What does your friend's family do here?" I ask David on the way to the rehearsal dinner.

"I think they own a local chain of gas stations or something," he answers nonchalantly.

Finding this unexpected tribe in an unfamiliar land makes me feel ordinary in the best way possible. I am not alone. There are pockets of us everywhere, in all sorts of fascinating multicultural combinations.

The wedding the next day is held at the sprawling Intercontinental Hotel in San Jose's most upscale area. It is, and will remain, the most extravagant nuptials I've ever attended. I had not expected the wedding to be so fancy.

Scrimping and hard labor in small businesses, much like my parents and grandparents, is how this Chinese family financed their daughter's American education and glamorous wedding, complete with Carnivale dancers, a full live band, and a chocolate fondue fountain.

The wedding guests are all down-to-earth and wholesome. I blend in seamlessly in my shimmery green bargain dress (from Ross, of course). David and I dance the night away in the Carnivale party procession, donning glittery party hats.

After the glamorous Costa Rican Chinese wedding, David and I hike around Arenal Volcano Park, spot wild toucans and giant spiders in rain forest tours, and breathe in the swirling mist of deafening waterfalls. The healing spring waters of La Fortuna soothe our tired muscles at the end of the day.

In Monteverde, we planned to zipline over the magnificent forest canopies, but when we arrive at the entrance of the forest tour company, there is a mandatory release form that is a pre-requisite to going on the tour. It says if we fall to our death, the company will not be responsible. Ever risk-averse, I hesitate, but David is too excited. He signs right away and waits for me. I shut my eyes and sign.

A winding shuttle takes us high into the mountains. The first few ziplines are low and manageable. I start to think maybe this won't be so bad. By the third zipline, we're somehow about a mile high above the forest. I am petrified, but there is no turning back without disrupting the dozen people on tour with us. I am too embarrassed to say anything and push onward. David is fearless, volunteering even to jump on the optional soaring rope swing that looks to me like a deadly pendulum.

"Michelle, you should try this too!"

"No way," I shake my head, looking at him like he's lost his mind. I know I am disappointing him, but I have my boundaries. The rope swing is high-risk, without moving us forward. That meant all risk, no reward. I don't take unnecessary risks. If we get hurt here in the rainforest, it would be hours before help could reach us.

Whipping through the air over breathtaking flora, I have an excellent time. Ziplining is fun and exhilarating once I get the hang of it. And when my feet are back safely on solid ground at the end of the tour, I say to David, "That was amazing, but I never need to do it again." And we laugh.

Though the hotels and hostels we stay at outside of San Jose are very rustic, our bed is often decorated at night with fresh tropical flower petals arranged into heart shapes, the towels rolled into swans. Every place addresses us as "Mr. and Mrs." We stop trying to correct them. We share many beds without ever touching one another.

David is relatively fluent in Spanish, and it helps our adventures in Costa Rica go smoothly. After Monteverde, we head for the coastal town of Tamarindo about three hours away, to relax on the beaches. At breakfast, my nose is in my thick copy of a Costa Rica travel guide. "So, should we travel by the $3-a-ticket Tico Bus, like the locals?" I ask David. "It sounds so charming. It's a refurbished school bus! We can do as the locals do. Really experience Costa Rica, you know? Pura Vida!"

David smirks and rolls his eyes. "I'd much rather pay for the $20-a-person, air-conditioned minivan shuttles that will get us right there."

"Oh, what's the fun in that?" I tease. "That's for foreign tourists only. Where's your sense of adventure?" I look at him with eyes open wide.

"Fine," he giggles, gently tossing a napkin at my face. "I don't care that much."

Despite the charming description of the refurbished old school buses in my travel book which had promised that it is reliable, the Tico Bus ride is violently bumpy and stiflingly hot. We are packed tight like sardines as we rumble down dirt roads with crater-sized potholes. After two hours on the road, David and I are dropped off with aching backs and necks in a deserted town in the middle of nowhere and mysteriously told to take a transfer to get to Tamarindo. There is not a soul around anywhere, which makes us nervous. The wind blows up gusts of dirt over our eyes.

We are at a bus stop with a handwritten sign. David deciphers that the next bus to Tamarindo leaves the next day. It is only mid-day, and the sun is burning hot above us. Suddenly, a lone taxi appears out of nowhere. The driver stops in front of us. We are eager for a way out. This could be our only chance.

David opens the cab door and asks him in Spanish, "How far are we to Tamarindo? Can you take us?"

The driver scratches his head. They exchange a few more words.

"He wants $100," David says to me, grumpily. He is clearly annoyed with me for my Tico Bus idea.

I am upset at being blamed for our predicament. I look around the vacant town, still not a soul in sight other than this taxi. "I guess we have no choice," I say to David. "We can't stay here until tomorrow."

We both get in the red sedan with our large backpacks, eager to be finished with this travel day. We ride in silence for hours on more bumpy dirt roads, sometimes having to wait until cows cross or children move, until we arrive in the beach town, ready to forget our stress and enjoy the rest of the trip.

Our hostel features impressive tropical trees and plants all around the courtyard with hammocks and bright-colored parrots happily perched in the center. We check in and drop off our bags as quickly as possible. We want to explore the beach, to see what we came all this way for. Making a rush decision, I pack my passport, digital camera, and jewelry in my mini backpack purse, afraid to leave it at the open-air hostel.

David is looking more tan than usual after our days here. He is wearing a white tank top and board shorts. I have my bathing suit under a soft, loose black Indonesian dress in Batik print that my mom received as a gift in her twenties. I love that dress. David and I are quieter than usual, but we're trying to put the unpleasantries behind us.

We wander toward the sound of the waves in flip-flops. As we near the empty beach, a family of small monkeys shriek at us from high up in the trees. David and I laugh. I snap pictures. David lets me pick our spot on the big beach. I'm indecisive.

"How about here?" I ask, pointing to a spot recessed from the water, bordering the greenbelt. "It's partly shaded, but partly in the sun too."

"Fine, sounds good," says David.

The cool waves beckon me, and I take off my dress to go in the water. David settles on the large beach towel for a nap. I leave my mini-backpack with him.

From waist deep in the ocean, I notice a tall man walk strangely close to where David is sleeping, but I don't say anything.

A few minutes later, I return from the water and don't see my bag.

"David, wake up! Have you seen my backpack? It's gone."

"No," David stands up drowsily and I tear away the towel. The backpack is nowhere. "I don't know where it is."

"My passport and my camera were in there." I gasp, panicking.

"What? Why did you bring your passport? Why didn't you leave it at the hostel?" David screeches.

"I thought it would be safer with me. You didn't notice anyone take it? I saw a man walking by. Did you see him?"

"No, I was asleep."

I cover my eyes with my hands, not knowing what to do. Our return flights are in two days, and my passport is gone.

"Please help us," David talks to a nearby shop owner. "My friend's bag was stolen."

I didn't have much cash in the bag and the jewelry was more of sentimental than monetary value, but the passport and my small digital camera are a different story. The possibility of being stranded here is making me panic. I would also be heartbroken to lose the hundreds of photos I'd taken on this trip.

David's passport is still safely back at the hostel. Throughout this exchange, he glares at me in frustration. We're not laughing anymore. We haven't for a while. I'm afraid to ask him if he will leave me alone in Costa Rica and fly back to the States by himself. Can I blame him if he does?

The people of Tamarindo are very helpful. The local economy depends on the tourism industry, and they want to do all they can to stop theft and crimes. David tells the shop owner, a woman with a baby on her back, what happened, about a tall man who walked by while he was sleeping. She seems to know exactly whom David was referring to. She gathers a crowd, taking our problem very seriously, and talks to the police in speedy Spanish that I cannot follow, not even a little. Looking from one speaker to another, I feel powerless. But it seems we're making progress.

The next day, instead of relaxing on the beach, we wake up early to take a taxi to a large white courthouse building the next town over. We spend all day waiting for the judge, hoping for an expedited processing of our case. The whole time, David and I feel like we only know maybe a third of what's going on. Not because of the language barrier, but because of what they are willing to tell us.

Fortunately, the police have recovered my passport and camera. The cash and jewelry are gone.

I am relieved I can fly home without any further complications or awkwardness with David and extremely grateful to not have to find out how eagerly he might have left without me.

On the final day and a half of the trip, David remains tense around me, even after everything is resolved. He is famous for his easy smiles, but he won't smile anymore. He won't laugh at my jokes. He is curt and dismissive about the things I say. I've never had David act this way toward me before, and I'm hurt that he seems to blame everything that has gone wrong with the trip on me. In turn, I am angry too.

We fly back to Arizona in silence and go our separate ways. I am not sure if we will ever speak again.

To my surprise, my anger dissipates before Christmas. I had been so hurt and angry, but within weeks, I am ready to put the events behind us. This is unusual for me, someone who holds epic grudges. I convince myself I could let things go so easily because of love. This is proof I am truly in love with David.

At this revelation, with my heart bursting, I pour my emotions into another handwritten letter. Since high school, I've written several versions of this letter, professing my love to David. I have never mailed them though. This time I will.

Sitting on the green carpet of David's aunt's condo that I call home, I scribble down everything with tears running down my face. My exact words are lost, but I imagine the letter contained the passion and drama of youth, of all the years of my pent-up, unrequited love. We had so many sweet memories together. David is the only person I'd ever made mixtapes for. The only guy, not counting my father, I'd gone on trips with alone. Images fill my heart: singing karaoke at my house, David holding out his hand to me to "Can't Help Falling in Love," all the movies in dark theaters, prom, driving around the desert, sakura blossoms in D.C., Costa Rican sunsets. All of my feelings, I pour into the letter.

With David, I never felt ashamed of my house or of its mismatched, messy interior, even though his house was always immaculately kept by his mother. I write that he must care for me too, even if he does not realize it himself. I offer up his faithful handwritten international correspondence, the "painter wife" comment from that time at the restaurant, and the fake fiancée living arrangement as evidence. I remind him of the magic, the laughter when we are together. I can't be the only one to experience these feelings.

I drop the letter in the mailbox before I run out of nerve. The metal handle closes with the weighty finality of a guillotine.

Several days later, David calls in the evening. I am sitting on the couch in his aunt's condo, still pretending to be his fiancée.

"I got your letter," he huffs. "How could you think this?" He sounds disgusted.

My heart is already crushed.

How could this be? I was so sure.

"You don't feel any of it?" I stare at the old TV across the room, trying to process what's happening. One hand is holding my small cellphone to my face while the other is picking at my hair.

"No, Michelle, I don't think of you that way," he says exasperated. "I thought we were on the same page."

"But what about...?"

"I don't think of you like that. I'm not attracted to you sexually. Your friend Leslie that we went dancing with, she is sexy. Someone like her, that's who I find sexy. Not you."

How could he be so cruel? He is dragging one of the Piggies, one of my closest friends, into this.

"Why would you lead me on all this time? Why did you say the thing about my painting?"

"We're just friends, Michelle!" His voice becomes sharp and defensive, like it had in high school when he tried to sound aggressive to fight against people calling him effeminate. "I think you just saw what you wanted to see and heard what you wanted to hear, but none of it is real."

Then, he softens. "Look, I already told you that I don't plan on getting married until I'm thirty or older. Maybe in time, things will change. Maybe we'll both change."

I interpret his statement the only way I can. I conclude that he means, maybe in the next few years, I can lose weight and become hotter. Someone who can be sexy to him. David confirms my worst fears and insecurities.

I am simultaneously burning with rage and ready to wither away from heartbreak. "Well, I can't do this anymore."

"Fine. When you're ready to be friends again, I'll be here." David merely sounds inconvenienced, while I am destroyed.

I end the call and move out as quickly as I can.

We have not seen each other or spoken since.

CHAPTER 39: Wisp

TUCSON, ARIZONA

"We need to go out. You need to get drunk this time," Teresa says to me. She has come to check on me in the cold room with two house-mates I rented in a hurry. The room is bare like the way I feel, it is also perpetually chilly and stony, even when it is warm and sunny outside. It suits me just fine.

I want to numb the pain and forget everything that happened with David. I am drowning in the sting of rejection I'd feared and avoided all of my life.

"Okay," I nod.

"Come on, get dressed!" Teresa urges. "You're gonna look hot, you hot, hot tamale!" Teresa's spiky short hair has grown out and softened into a chic bob. She looks so much more grown-up than when we were in college.

I put on tight-fitting checkered slacks with a low-cut black tank top. My favorite maroon velvet blazer finishes the look. Most of the time, I don't wear makeup, so my maroon lipstick and dark eyeliner makes it feel like a special occasion. I don't feel sexy, I never do, but it's the best I can manage.

Teresa drags me to a bar and then a club. I keep a bottle of cheap champagne with me all night and force myself to gulp until my vision blurs. As the night wears on, sadness seeps from every pore of my body. In a dirty stall of a bar bathroom, I fall like a pile of rocks next to the toilet, utterly defeated. Suddenly, Teresa is there. She hoists me up, and I am overcome with gratitude for her love, tears silently streaming down my cheeks until I lose consciousness.

The Piggies urge me to put myself out there, but I don't know how. Nothing ever happens organically like it does for them. I'm tired of one-sided crushes. I'm 24 years old. Too old for that stuff. Too old to never have gone on a real date and never been kissed. Too old to be a virgin. I don't fit the stereotypical mold of the sexually desirable Asian woman. At 5'9" and hovering around 200 pounds, I am not delicate, demure, or submissive. I am bigger than most Asian men, and I do not fit into the fantasy of any non-Asians, not that I ever want to be anyone's fetish. I want to be seen and loved for who I am, but more than that, I want someone who will let me love them. I am desperate for the opportunity to prove myself a great partner, but at this rate, I feel like I'll never have the opportunity.

At night, I dance alone in my room, with the stereo turned up on the *Pussycat Dolls* "Stickwitu." It's a silly, catchy love song but I apply the chorus lyrics to loving myself. I am trying to learn the lesson that I can't rely on others to feel loved and whole. I must love myself first.

But, in darker moments, the status quo is unbearable enough to push me out of my comfort zone. I try internet dating in its infancy and go on a couple of typical bad dates. When a colleague from work asks me to join her for a speed dating event, I agree. I dress in head-to-toe slimming black, with accents of red jewelry. Of the dozen or so guys I talk to, I match with two. The only two Asian guys in the room. One turns out to be almost a decade older than me and is shocked to learn my age when we meet for coffee. We never contact each other again.

The other is a Japanese American guy who is training for the

Ironman triathlon. The first time we meet after the speed dating event, he stares at my stomach for far too long and it makes me want to hide. He is intense, has severe social anxiety, and is constantly being coached by his older brother on dating. I am a head taller than him. The conversation never flows. Still, I want it to work. The Ironman is handsome, employed, and nice enough. I want to try.

Back then, I tell my parents everything about my life. I tell them everything about why David and I are no longer friends. "You should never have introduced him to your pretty friends, ah!" Baba scolds me. "Let that be a lesson for next time."

My parents waste no time in asking me if there is someone new. Excitedly, I mention the Ironman, thinking they might be happy I am seeing an Asian American.

"A Japanese person?" Baba shakes, offended. "Why must you pick someone I detest?"

I am painfully aware of the trauma caused by the Japanese government in Korea and China, but we also have family friends who married Japanese people. Baba and Mama seem to like them, so I am blindsided by this reaction. Baba does not acknowledge how difficult it is for me to date, even though he's witnessed me cry so many times over feeling unlovable.

One of those instances in high school, I was crying in my bed, the same twin bed that caused Baba to call me Snow White for appearing too big for it. "When you're old enough, I'll march you down a busy street in Beijing with a fat check on your forehead," he had said, trying to comfort me. "We'll see how many men will line up to marry you then."

I'd wept even harder. Was I so disgusting that my own father believed he would need to pay someone to marry me?

I am exasperated by Baba's opposition to the Ironman. My wish is to simply date, like every other young American, but it seems not in the cards for me. Trying to date while fat and Asian in Arizona and living with bipolar disorder is tough enough without additional restrictions from Baba. Seeking approval from my parents is pointless.

I promise myself I will not do it moving forward. Finding love, which is near-impossible already, will be my priority.

The Ironman and I do not work out. Neither of us are confident enough to be the partner the other needs. He has not yet healed from the severe past traumas of his own, including an attempted suicide in college. I take every hesitation on his part as an attack on me, due to my own insecurities, projecting what happened with David onto him.

A few weeks of dating brings us no closer emotionally or physically. He just doesn't seem that into me, and the wall between us is so thick that I don't think I'm into him either. We share a few chaste pecks when saying good night, but there is no romance. Finally, one night on the phone, the Ironman says to me, "My brother thinks we should go with our friends on a party cruise."

"A party cruise?" I nearly drop the phone. I have never even heard of such a thing.

"Yeah," he continues. "With your friends and my friends, we can all have a good time."

Unlike him, who works in a well-paying corporate job, I am recently out of college and working for a nonprofit. Coming from a family who never takes real vacations, this suggestion is ludicrous. David's words about how he found my friend, not me, attractive rings in my ears.

"Why do you want to spend time with my friends?" I'm seeing red again.

The Ironman does not have answers that can satisfy me. "I don't know. I just think it would be a good time."

He digs himself a bigger hole. I conclude he wants to use me to get to my more attractive friends.

After that, I don't take his calls. He calls several times and then never again. Living in fear that men do not want me, I end it before he can hurt me like David had.

CHAPTER 40: Fire

TUCSON, ARIZONA

Things need to change... age 25
Date: 2005-12-28, 3:29 AM MST

Well, im kinda tired of this online dating attempt... I mean most females want a settled, decent and caring guy... no other criterion... however upon delving further they seem to have preferences not listed... im specifically talking abt race... yes that's right im not caucasion or a African American or a Hispanic or an Asian for that matter.... Well other than this im pretty normal. im 25, 5ft 8in tall, average/lean body. Luv to sing and dance... and enjoy all kinds of music other than hard rock, holding 2 graduate degrees... and fairly intelligent... I am very decent to look at... I believe in traditional values... and am not looking for a person to hop in the sack with... I have no bad habits... don't do drugs and don't drink (maybe a beer once in a while)... I live alone and would like to meet someone for a coffee or something... reply and u will not be disappointed...pls no mind games... and I don't mind sending u my pic once we get to know each other a little bit more...

Internet dating before it becomes the default method of dating, before it evolves into countless apps and websites, is just as overwhelming. I am reluctant to share my photo first, wanting to find a guy who isn't so hung up on appearances. This helps weed through most of the responses and posts because ninety-nine percent of the men want pictures without wasting any time on niceties. Many men who want to meet me in earnest are recent immigrants from India.

Though I have no trouble picturing myself dating American-raised South Asian men, the idea of dating a recent immigrant is honestly a challenge. I reckon with my own long-held biases. I recall Indian immigrant customers at our restaurant who treated me and my parents as less than human, who constantly made unreasonable demands and complaints. The pattern is difficult to dismiss, but I refuse to be a hypocrite. I am not a bigot and want to undo the prejudice in my mind. If I want someone to get to know me for me, I should do the same.

Zach's rambling, cringe-worthy, stream-of-consciousness message intrigues me. It honestly stands apart from the rest. He allows his vulnerability to show. The lack of ego is refreshing. I can relate to his struggle with race identity in dating. Finally, I love that he also doesn't want to share a picture until later. His yearning mirrors mine.

We make plans to meet at the coffee shop in Borders. He looks shorter than 5'8", but his large eyes under the thick glasses appear gentle. Sitting slightly hunched in a collared shirt and lightweight tan jacket, he looks unintimidating and unremarkable.

We make awkward small talk that seems to be going fine, but I am distracted. On the way to the date, a friend had called me crying. She has been struggling, teaching preschool by day and dancing at a strip club by night. There is a lot going on with her, and tonight, she is in crisis. She calls several times during the date as I am trying to talk to Zach.

Finally, I tell him, "Hey, I'm so sorry to have to do this, but my friend is having an emergency. Would it be okay if we meet again after the holidays?"

At this request, he looks as if I'd punched him in the gut. He seems completely crushed, which I find both endearing and an over-reaction. I have every intention of meeting up with him again, as long as he is willing. I have no idea "a friend's emergency call" is a common out that women use on blind dates.

About a week later, when Zach still hasn't contacted me, I write him an email apologizing again for having to leave. He is ecstatic to hear from me, and we make plans to meet again. Zach loves going to the movies. He'll go to three movies per week easily, and it is nice to go with him when, for so long, I have wanted nothing more than a boyfriend to watch movies with.

Zach confides that he had brought me flowers on our first date, but felt too stupid to bring them into the bookstore, so he'd left them in the car. As I left abruptly, he'd tried chasing after me in the parking lot, but I had already gone.

I melt a little.

After our second date, Zach begins calling nonstop. Once, he calls while I am driving with my friend Shermayne. She and I just left Tucson Mall and are happily chatting up a storm. I let it go to voice-mail. He calls again and again. Zach calls four times consecutively.

Shermayne and I look at one another surprised. We are equally alarmed and just a bit impressed. Dating doesn't come easily to Shermy, either. Though gorgeous and brilliant with a Master's degree in music, her open vivaciousness often intimates men. My friend doesn't know what to make of Zach's forwardness either.

Rule number one of dating seems to be "be careful not to seem too eager," especially for guys. Even I know that. After years of not being noticed, the persistent calls give me a rush. Whether I am near or far, Zach is in desperate need of my presence and connection. I am almost twenty-five and for the first time, I feel desired.

When we *are* together, Zach constantly asks if I need anything, jumping to bring me a glass of water or brewing chai tea in his mismatched pots and pans because he doesn't own a teapot. When I arrive at his messy bachelor pad of an apartment for the first time, he asks me to sit and proceeds to remove my shoes for me. It is excruci-atingly uncomfortable and strange. This dynamic is entirely foreign to me, but having never really dated, I don't know what to expect. Zach insists on paying for everything and often brings gifts he won't let me refuse.

Before seeing a movie at the mall, he steers me to the stores. I initially think we are just killing time walking around, but he stops in front of a watch counter.

"I want to buy you a timepiece," he says.

"Oh, no. I don't need a watch, really, but thank you for the thought."

"Just throw it in the garbage if you don't want it," he says, thrusting the pretty silver watch into my hands.

His gift seems to have symbolic meaning. A timepiece for more time with me. A bottle of perfume, to remind me of him even when he's not around. I have never purchased a full-priced, full bottle of perfume at a department store makeup counter before. It is a strange feeling, being wooed like this. I don't think most guys I know from college do this type of thing, unless it is with a longtime girlfriend. Zach and I have barely been seeing each other for a few weeks.

He seems anxious at all times that I will disappear. Zach worries each time we see each other will be the last. He leaves big-price items, like his laptop, at my place with silly excuses like "it needs to cool down" to ensure we'll see each other again.

Zach is unafraid to show affection. He flaunts it. The silly pet names and affectionate touching begins almost immediately. He kisses my shoulder throughout the many movies we watch together. He calls, texts, and instant messages me all day long, every day, even when we are both at work. I don't know how to draw boundaries; I don't know I need them. Within weeks, we are addicted to each other, needing to share every thought and happening with one another.

The Piggies are hesitant when it comes to Zach, but they tell me he'll be a good "starter boyfriend." I don't know what that means. To me, his complete disregard for playing it cool is charming. More than anything, I want to be able to refer to someone casually as my boyfriend. After over a decade of yearning on my own with one-sided crushes, I crave for someone to belong to and for them to belong to me. I finally have what I wanted. I will pay any price.

CHAPTER 41: Caught

TUCSON, ARIZONA

My first real kiss is with Zach, about a month after we begin seeing each other. When I go to the bathroom afterward, the tissue pressed between my sore lips comes away spotted with blood. He'd bit my lips and rubbed my face raw with his thick stubble. I don't know if this is good or bad. I don't know how it is supposed to feel or what I like, but I want this passage into adulthood. I want to feel chosen so badly I don't care.

That same night, he insists that I sleep over at his place. "You can stay in the bedroom, and I'll be on the couch. Nothing to worry about."

"No, I should get going," I counter. But Zach had insisted on picking me up for all our dates after that first meeting, even though I lived clear across town, and I had let him, thinking it chivalrous.

"It's late. Why not just stay? I can run out and buy you pajamas if you need," he begs.

Zach is nothing if not persistent. Not needing to seem cool and aloof means he is an expert at begging. I feel bad asking him to drive me back. In Tucson, there is no reliable public transportation, especially late at night. There are no rideshare apps yet, and no easy or affordable way to get a taxi. His urgent need for my presence is heady, so I relent.

I am in a deep sleep, when I am awoken by the weight of Zach on top of me, grunting. He is humping my body over my clothes. He is not wearing pants. His eyes are focused on mine, glinting in the darkness. The meek and polite persona is gone. My mind is cloudy, my eyes barely open.

"Tell me not to stop…" he whispers breathily, barely audible, as if he is in pain.

Confused, I try to sharpen my mind. His penis is the first one I've ever seen up close, let alone one that is erect.

"Tell me not to stop…" he repeats.

I scramble, speechless and stunned. I don't know what I'm supposed to do.

He looks at me, questioning my lack of response. He seems to take my silence as an invite. He expertly pins me under him, his knees prying mine open, like a dead frog readied for dissection. I am surprised by his strength.

This is my own doing, I think. *I am here in his apartment, in his bed of my own volition, in the middle of the night with no transportation. What did I expect? How could I have been so naïve?*

Weak and confused from sleep, I try to do damage control. I ask, "Shouldn't you get a condom?"

He gets up immediately.

When he returns with the condom, I am more awake. "Wait, I don't know…"

He looks away. A flash of annoyance. He scoffs, pushing air through his nostrils, giving his head the slightest shake.

"What?" I ask.

"It's just…Nothing…It's just… I've never been asked to put on a condom and then to stop."

The guilt trip works. I feel sorry. I don't know how any of this works. I might lose this first relationship. I had waited for so long to begin dating.

As soon as it begins, I scream. Steaming tears gush down my face, pooling in my ears. The weeping seeps out from my insides, unstoppable, guttural, and animal. "Ow, ow, ow." I shake with pain.

He keeps going through my cries, each movement excruciating.

When he finally stops, I ask through loud sobs, "Was it good for you?"

My first concern is that he had enjoyed himself. I want to please him. I want to prove David wrong. I don't want to be thrown away.

"Yes...but are you okay?" he asks, worried now. "Why are you crying?"

"It wasn't supposed to be this way...It wasn't supposed to be this way...It wasn't supposed to be this way..." I repeat, inconsolable.

"What do you mean?"

"I always thought my first time would be with someone I'd been friends with for a long time..." I am shaking.

Soon after we met, I had told Zach that I'd never had a boyfriend and that he was the first person I'd dated seriously. It never occurs to me that he might not have believed me until this moment.

He pauses before saying earnestly, "I love you. I really love you."

I peer at him through my tears, aghast and speechless. Does he think that is what I want to hear? I know this can't be true. We do not know each other enough for love. So why is he lying?

My grandmotherly therapist listens quietly when I tell her about how I couldn't stop crying during my first sexual experience. She never questions if there was consent. She never asks how it happened and whether I had wanted it to happen. She smiles wistfully and agrees that crying during the first time is not unusual, and she is happy for me that I am in an adult relationship.

Reeling from what had happened, I need a male friend's perspective and confide in someone I trust. I turn to Ben, the fellow Flinn scholar who had traveled across Europe with me. By this point, we had lived in the same honors dorm, and, later, in the same apartment building. He is popular, compassionate, funny, and always makes time to listen to me. Even in parties packed with people, he talks or dances with me every time, making me feel like I matter. In turn, I stick by him through some of his toughest times. Our bond is strong and platonic.

Floor-to-ceiling photos of models in bikinis on the beach hang in Ben's bachelor pad. This is new.

"My friend is the photographer," he says when he notices me looking at his new décor. "Isn't he talented?"

I don't know what to say and scrunch my face and laugh.

Ben giggles with me, and we sit down on the second-hand couch and sofa in front of the gaze of the giant, near-nude models.

"So, what's up?" Ben asks. It has been a while since we've talked like this. Probably not since we'd lived in the same building.

"You know I started seeing this guy, Zach," I say. "Things are going well. Moving quickly, but going well. He seems like a nice guy. But I don't know why I am so sad and panicked when I should feel happy. I have wanted this for so long, right? A boyfriend?"

Ben is a great listener and has listened to me a lot over the years. He is listening more intently than ever as he leans in from the worn, brown seat.

Nervous and embarrassed, I work up the courage to ask, "I cried during our first time, really hard. Is that normal?"

We've never talked about sex before. Not like this.

"Has this ever happened to you?" I ask, thinking of the women he's been with.

Ben laughs out loud, so loud I jump in the quiet night.

"No, I have never cried during sex." He keeps laughing as if it is the funniest thing he's ever heard.

I don't blame Ben, but this was a mistake. I shouldn't have come here.

Growing up, I loved watching Korean and Chinese dramas with my parents. After we immigrated, these soap opera-like drama series became even more significant to our family because they anchored us to our past lives. Before the internet streaming and satellite dishes were readily available, Baba rented small cardboard boxes of VHS tapes of K Dramas at $1 per tape. We'd binge-watch them together, indulgently staying up way too late.

Rape was sometimes part of the plotlines, and it led to two inevitable outcomes for the victim. She would either be forced to marry her attacker, who had marked her as his, or she would kill herself to reclaim her honor.

Over a decade will pass before I begin to comprehend that what I experienced was rape too.

CHAPTER 42: Wound

ARIZONA

After the first night I spend with Zach, I feel all my confidence drain away, replaced with an insistent sense of danger. I feel certain doom, like the earth beneath me will give way at any moment. Constantly worried that he will reject me, I no longer feel myself. To rid myself of the worry, I must confess my deepest shame. If he will leave me once he knows, I would rather it happen sooner rather than later, to abbreviate my torture, and so I don't get more attached.

About a week later, in Zach's apartment, I take a big breath. "Hey, I have to tell you something," I say. "It's important, and you may not want to be with me once you know."

"What do you mean?" answers Zach, immediately dismissive. "There's nothing you could say."

"I have bipolar disorder." I can't meet his eyes.

"It doesn't matter," he says. "It's not a big deal. I don't even believe it's a real thing."

"Are you sure you know what bipolar disorder is?" I can't

comprehend his response. I had expected him to be horrified.

"It's something that only happens to Americans. Don't worry. I'm sure it's nothing."

Zach shushes my further attempts to explain. My mental health condition is irrelevant to him. I don't know whether to be relieved or be more weighed down. I will continue to harbor the gravity of my condition alone, holding that Pandora's Box. Only I know what it is, what havoc it has wreaked, what it can do.

Zach chooses to ignore its presence instead of trying to understand it. Though I confessed, his indifference gnaws at me all the same, leaving me in the state of insecurity.

Maybe I need a little distance from Zach, who is suddenly always next to me. The following weekend, I go home to Phoenix. I don't understand why I am regularly losing control of my bladder. It is both scary and painful. I explain my symptoms to Mama, who, of course, immediately tells Baba. She never keeps anything from him. I should have figured, but at least I don't hear from him until I am driving back to Tucson.

About an hour into my journey on the long, bright Interstate-10 Eastbound through desert landscape in my white Honda Accord, Baba starts calling nonstop.

"This is not something that happens to virgins!" he screams through my speakerphone, referring to what I would later learn to be a urinary tract infection.

"Why are you doing this to me? It's like you're purposely choosing people I hate. First, a Japanese guy and now an Indian? And you've slept with him?" he yells. "I will come down there and shoot him! I will destroy him."

Baba loves guns, and always has, since the days back in Korea when he would shoot city birds with his BB gun. But, unlike in Korea, where the right for civilians to bear arms does not exist, his lifelong fascination blossoms into a hobby in Arizona. He buys several hand-guns and goes to shooting ranges regularly. Customers call him the Chinese cowboy because he loves country music (playing it every day at the restaurant) and wears a large, shiny belt buckle (a gift from a regular customer). Still, I know Baba well enough to recognize the emptiness of his threat. The 140 miles between us also serve as a security blanket—not to mention, the fact that Baba doesn't know where Zach's apartment is and that's where I am headed.

Mama's tears, though, are harder to ignore. "I'm worried he'll take you away from me, Beautiful Jade. He could take you to India, where women are treated worse than cows, and I will never see you again."

There is not much I can do but embrace her the next time I am home, absorbing her tears on my shoulder, and wrapping her warmth into mine. "Mama, that won't happen."

She continues crying for weeks.

A couple of months after I meet Zach, when the intense heat returns to Southern Arizona, Didi—by now a strapping six-foot tall man of twenty-two—confronts my new boyfriend alone in the parking lot outside my apartment building. He flashes an old revolver and speaks in a deep, firm tone, "If you ever hurt my sister, I'll come for you."

I notice Zach's blanched face right away as he enters the apartment. "What's wrong?" I ask.

"Nothing. I am impressed," he says, slowly nodding with his hands in his pocket as he tells me what happened outside.

"Oh, my god. I'm so sorry." I bury my head in my hands, mortified.

Baba soon demands to meet Zach. We make a plan to meet at our family's favorite Korean restaurant in Phoenix.

"I'll leave the restaurant with you if they become unreasonable," I tell Zach in the car ride to Phoenix as I sense his growing nervousness. "We can just walk out, I promise."

"No, we won't do that. You have to stay no matter what happens."

I appreciate Zach's old-school reverence for family. As a recent transplant to the U.S., he is far more traditional than I am.

Zach is appropriately deferential, and Baba keeps the peace. Though tense throughout, the meal goes more smoothly than we feared. We don't even need to consider storming out.

"I had to be polite to him because it will affect how he treats you," Baba later tells me.

My parents could build up a solid case against Zach if they could look past his skin color. Instead, they fixate on his ethnicity, the stereotypes, and see nothing else. They miss the bruises on my arms and do not detect his possessiveness. They press me to end the relationship only on account of his Indian nationality—Baba with fighter urgency and Mama with grief-stricken guilt trips. Predictably, their opposition pushes me closer to Zach, making ours a forbidden romance.

To be clear, even years later, I don't believe there is anything my parents or anyone else could have done to tear me away from Zach. I don't blame anyone but myself. The decision to stay was mine.

Zach leaves bruises shaped like continents where he grips me to make me feel his rage. His love leaves my breasts and shoulders in shades of black and blue. When doctors and nurses ask questions with concern, I giggle and answer, "Oh, it's nothing. I bruise so easily," parroting what Zach says.

My fault. I bruise easily. Me. Not him.

Zach becomes jealous if I see friends without him. He shows up unannounced at my work and throws tantrums outside my building. Within inches of my face, he yells. His voice sharp as razors.

I can never anticipate the things that will set him off. Once, it is because I purchase a laptop without consulting him, even though it is with my own money, for my own use. Another time because I didn't follow his advice about my work's website.

But I am not afraid of Zach like I am of my father. He isn't huge and hulking. Zach grips my arms so hard that I yelp, but he never hits me. For all of his wrath, the most he can muster from his medium frame is nothing compared to what I was trained to withstand from my six-foot-three tornado of a father. I assess Zach's rage with detached calm and curiosity at times and acute annoyance at others. Are his tantrums a sign of how much he cares? I want to believe it.

In the ignorance of my mid-twenties, without the years of ther-

apy I would later undergo, I do not see that it is about control. All I
see is a man who wants to look out for me.

I apologize for annoying him. I let him touch me whenever, wher-
ever, because he makes me feel wanted.

"Hey, buffalo, what is this?" Zach grabs my belly fat, just like Baba
had. My tears gush instantly, as if by some biological trigger.

"What? Are you seriously crying?" he snaps. "I can't take this,
Michelle. You are too sensitive for me."

I am too sensitive. Baba always says so too. I recognize the unde-
niable similarities between Baba and Zach. The volatility is all too
familiar, but if no other man will love me as much as Baba, is this
what love is supposed to feel like?

Around this time, I am awarded YWCA's Woman on the Move
Award alongside one of my idols, State Senator Gabrielle Giffords. I
am a Flinn scholar alum, a non-profit leader, a fun-loving member of
the Three Piggies. I am an empowered, educated young professional
with many friends. I do not look like or feel like a domestic abuse
victim. I have no awareness about it. So, I cover up the bruises, bury
the insults, and swallow the sobs.

When I was twelve years old, I watched the Julia Roberts movie *Sleeping with the Enemy* with Baba. Though he was in his late thirties, his
hair was still jet black. The tough three years working in Chinese
restaurant kitchens in America had not yet caught up with him.

It was late at night. Mama and Didi were already asleep.

"But the husband really loves her. Why is she running away?"
he asked.

"Because he was beating her," I gasped, not understanding his
confusion.

"But that's just a bad habit," my father said dismissively. "What
matters is he loves her."

Indeed, in the K-dramas we watched at that time, domestic

violence was often presented as comic relief. In Baba's Korea, which is the world inside Baba's head, domestic violence will not be declared illegal for years.

Zach's best trait is his gift for nurturing. He volunteers at my adoption agency work events during weekends and is quick to move tables and chairs and carry boxes without being asked. He jumps at every opportunity to be as helpful as possible, impressing the adoptive families who have become my good friends. Zach has what Koreans call nunchi—he can read a room, and anticipate the needs of others. I try to focus on the good. He tells me constantly how much he loves me with excessive tenderness. I savor our coupledom. We take a road trip to watch the dolphins on the beaches of San Diego, visit the largest rose bush in the world in Tombstone, and join The Piggies and their boyfriends for regular outings. Dreams I've been collecting since I was young, the dates I've wanted to go on when I have a boyfriend, are realized.

In a dimly lit theater before a movie starts, Zach shows me faint, small swirls of scars on his wrist. Back in India, Zach had burned himself with cigarettes after a bad breakup with a girl whose family wouldn't accept him because of his caste and his acne.

I can see him clearly then: a gaping, festering wound, still running from his past.

CHAPTER 43: Reckoning

ARIZONA

Every face in the room turned to me in shock. One dozen pairs of eyes narrowed on me with concern. Humiliation burned my cheeks. I looked away and swallowed hard, having accidentally outed my ignorance. I'd expected everyone to agree with me, maybe even applaud me for calling bullshit on this unrealistic list. Instead, a pregnant silence laid claim to the room.

This was during my freshman year in college. My friend Lauren told me about Beyond Tolerance, a student organization that shared the same mission and founders as Anytown, U.S.A. I joined immediately. Many of the officers in this club were Anytown alumni. We formed a kinship and a safe space. Together, we facilitated healthy, often emotional, dialogue around campus about racism, discrimination, and stereotypes of all kinds.

A guest speaker was giving a presentation about domestic violence and abusive relationships. She'd handed out a flyer that called out warning signs: possessiveness, jealousy, put-downs, threats, and violence. "Have you ever experienced these in your relationships?"

Having never been in a relationship at the time, I applied the questions to the relationship I know best: my parents'.

The more I listened, the more my eyebrows raised, until my skepticism could no longer be contained. I raised my hand and asked matter-of-factly, "Aren't most of these just a part of being in any relationship? I mean, not the violence, of course, but many of the others called out, aren't they just a part of life? No relationship is perfect. Don't some things need to be overlooked for a relationship to last?"

That's when one dozen shocked eyes met mine. I was alone. My parents' marriage had conditioned within me a set of expectations. This discussion scratched the foundation of my conditioning, but it was not yet broken. I remained a daughter who believed her parents' marriage was imperfect but good enough. Unlike most of my friends' parents, Baba and Mama stayed married. Certain sacrifices were required for the longevity of a relationship.

"Wan go la! So, he's grown tired of playing you," Baba says.

I feel as if I have been stabbed. The living room of my parents' is stifling all of a sudden. It is if I'm caged, and I wish I could fly away.

Baba won't look at my face. As if he is ashamed and disappointed in what I have done.

"No, Baba. He is just taking a job in Seattle." I am defensive. I hate that he has gotten to me.

"Same difference. He's leaving. That means he's tired of using you."

Using me for sex. Tired of my body that he'd used as a toy. Zach and I have been together for over a year. To my parents, though, sex is all it was. I'd stupidly allowed myself to be used and discarded. Baba's words pierce me with paranoia and worry. I wonder if what Baba says is true.

Arizona is my home, but Zach is a foreigner on a work visa. During our relationship, I am the one who has more occasions to leave town, to see family, travel for work or with friends. Whenever I am away, he'll call and text even more frequently than he does when I am in town. This is our norm. I always take his calls, answer his texts.

Some months before Zach decides to move to Seattle, he is elated when a few of his college friends who are scattered across the country plan a reunion in Florida. Dropping him off at the airport, I wish him a great time, fully expecting us to stay connected as usual.

But Zach doesn't call and is curt and impatient when I text him. I take the hint and leave him alone. It is the longest we've been apart without constant communication. I don't know what to do with myself. I reach out to friends last minute to see if they can hang out without much success.

Upon his return, the change is immediate.

"What's the matter? Are you okay? You're acting weird." He avoids eye contact. Things were normal before he left. "What happened?"

"My life doesn't look good," he answers, still not looking at me. "My friends have better jobs, better homes, better lives. One even has a blonde girlfriend."

I am speechless.

Zach and I have been living together for over six months, though I keep my own place. After the trip, he begins applying for a new job, and a few months later, he lands a role in Seattle that is far more prestigious than his current one in Tucson. He doesn't ask me to move with him. Our relationship isn't perfect. This feels like a natural and humane end.

I say the actual words. The break-up is inevitable. Zach agrees easily.

After he leaves, the Piggies remind me he was a fine starter boyfriend, and that I can do better. I don't believe them. They don't know what it's like to live in my fat, crazy body. I haven't told the Piggies about my bipolar disorder, about how damaged and insecure it all makes me feel.

CHAPTER 44: Excuses

ARIZONA

Zach calls me as soon as he lands in Seattle and keeps me updated about every detail of his new life. He talks to me like himself again, before he went to Florida. The affection and intimacy return. He calls every day to say goodnight. The texts and instant messages throughout the day resume.

I had not expected this. We are broken up and living across the country from each other. Because I believe the long distance will eventually separate us for good, I do not draw any boundaries. It seems harmless. He is over a thousand miles away. We had agreed to remain friends.

Months pass like this, and I realize Zach and I are treating each other exactly as we had when we were together, except now we do not have the label. He is still taking up all the emotional space. I don't feel the need to look elsewhere or to date anyone else.

I still love him, I begin to think and wonder why we had broken up if we are still so attached.

"Do you notice we've been carrying on like we never broke up?" I ask him during one of our calls. I'm walking in the cool desert night under the stars in my apartment complex. Outside, I feel closer to Zach.

He mumbles something incoherent.

"I think we should get back together," I say confidently, thinking it is a no-brainer. He is the one calling me all the time. I had thought he would agree right away. "We seem to be doing this long-distance thing, whether or not we're calling it that."

"Let's talk about it later."

Though his response surprises me, I don't push the matter. I don't bring it up again. The chances of us living in the same city again seem very low. By this time, I've applied to a handful of MBA schools, including a program in Seattle, but I want to move to California. Other romantic prospects aren't knocking down my door, and I am not looking either. It's easier not to be looking and yearning. I am okay with the status quo, at least for now. I have been on my mood stabilizer for my bipolar disorder for over five years and am generally doing well, but I am still susceptible to anxiety and depression. Work stress and seasonal changes still affect me. Big decisions about graduate school are ahead. On the brink of many changes, I want stability and support. Zach is always available. I don't think too hard about remaining reliant on each other during our transitions.

Before Zach moved to Seattle, for weeks leading up to my GMAT exam, I had locked myself in my apartment to study. Except for going to work, I did not allow myself to leave for any reason until I had a practice test score that satisfied me. Zach brought takeout over and kept me company while I studied.

He and I spent every day together until he moved, so he was with me the day I took the exam and with me the day I got my score.

"Zach, I did it! I got a 700!" I was jumping up and down.

He took my results from my hand to see for himself and looked genuinely shocked. "Are you serious?"

"Yes, why?"

"That's a really good score."

"And?" I didn't know why he was so surprised. He'd been witness to all my exam preparation.

"Good job. Congratulations. Really, I didn't think you could do it."

"Wow," I glared at him and stomped off.

Zach trailed after me, laughing.

Earlier in our relationship, in the context of talking about his graduate school friends, he told me he believed no woman could inherently be as smart as a man, let alone smarter. Zach had thought all the women in his program relied on their male classmates to get by.

Tucson is a progressive, queer-friendly city. It is one of the reasons I love living there. I naively assumed that most people in their 20s like me shared my views politically. I was shocked when Zach, my own boyfriend, declared, "There are no gay people in India," with all the confidence in the world.

"There are over a billion people in India! How can you say there are no gay people there?" I retorted.

"Have you been there? There are no gay people in India."

I was infuriated by his belief system then and was again at his response to my GMAT score, but I hoped he would become more progressive after years of living in the U.S.

I should have known better.

As Zach settles into life in Seattle, he begins mentioning "Canadian friends" in gender-neutral terms on our calls. I don't know why he doesn't want to tell me they are female friends. I am happy for him to make friends. I trust him to tell me if anything develops that would preclude us from being so close.

My colleagues are impressed when Zach flies back to Tucson for my work holiday party. I appreciate him being there. We are familiar, yet new. At night, in the quiet privacy of my first apartment without roommates, we fall hungrily on one another. Our reunion is so intense that it resets our relationship.

Not long after he returns to Seattle, Zach calls me, beating around the bush with flowery words in an anxious way that indicates when something big is about to drop.

"Michelle, we can do this together. I will help you," he says earnestly.

"What? What are you talking about?" I'm already frustrated.

He takes a deep breath. "My parents," he continues. "They're coming to visit from India in June. That's six months from now. If you can lose thirty pounds before then, you can meet my parents."

"What in the hell?"

"You can do it, Michelle," Zach adds. Could he be completely unaware? "I believe in you. I can help you."

I was seven years old when Baba first took away my rice bowl as the family sat down to eat.

"You are too fat. Don't eat today," he roared while I sobbed. Didi and Mama watched in choked silence.

This happened throughout my childhood, like earthquakes—difficult to predict but the possibility forever present below the surface. We lived on the fault lines. After we immigrated, I gained more weight. By middle school and high school, Baba had tried everything to shrink me, reiterating that men only want women who are thin and beautiful.

When Zach asks me to lose thirty pounds, all memories of Baba torturing me to shrink my body blind me with anger. Before this call, though Zach teased me about my weight, he'd never asked me to change my appearance. He never had the gall to ask me to cut myself down to size. Thankful he can't see my tears, I hope the phone line will carry across only my rage and none of my heartbreak.

"If I could lose thirty pounds, do you think I would be with you?"

I hang up.

CHAPTER 45: Rain City

SEATTLE, WASHINGTON

I can't explain what happens in the time between that phone call in January and April, when I fly to Seattle for the MBA preview weekend at the University of Washington.

Zach is extremely good at groveling. He is shameless and persistent, the best groveler I have ever met. Somehow, I've forgiven him enough to let him pick me up from the airport and drive me to my hotel. Maybe it is weakness, maybe I convince myself I can be emotionally detached, maybe I think I can use him like he had used me. I am not proud of it, but I let him back in.

The University of Washington's program impresses me—especially the kindness of the program recruiter, who'd been supportive since they reviewed my application, and the more down-to-earth nature of many of the prospective students. Arizona State University and the University of Washington are the only two programs that offer me a significant scholarship. The former is not as viable of an option because I want more independence and a new city, and it is geographically too close to where I grew up.

My career aspirations change from a career in diplomacy to one in nonprofit management, due in no small part to my experience at the adoption agency. Pursuing an MBA to work in the nonprofit world is an unusual path, but I learn from experience that business skills are vital for any thriving organization. I consider a Master's in Public Administration or Social Work, but I reason that the skills most lacking in the nonprofit sector are business acumen.

Unlike most of my classmates, I have no real interest in business at that time. Pursuing an MBA is nerve-wracking and risky. When visiting various programs, I worry about fitting in. Horror stories about the ultra-competitive culture of some programs where students hide reference materials from one another get in my head. Avoiding that kind of environment is a top priority.

Having written about my nonprofit management career goals in my application essays, I am grateful for UW's choice to invest in me. The prospective return on investment for my scholarship is low to none, not to mention my nonprofit income will likely reduce the average salary of graduating class statistics. Schools depend on those numbers. The UW program shows me its heart and authenticity, and that matters a great deal.

I return to Tucson with a plan to attend UW in the fall. In the three months before the big move, I internalize the falling out with Zach about my weight, negotiating a narrative with myself in which his request is not so unreasonable. My fatness has been a lifelong problem for everyone around me for as long as I could remember.

I join Nutrisystem. I eat unappetizing, tiny portions of prepackaged, processed foods every day until I lose twenty pounds, reaching my lowest weight since puberty. I promise myself I am losing weight for no one but me, for my own new beginning. I don't want anyone else to use my weight to hold me down.

The three months after the MBA preview weekend pass quickly. In the late summer of 2007, I move to Seattle, convincing my friends, family, and, most of all, myself that I am not moving there to be with

Zach. He just also happens to be there. Zach hosts me at his home while helping me find housing. His familiarity calms my anxiety at a time when everything is new and changing.

Business school is daunting. The subjects are not my natural strengths or interests. I am forcing myself to get through the degree. I tell myself I can do anything for two years. Everything is demanding—the classes, the weather, the bus commute. Figuring out and setting up campus health appointments, retelling my mental health history, building trust with new providers drains all of my energy. There is little time for respite, for sleep. I am always behind. My relationship with Zach is honestly easier to let be than resist. I can cocoon myself with him in a less complicated, less demanding escape.

This time, I will set the rules, I tell myself, steeling to avoid emotional entanglement. I am determined not to get hurt.

"We don't have to be boyfriend and girlfriend. We don't need labels," I say to Zach on a rainy drive to his place across town in my first month in Seattle. His car is small. I don't like driving in Seattle yet, and am grateful he is always willing. "But if one of us becomes interested in someone else, we have to tell the other person, okay?"

"Okay," Zach agrees readily, nodding.

The rain is coming down so hard that I can't see out the windshield, but Zach does not turn on the wipers. Feeling afraid, I reach over and do it for him.

He turns it off after one wipe.

The dumping rain blinds us on the freeway again. I reach over again to turn on the wipers. He swipes away my hand firmly. "Stop," he says.

Swallowing my fears, I stop.

CHAPTER 46: Face

SEATTLE, WASHINGTON

Zach's friends tease him about having a thing for East Asian women. I don't know how to feel about this. Is an East Asian fetish a thing if the guy is South Asian? He is unabashed in his admiration for my lighter skin, gori, but is that enough to be deemed a fetish? As far as I know, Zach has only dated two women before me, one of them was an East Asian adoptee and the other was Indian. I tell myself that is not enough data for a pattern.

One of the "Canadians" Zach befriends not long after moving to Seattle is a woman called Grace, who also happens to be East Asian. The two have clearly grown close in the time before I arrived in town, but I have no reason to suspect that their friendship is anything but platonic. Grace moves back to Canada the same month I move to Seattle, but she and I meet once when she swoops back into town for a visit. At Zach's apartment, she's strewn her bra and panties across his bed and is taking a shower in his bathroom when I walk in. I feel territorial and uneasy, but Zach swears to me they are only friends.

Evidently, I am emotionally invested despite my efforts. I don't know how not to care.

Zach stops saying "I love you" when I move to Seattle, but I still slip sometimes. I can't help it.

Months pass in relative peace. I try not to drown in my demanding graduate school program. I try not to let the gloomy weather get to me and instead appreciate the evergreen trees around me, the Olympic mountains in the distance, and Mount Rainier on clear days. Most of all, I promise myself that I would never take for granted all the water around me, the Puget Sound and the lakes, which feel like mothers all around me. After living in landlocked Arizona for two decades, I want to drink it in forever.

As my winter quarter begins in January 2008, I'm hanging out at Zach's place in West Seattle, doing what I always do on weekends. Textbooks are spread out in front of me in the kitchen, papers are scattered all around me—I'm trying to keep up.

Zach steps inside after a smoke break and shivers, shaking tiny droplets of rain from his hair. Since our first dates in Tucson, he has long since stopped trying to hide his habit. He sits down in the chair across from mine.

"Grace is coming to town again and needs to crash at my place." Zach is not looking into my eyes, though he is trying to sound nonchalant.

This time, I am prepared. I am firm and direct with him.

"Why does she have to stay with you?" I ask. "Grace lived here for years. She has plenty of friends in Seattle."

Zach scrunches up his face, which is covered in a full beard. He makes the face of his that shows I'm torturing him, but says nothing.

"As long as you and I are sleeping together, I don't want her or any other woman staying the night at your place," I say. "You're welcome to hang out with her as friends. I don't see why she must crash here."

Moments pass in silence. Zach runs his hands through his thick, black hair, sighing and making troubled expressions, but he agrees, nodding slowly.

Trusting in our agreement, I forget about Grace's impending visit.

Another month or so passes, and signs of spring are just beginning to show in the tender buds that poke through the rich, volcanic soil and in the early blooms on the few flowering trees more impatient than their peers.

It is late on a Saturday night when Zach appears at my doorstep in the Sandpoint neighborhood house I rent with two roommates. He is clean-shaven this time, still wearing his thick glasses, of course, but also wearing that fitted tan jacket he favors and had on the first time we met.

"I can't spend the night," he says as he takes off his shoes. "I have to go in the office."

This is unusual. Zach routinely brings work with him over the weekend, but I don't think anything of it. After a few quiet hours together, he falls asleep after midnight, and I decide not to wake him. It is Saturday, after all, and very late. Technically, it is already Sunday. I'm sure work can wait.

"Shit! Shit! Shit! What time is it?" Zach shoots up in bed next to me at 7:39 AM. "Why didn't you wake me? I have to go!"

"What? Why?" I mutter, rubbing sleep from my eyes.

Zach gathers his things in a panic and runs out the front door without shutting it or saying goodbye.

He makes it to the end of the driveway before turning back. "Can I borrow your phone? I'll bring it back in a few hours. My phone is dead."

Without a word, I hand it over. *Is it some sort of work emergency?* I'm confused.

That evening, I'm studying with a friend from the MBA program at my round dining room table when my phone, which Zach returned earlier, rings from a number I don't recognize.

"Hi, this is Grace Lee. Zach called me from this number earlier?" Her voice sounds scratchy and deeper than I remember.

Surprised by the caller, I excuse myself and step out to the front porch to continue the call.

"...Hi...Yes, this is Michelle. He borrowed my phone this morning but didn't tell me why." It's cold outside, I didn't grab a jacket, but the fresh air feels good in my lungs. Holding the phone to my ear with one hand, I hug myself as best I can with the other.

"He was supposed to take me to the airport this morning, but he never came back last night," says Grace. "I called him so many times. I almost had to call a taxi."

"Zach spent the night at my place, and his phone died," I reply. "I didn't know you were in town this weekend. You were staying with him?" I look out over the lush front yard in the twilight. The center-piece is a gorgeous fig tree, yet to bear fruit since I moved here.

"Yes, I was. Zach told me he fell asleep at work and his phone died, so he borrowed the security guard's phone, but I didn't believe him since the area code was from Arizona."

When Zach returned my phone, I had checked the call records but found no calls that he had made. He must have deleted it.

"Right. He didn't tell me you were staying with him," I say, solemnly but also exasperated. "I told him I wasn't comfortable with that as long as he and I were still together." I always laugh when I'm uncomfortable. I can't help but think this horrible situation is a bit funny.

"You two are still together?" Grace asks.

"Yup. We have been seeing each other. How about you? He always told me you were only friends." I'm getting really cold now, and I step inside the threshold.

"We have been seeing each other, too. Pretty much since we met when he first moved to Seattle. He told me you two broke up when he left Tucson."

Grace and I are eerily calm throughout the exchange as we connect the dots, filling one another in. As awkward as the situation is, we are both smart enough to know to whom to direct our anger, and it's not one another. We have both been played.

For the past year, Zach has been lying. In Seattle, each time he stepped out for a smoke, he told me he had been talking to someone different—a cousin, a co-worker, a friend. Now, I wonder if it has been Grace all along. When I was in Arizona, it was so easy for him to omit the extent of his relationship with her. Was he making a goodnight call before he snuggled up with me, just as it had been the other way around with her when I was in Tucson? How was he so bold that he was carrying on right under our noses? He even dared to introduce us to each other on his last birthday, the time she threw her bra and panties on his bed. He must have felt like such hot shit juggling the two of us.

I step into my house while Grace is still on the phone. My friend is still at the dining room table. She looks at me questioningly. I'm sure she can't concentrate on studying. The look on her face tells me she had overheard enough.

"Grace, I'm glad you called me to check," I say. "I'm glad we know now."

After that, it is a blur. I don't remember how the call ends. I don't feel particularly angry. That part will come later. The overwhelming feeling is that of finality. I am done.

On a humid, sunny summer day in Incheon, Baba and Mama loaded four-year-old Didi and seven-year-old me into the car with the promise of a trip to the pier. Family days out were uncommon and precious, even in those days back in Korea. My parents have always been frugal and do not spend money on fun and frivolities. Mama dressed me in a white and blue sundress with pigtails and Didi in a denim blue shirt with matching shorts. My brother and I looked forward to a day strolling the boardwalk and enjoying ice cream cones, maybe even going on a few rides if we were lucky.

About five minutes away from the destination, we rolled up to a red light.

"Look, it's Second Uncle!" Didi shouted, pointing out the window at my father's second eldest brother.

The rest of us turned our gazes to find Second Uncle in his car inches away from us in the next lane. A slim, twenty-something woman with long, pretty hair, also wearing a sundress, sat in his passenger seat. A pretty young woman, who was not his wife, the mother of his three teenage children.

"Don't look," Baba shouted as if he'd be shot. "Pretend you don't see them. I'm sure he saw us already. Second Uncle has eyes like an eagle."

From the back seat, I sneaked a peek anyway. By the rigid way my uncle and his lady friend were seated, staring straight ahead without speaking, I knew Baba was right.

"We can't go to the pier and risk running into them," Baba said. "We'll go somewhere else."

Didi shrieked, breaking down into a full-blown tantrum. I pouted with my arms crossed. It was so unfair.

From eavesdropping in the whispers of my parents and other grown-ups, I would learn that cheating is common, even expected, especially for powerful men. They talked as if men couldn't possibly be expected to remain faithful.

Not me, I promised myself. I crossed my brows and my arms every time I heard a story like this. I would go outside and sit on a cement stoop, roll pebbles under my worn red sneakers, stare at the tiny ants at work, and sigh at the injustice.

When I grow up, I will never put up with a partner who strays.

I don't recall how Zach finds out about Grace and my phone call. I don't remember talking to him, so maybe she tells him. He shows up at my door that night and rings my doorbell nonstop. I am mortified in front of my two sympathetic housemates who must turn him away for me. He stands outside my house shivering for hours in the dramatic spotlight of his car headlights, waiting for me to come out. When that doesn't work, he leaves me long, sorrowful voicemails, begging.

His tactics switch from trying to make me feel guilty, to attempting to draw out pity, to that of coercion.

"You've made me sick from standing outside your door…"

"I'm drinking this whole bottle of wine alone. I'm so messed up right now."

"I'm so sorry. You're such a good person. I'm lost without you … [sobs]"

"Was this all that I meant to you? After all the times I was there for you? So, you're just not going to talk to me anymore? Don't I deserve at least a chance to explain?"

I wasted enough of myself on him. He doesn't deserve a moment more of my time. I cut him off completely, block him on my phone and on social media. I ask all my friends to do the same. I do not want to be like my aunts who have no choice but to turn a bitter blind eye to the affairs. I do not waver. Not even for a second. I learned from my elders.

"Is everything alright? Is something going on at home?" a middle-aged classmate asks me in Korean. He is one of the many international students in our program.

For weeks, I'd been in my classes crying, face red and puffy. Most people do not seem to notice. Only my best friend in the program, who'd been at my house studying with me during the call with Grace, provides support. No one else says anything, which is what I think I want—to be left alone.

When the Korean international student whom I don't know very well shows me concern, I am too upset to answer. Even though I rush away wordlessly, I am grateful someone notices my pain.

Every night, from my small bedroom, I call any friend who will listen, looking to fill the gaping hole in my life where Zach had been. My cell phone becomes water-damaged from my tears.

I tell Mama and Baba too, heartbroken. I still talk to them both multiple times a day.

"I told you so," says Baba between my sobs, who can't seem to help himself.

A couple of weeks later, when my depression refuses to lift, Baba calls me as if he's had an epiphany. "You should ride a horse to catch a horse," he says, almost gleefully.

I am driving home from campus and had put my dad on speaker phone, but I pull over on the winding road hugging Lake Washington from the sheer shock. "What are you saying, Baba?"

"Go back to Zach. Be with him until you meet someone else. It's easier to catch a horse when you're already riding one."

I lean my head onto the steering wheel. I'm not sure if I should be touched that Baba overcame his distaste for Zach to give me this advice or just feel plain appalled. It doesn't matter. There is no way I'll go back to Zach again. This is the single worst piece of advice Baba has ever given me, and he will never recover his credibility with me.

I spend Valentine's Day with girlfriends from business school watching romcoms at my best friend's apartment. When I come home late that night, a card from Zach is waiting for me at the door. It is filled with his tiny, neat script—all meandering, cowardly words. He had tried to catch me in a moment of weakness.

What an ass, I think, shaking my head, relieved I hadn't been there to see his sorry face.

PART
四

CHAPTER 47: Bold

INDIA

"Are you really Irish?" my MBA classmate Reno asks me as we board our flight.

"No," I answer with a mischievous smile. "And you shouldn't trust me either."

"Oh, is that how that works?" Reno blushes, after a pause.

I'm wearing my "Trust Me, I'm Irish" shirt in honor of St. Patrick's Day, the day we are departing on an MBA spring study tour to India. I'd registered well before my relationship with Zach imploded.

I did not expect Reno to blush, and it is adorable. He is very confident, is covered in tattoos, and loves to talk about music and the fact that he is a drummer. I am surprised I can draw this reaction from him. I like it.

Reno somehow manages to play in both a skate-punk band and an indie band during our rigorous program. With his short, brown hair dyed purple, eyebrow piercing, and tattoos, he certainly stands out in our class of one hundred MBA candidates. Of course, dyeing his hair purple during orientation week to match the school color is extremely nerdy in addition to being punk rock, which, as it turns out, is what he was going for. Reno never hesitates to raise his hand to ask questions in the large auditoriums of people. With his background in music education, he and I are the minority among classmates who mostly come from business backgrounds. I am looking forward to getting to know him better on this trip.

We land in Mumbai on a balmy, breezy night. My first impression is that the entire city is in different stages of construction. Both sides of the streets are lined with people sleeping shoulder to shoulder in the warm spring evening practically the entire shuttle bus ride from the airport to the hotel.

The next morning, a dozen of us set out to explore on foot after a luxury breakfast buffet that includes everything from saag paneer to congee, before the first company visit on our itinerary. During our week-plus trip in India, we are to visit several corporations and businesses in exchange for course credit. We all end up following Reno's lead. He walks boldly, his red and black shirt starkly contrasting with the rust and golden hues of the architecture around him. Reno leads us further and further into the deep alleyways.

"Um...Do you think this is a good idea?" I catch up to him at the front and interject. We are a large, conspicuous group of foreigners, now far removed from the public view of the major street, and none of us know where we were going. "Shouldn't we turn around now?"

Reno thinks for a moment. "You're probably right," his face flushes as he smiles at me. The group reverses directions with Reno and me at the back end now, strolling back to the beach in front of the city street where our hotel is located. We dip our toes in the warm surf and bask in the morning sun.

Later, on the long bus ride, Reno doodles a detailed cartoon map of the hotel, the main street, the beach, and the cluster of corridors, which he marks "Reno's Bad Idea," and gifts it to me. After this, I look for every excuse to spend more time with him. I wait for him to board our chartered bus and try to follow immediately after so I can sit next to him, grumbling under my breath if someone beats me to the seat or if foolish Reno chooses a seat next to someone else. Other times, I'll get on the bus first, my heart thumping in anticipation that Reno may sit next to me. We begin sitting together for almost every ride, and I give up any pretense of making it seem accidental.

The traffic in Mumbai is nothing like most of us have ever experienced. A drive a few miles across town could be stalled all day. The tour leaders, fellow MBAs from a year ahead, pack cases of Costco granola bars in preparation. My conversations with Reno are amusing from the start and flow naturally—we talk about everything from the giant billboards all over town advertising *RACE*, the new Bollywood movie premiering that week, to the slow-moving, confident cows in the streets, to all the colorful people and sights around us. We are so absorbed in each other that I look forward to the traffic. Our classmates quickly take notice, eavesdropping on our conversations and then turning to look at us, some smiling with blatant knowing expressions while others steal backward glances through faked stretches.

My head swirls with the possibility of romance. No prior attempt at flirting had been this effective for me, so it is hard to trust my feelings. But Reno is so receptive and reciprocating, I find it hard to accept that it could be one-sided again this time. Our interactions are organic yet intoxicating. I haven't felt this way since my memories with David, which have yellowed into bittersweetness.

As much as I love traveling, it poses major challenges for my mental health. As with my Europe Flinn trip, I have not been sleeping well. The drastic time difference, change in climate, and sleeping in unfamiliar places with a roommate I don't know well are all not conducive to rest. The malaria medication I am prescribed has since been outlawed by the Food and Drug Administration for causing mania in people. I am unaware of this risk at the time. Knowing when to take my mood stabilizer medication is also a challenge because we are on the move so much with full days of programs.

My interactions with Reno make me feel like a helium balloon.

I'm okay, I'll be home soon, I tell myself.

The possibility of something happening scares me, but I am emboldened by mild mania, feeling a bit invincible. The sense that the universe has ordained our connection hovers around me. I want this thing with Reno to be real. I know the risks, or think I do. *Everyone in the class will know… What if he ghosts me after we return to Seattle? What if, to him, it is harmless spring break flirting? How much do I really know him? He is a musician with tattoos and piercings. He probably goes through women in droves.*

There are plenty of reasons for not getting involved with Reno, but playing by the rules before left me heartbroken and depleted. In the past, I had waited and waited to be approached, pining silently for years. All of my frustration and impatience ignites a desire to take a risk. This chemistry with Reno is genuine. I always play it safe. I don't want to any longer.

In our travel group of twenty or so students, there has been talk about going dancing. I think it might be the perfect chance to engage Reno.

"Are you going to go dancing?" I ask Reno eagerly in our hotel lobby in Mumbai. The place has seen better days and reminds me of places I've stayed in Taiwan with my family. Not at all fancy, no-frills, but fine. The smell of meals past forever clings in the air.

"I don't dance," he answers, smiling sheepishly.

I think quickly, changing course and undeterred. I want to get to know Reno and free time is rare in our full itinerary.

"How about that movie, *RACE*, that just opened?" I ask. "I found a theater nearby where it's playing."

He looks taken aback but in a good way. "Sure, that sounds fun. Should we get a group together?"

I widen my eyes and glare at him.

"Or…not…" Reno's eyes round in understanding. He mumbles, "Or it can just be the two…of us?"

I smile. "That sounds nice. Great idea. I'll meet you outside in an hour."

When night falls, Reno and I meet in front of the hotel. On the busy street, he hails a yellow and black rickshaw. I tell the driver the name of the theater and ask, "How much?" The driver gives us the foreigner rate, and I open my mouth to haggle, as it is the way my family taught me in Taiwan and Korea shopping in street markets. In India, it is no different. We see haggling take place and were taught about it before our trip in our preparation session.

"That sounds fine," Reno interrupts me before I can say anything. He nods to the driver.

After we crouch our too-big American bodies into the rickshaw, I ask him, "Why didn't you let me haggle? I think we're paying too much."

Reno says, "The amount we'd haggle makes no difference to us in the long run, but it might to him."

As the rickshaw weaves through the noisy cityscape to deliver us to the movie theater, I am happy to squeeze into a tight space with Reno. We swerve in the tin can of a vehicle, giggling as we're thrown about.

The theater, though, is gleaming and modern. It is yet another example of the wealth and poverty that exist side by side throughout our travels here. The theater lobby features a chocolate fondue fountain and all the concession options.

The film is entirely in Hindi, save for a few phrases in English, and there are no subtitles. The dramatic twists are difficult to follow, but the big musical numbers are fun to watch. Other moviegoers answer calls on their cell phones and talk loudly throughout the three-hour movie. We chuckle. We don't care, gleeful to have this stolen night alone.

After that, Reno becomes more endearing with each idiosyncrasy I observe. He carefully averts his eyes when women in bathing suits are around. At restaurants, he pulls out his chair as quietly as possible to not disturb the other diners when the rest of our conspicuous group is careless and boisterous.

We are walking about a busy shopping district in Bangalore, shortly after arriving in the new city. Everyone in our group is trying to adapt to the humidity and the heat that is so different from the Pacific North-west when we come upon a musical instrument store. The shop is not too big, but two stories high and brimming with all kinds of shiny rock instruments. All of us enter and begin looking around.

I follow Reno up the tiny spiral staircase and get a clear view of the tattoos on the back of his calves below his Dickies shorts. "What do these tattoos on your legs mean?" I ask, but I am too late. Reno has found what he has been looking for and is entranced like an insect drawn to the light—a small silver drum set. He sits down on the throne and plays as if he has been parched. The rest of us surround him and become his audience, taking pictures.

"That should tide me over," he says afterward. I can see the glowing effects of the relief on his face and his presence. "I don't usually go for more than a couple days without playing."

I nod and smile.

"Oh, and about the tattoos, sorry I was distracted," Reno says and answers my questions. I'm impressed that he remembers my question despite the drumming intermission. I also note his urgency to play, as if he can't live without it.

India is a place of great contrasts: extreme poverty juxtaposed against unimaginable wealth, brilliant red and orange hues refusing to be drowned out by the greys and browns. Cows grazing in bustling city streets near the IT capital of Bangalore.

The next day, walking onto the grounds of the Infosys campus is like entering a detached dimension, with its striking glass pyramid, steely modern architecture, and immaculate landscaping as far as I can see.

On this company tour, our crew is baptized by a sudden monsoon shower, which thoroughly drenches our business suits. The group rushes back to the hotel where we are expected for a guest lecture, requiring a quick costume change. I peel off my wet clothes and slip on a bright red peasant shirt embellished with gold thread, newly purchased from a street vendor. I return to the meeting room in the hotel within five minutes.

"Wow," Reno gasps loudly when he sees me.

Our classmates giggle, and we both blush this time.

Since the movie outing during the first days of the trip, Reno and I continue flirting, but nothing else happens. With the trip wrapping up, I don't want to go home and have everything that happened here feel like a dream. Three nights before our flight home, Reno, another classmate, and I go into the city to shop for souvenirs. On our walk back to the hotel, our classmate is ahead of us, and I walk alongside Reno, who is holding a heavy shopping bag. He is passing it back and forth from his right hand to his left. I try to work up the nerve to hold Reno's hand for what seems like over an hour, trying to find the right time when his hand would be open on my side. Finally, I grab at my next chance. His hand is soft and warm. Not callused like I thought it might be.

Reno startles, looks at me, and does not let go.

Our last stop in India is a dreamy, historic beachfront hotel in Kochi, Kerala. Our trip organizers, all MBA students themselves, believe we need a few days to decompress before heading back to the intense pace of the program, and we are grateful. It is by far the nicest hotel we've stayed at during the trip. Beautiful, ornate wood carvings adorn the hotel lobby and the grounds. A glittering, clear blue pool lies parallel to the beach, a feature I've only seen in movies. Dolphins dance before a glorious backdrop of ginger-spiced sunsets each evening.

Reno and I haven't had the time to talk alone much, certainly not since our night walk hand-in-hand. We get the opportunity on the final night at a dinner with just the two of us. Even though we are at the hotel restaurant, this is the first time we can talk without being in earshot of classmates.

The conversation flows easily.

"I'm half Maltese," says Reno, who I only knew to be from the Midwest. "My mom's whole family emigrated from there."

"Wow, no way. One of my friends from Tucson is Maltese," proud to have known anything about the small island nation in the Mediterranean.

"That's awesome. Most people have never even heard of Malta," Reno laughs. "They think I'm talking about the little dog or the falcon."

"So, tell me," I ask. "What's the reason you don't drink?"

"Do you have a guess?" He smiles.

"Well, there are rumors," I say. "Are you a recovering alcoholic? Or straight-edge?"

Reno laughs heartily. "I can see why people would think that, but no. Drinking just never appealed to me."

"Never?" I am dubious.

"Never," he answers. "I don't like the taste and never felt the need."

Huh. His straightforward self-assurance—unyielding and unconcerned by pressures to conform—is as refreshing as it is admirable.

This reason is much more boring, but I like it.

After the simple dinner, we stroll around the hotel. Though the immediate grounds are lush and well-kept, we find that immediately outside it is quiet. The plain streets are not well-lit, and are unremarkable and empty. The desolation seems to be the perfect backdrop for me to tell him about Zach, about how that relationship just ended.

"I have no interest in being your rebound," he says earnestly.

I smile and turn toward him, detecting his vulnerability. "I don't do rebounds."

"To be fair, you don't know that if you haven't dated before," he says. We keep walking down the dark, unfamiliar street hand-in-hand.

"I guess you're right," I answer honestly.

Though there's nothing more I can say, this doesn't feel like a rebound.

We step back into the brightly lit garden of the hotel, back into the dream. We sit on the intricately carved wooden swing chair facing the rhythmic ocean waves. It feels too magical to be real.

"Can I kiss you?" Reno whispers.

I nod.

At this precise moment, the crystal ball lamps on either side of the swing chair switch off.

We lean into each other in the warm, salty breeze.

CHAPTER 48: Falling

After long, bashful kisses on the swing chair, Reno and I walk hand in hand to the elevator, where we kiss all the way up to my floor. When the doors ding open, Reno wishes me goodnight.

"Good night," I reply reflexively as I walk out. *Should I have invited him into my room?* I hadn't thought that far, and I was caught off guard by his goodbye. I wouldn't have minded more time alone with him, away from the prying eyes of our classmates.

It is still early, around 10:00 PM. I am alone in bed, and I feel like I'm going to burst into flames with energy. My roommate is still out. My mind and body tingle like I am at a strobe-lit disco. I can't sleep a wink. *Love. India. Reno.* The thoughts rush around me in a cyclone.

By morning, the intensely euphoric spell is broken, replaced by a forceful black vacuum threatening to consume me. My feelings for Reno haven't changed, but instead of hope and sunshine, a dark, inescapable fear drains me. I can no longer see the rosy buds of new love. Instead, I am paralyzed by the impending rejection and loneliness threatening above my head. I am petrified of losing it all.

Though I was taking my medication as regularly as my travel

schedule allowed, the mood stabilizer is no longer powerful enough to still the rocking waves in my head. My judgement and connection to reality is breached. Like the waves, my mood ebbs and flows between joy and despair. In moments of lightness, spirituality and the universe are guiding my path again. In darkness, I am exposed, judged, and despised by all.

"So did you and Reno...?" a woman from the program asks me on the same swing chair the next morning. She tilts her head full of shiny curls, releasing two clicking sounds out of the side of her lips.

I am caught unprepared for her bold questioning, and in my sleepless fuzziness, I am too dense to understand what she meant. "What?"

"So did you and Reno...?" she clicks twice again.

I am too confused. I don't know what the clicking means.

"Yes," I answer, choosing to interpret her question broadly, emotionally. I smile softly, not knowing what else to say. I don't know why I answer at all. My mind is leaving me, and I am having grandiose thoughts again. I suspect she is a holy messenger, and I have to convey my commitment to Reno, so I say yes.

Having never dated anyone within my social circle, the idea of everyone at school knowing about us strikes profound terror. I spin out. I need to hold onto Reno, to make it feel real. I am afraid to leave his side and do not let go of his hand. I even wait outside the bathroom for him at the airport, grabbing tight to his hand as soon as he comes back.

When introducing a new fish to an aquarium, you're supposed to open the plastic bag and place the whole thing in the tank, allowing the water from the bag to mix slowly with the water from its new environment. This allows the fish to adjust to the new temperature and chemical balance gradually, to avoid shock. When humans travel between worlds, there is no gradual adjustment period. We are plucked from warm South Indian breezes beneath a blazing sun and dropped in the inescapably chill air under a black peppery sky in Seattle.

I am afraid I'll wake up to discover the past week has been a dream. *Was the kiss on the swing chair before the orange setting sun only in my head?* I need to be with Reno, to absorb the solidity of his hands.

The first night back from our trip, I drive to his studio apartment near campus. It is my first time at his place, and I find its snugness comforting. After we flip through his DVD collection, Reno talks me into watching the classic *Ghostbusters*, his favorite. We wrap ourselves around each other in his bed because there is no other place to sit. The studio is nothing more than a bed, desk, and television. Dizzy from the intimacy of the moment, we allow our bodies to connect. By the time the movie ends, Reno is sound asleep. The two of us try to fit in his twin-sized bed. He is mostly hanging off of it, and I am given more space, but I am still uncomfortable.

I sneak out of the room. This is the first time I leave someone's place in the middle of the night like this, and I'm overcome with doubt and shame in the quiet of the night. *What have I done? Is this who I am now?*

"Are you awake? Can we talk?" I send a text to Leslie as I walk to my car. It is past one in the morning, but she is awake. I put her on speaker phone and turn on the ignition to my white Honda Accord.

"I am so scared," I tell her. I am shaking a little. "I just slept with a guy from my program after our trip to India."

"What are you scared about?" she asks patiently.

"What will people say?" I spiral in my thoughts as I drive on the dark winding road back to my house in Sandpoint. There is no one else on the quiet street. "What if everyone finds out at school, and what if people think I'm a slut?"

I am nearly twenty-seven years old by this time and without any awareness about how immature this concern is. *What would my parents think?* I panic.

"Oh, Michelle, I'm so happy for you," Leslie soothes in her calming voice. "What happened is totally normal. I hope you can enjoy it, and try not to worry so much."

I don't know what I expected her to say, but I did not guess that she would be happy for me. In my negative spiral of racing thoughts, "normal" had not entered my consciousness. The word jolts me out of my misery, but my stomach continues to roil.

CHAPTER 49: Wo Hai Pa

SEATTLE, WASHINGTON

"Good morning, Sunshine!" I text Reno the next morning when I can wait no longer.

I realize how obnoxious and desperate this sounds, but I can't help it. I feel entirely exposed.

Sunshine returns to the rainy city like a celebrated guest that weekend. The famous Japanese cherry trees in the Quad at the University of Washington are in bloom. Gusts of wind sweep confetti clouds of tiny pink and white fluttering petals all around me and Reno when we stroll together, reminding me of a perfect scene in a Disney movie. Everything is surreal and bathed in golden light. Reno removes his black peacoat and lays it on the lawn like a blanket, inviting me to sit close. We savor the touch of the tender grass, the fragrant blossoms—a festive rebirth of spring. My very own real romance. This level of bliss had seemed unattainable, not for me.

But like the cherry blossoms, my euphoria is fleeting. The black vacuum returns, a massacre of delicate hope butterflies. Reno isn't just anyone. He is a classmate in our relatively small program. For me to continue seeing Reno, I will have to tell him about my condition, my skeleton in the closet, my mental illness, which I have kept secret for as long as I have known about it.

And then everyone will know.

What if he rejects me once he knew the truth about me?

I will feel like trash. Like a piece of defective garbage.

I gasp for air. It feels like the end.

I spin into full panic and then into despair. My mood stabilizer is still not working to steady me quickly enough. Once there has been a disturbance in the water, it takes a while for the waves and then rings to calm and still.

I need to get back to the doctor. My mind and heart battle over whether or not to confess to Reno about my condition as soon as possible.

"Wo hai pa," I call Mama on the phone from my bedroom, peering out my window. I'm scared, a worried child again. The sky is grey once more. My parents know "wo hai pa" as my quiet but chilling call for help. My mental health is crumbling.

"Ze mo la?" Mama answers, full of concern. "Yeo se mo se?" What happened?

When spring quarter starts days after we return from India, I don't go to class.

I am afraid to leave my room again.

I stop eating. My thoughts race.

I am a complete fraud.

The school will kick me out anyway.

Why did I think I could earn a Master's degree?

Everyone hates me.

No one thinks I can cut it here.

Reno will regret getting involved.

I don't deserve to breathe.

I am the worst person.

I don't deserve to live.

I stop answering calls from Reno, from anyone.

I don't want Reno to see me differently. I don't want my peers and professors to know my secret shame. My instinct is to run away. Drop out of the program. I am too afraid, too weak to fight.

Leaving would mean thousands of dollars wasted and going back home to Arizona a failure, but I could take my secret with me and lock my crazy self away in the proverbial attic. I could disappear without explanation.

"Mama, wo hai pa."

Mama deploys our only distant relatives in the area to help me. This time, within hours, my second cousin Uncle Howie and his wife appear at my door with a takeout box of steaming, spicy and salty Malaysian rice noodles. It is the only real food I've eaten in over a week. I lose over ten pounds in days. I gulp down the nourishment, hardly chewing.

"Slow down," they say in unison, unable to hide their shock. "Eat slowly."

I am no longer the confident and independent person they met a few months earlier, who moved across the country with seeming ease and limitless ambition. I am a shell of my prior self, unsure of my every movement and every breath. Any simple decision or question debilitates me like they had during my episodes in high school.

My uncle and aunt coax me to come with them back to their peaceful house in the suburbs. I agree, nervous but relieved. With a belly full of food, away from my rented room which I'd come to associate with many kinds of stress, I breathe easier. I am thankful not to be alone and to be under the protection of family.

Their neighborhood in the Issaquah Highlands is so picture-perfect that it looks fake. So many Asian American families live there that it seems to be made up of mostly Asians. Their house is beautiful, though sparsely decorated. It's very clean. I wonder who cleans it.

My kind aunt and uncle set me up in a guest bedroom upstairs. Its blank walls and the sterile scent are comforting, like the beginning of a fresh start. In the stark, white bathroom across the hallway, my aunt asks me, "What happened? What's wrong?"

I don't know how long my aunt and uncle have been married, but it can't be long. Uncle Howie is only four years older than me. They don't have children yet. My aunt is genuinely sweet, with wavy hair and a smile that lights up a room. I feel I owe them an answer for taking care of me.

"I have bipolar disorder," I spit out, the shame pulling my eyes to the cold tiled floor. My confession clunks like an anvil. I have never revealed my secret to any extended family member, let alone this young, pretty aunt by marriage whom I don't know very well. This is also my first admission during an episode.

She looks up at me in alarm, the information registering. Without a word, she turns around and walks out of the bathroom, presumably to tell my uncle what she's learned.

I want the cold floor to swallow me up.

My kind relatives take good care of me. I don't remember if we talk anymore about my illness, but peace finds me in their quiet guest room. I sleep for a long time.

When I awake, I am distraught.

"I can't keep missing school," I say. "There's a club meeting today, and I have to be there. I'm the president. I run the meetings."

My aunt and uncle try to calm me down. I am panic-stricken and in no condition to go to school, but the idea of just not showing up, where my absence would definitely be noticed, is unbearable. But I also know I can't go to school like this, when I can't think straight and my head is spinning. That would be worse. I don't know what to do.

In the end, I ask my uncle to send an email to the club listserv from my MBA email account:

"Michelle is sick and cannot come to school.
-Michelle's Uncle Howie."

The ridiculousness of this email, especially coming from my school account to all the members of the club listserv, is not lost on me, but I have no other option. I can't leave a room full of people waiting and asking questions.

Reno, along with my best friend in the program, both worry about my absences. They call me and check in with one another as I continue to dodge their contact. I can't bear to face them.

Mama arrives in Seattle a couple days later and cocoons me. In her embrace, I am grounded. The next day, she accompanies me to my appointment with the campus health psychiatric nurse practitioner, whom I have been seeing since starting the MBA program. We take the city bus and disembark near the old campus health building. Its cozy, collegiate look with red exposed bricks and ivy is comforting.

We wait in the bright lobby. I am uneasy as I lean on Mama, drinking in her love and shelter. Sharon beckons us into her office. Even from her appearance, she is tall and sturdy and does not look like someone who would get pushed around. Sharon is wise, no-nonsense but empathetic, and one of the best mental health providers that I have ever worked with. She also is Black, and she understands my experiences better than other mental health providers. Sharon is my first non-white provider. Her urgency to help me get back on track matches my own. Sharon looks sad and compassionate while speaking to me, but never angry, which is different from my past experiences with providers. Fear often manifests as anger. She is not afraid.

I tell Sharon what happened on my India study tour.

"I'm so scared," I say, not able to look her or my mom in the eyes. "I am worried I will need to drop out of the program and go home to Phoenix."

"No, that is premature," Sharon says kindly, but firmly. "But you should take at least another week off of school to recover."

"But that will mean missing the first two weeks of the quarter," I look up at her, alarmed. "Will the school allow that? Won't they kick me out?"

I don't know how I will ever catch up with my challenging

course load. The stigma I hold inside is so strong, I am still afraid that my program will expel me if they find out about my bipolar diagnosis.

"Don't worry," Sharon soothes. "I will write a letter to the dean excusing you from your classes."

Like the instance with Dr. R back in Phoenix when he suggested I take a semester off of school, the possibility that I can take two weeks off hadn't occurred to me. Knowing she has the power to medically excuse me eases my mind somewhat.

I take a deep breath.

"I'm also going to increase your dosage of Depakote," she adds. "You can taper up, but it should help you stabilize."

"Thank you. You good doctor," Mama says to Sharon with tears in her eyes, offering the few English words she can.

For the next several days, Mama hides me from the world in my Seattle home on Sandpoint Way. She cooks my favorite dishes— simmering potato and beef soup she learned to make from her grandmother, stir-fried tomato and eggs, and tangy, and rich kimchi soup that heals me from the inside. Mama strokes my hair each night, my skin tingles with the love of her tender gaze. Under her protection, I slowly regain my strength and find my center.

Waking up from an episode, I climb out of the ashes, naked. I must survey the damage and muster the strength to show my face. Because I'm now fully in control and entirely conscious of the mess I've made, the shame is all-consuming. I'm ashamed for having burdened loved ones with worry. I'm embarrassed for disappearing, for losing touch with reality.

My last severe episode was seven years ago in China. Each time I suffer an episode, I pray it will be my last. I grieve the false sense of security I held about being better.

The next time Reno calls, I answer. It is evening, and I am alone in my room, sitting on my double bed, which takes up almost all of it. My knees are bent, and I pull my blanket up to my chin. I pick up my cellphone with dread, fearful this will be the end.

"Are you okay?" he asks gently. His voice shakes. "Where have you been?"

"I'm sorry," I say quietly. "I'm doing better now."

"What happened?"

Shrinking into a pebble, weighty yet small, I wish I could bury myself deeper in dirt, but I can't.

"I have bipolar disorder," I utter clearly.

I do not want to lose Reno, to be forced to let go of this organic, romantic connection. We will end before we began, but I have no other option. I have to tell him.

"I might drop out of the program and go back to Arizona," I say in a voice so feeble it is barely audible.

Once Reno knows, he will not want me.

Why would anyone want me?

I do not want me.

"I understand if you want to stop seeing each other," I quiver in defeat, bracing for the inevitable blow to finish me.

"Oh," he pauses. "Someone close to me also has bipolar disorder. I understand. It's not a deal breaker for me."

I process this unexpected response without optimism. I still hate who I am.

"If you know what this is like, why would you want to invite more of it into your life?"

"Because..." says Reno firmly, "did you ever consider that you are worth fighting for?"

His words somehow break through my numbness and despair.

I am worth fighting for.

I am reminded of the person I had been and wanted to be again.

Once we say goodbye, I stand up and stretch. The weight of Reno's words and sentiment sinking in.

I still feel like shit, but I am reminded this is not permanent.

I will be me again.

I feel lower than dirt, but that is my bipolar talking.

I will get better. I can rebuild.

I am still me: Flawed, imperfect, but strong and worthy.
My spirit took another beating, but I straighten my spine.
I begin mending, reborn again.
I will not run.
I will fight.

CHAPTER 50: Summer

SEATTLE, WASHINGTON

University Avenue is lively when Spring Quarter is in session. Reno and I sneak away between classes to our favorite quick lunch spot, Yummy Bites. With Korean American owners, their diverse menu allows me to order comforting soondubu and Reno to order a Caesar wrap. Afterward, we stroll back to campus, taking our time. The cloud cover is a near permanent fixture this time of the year, but we don't mind.

"I know we haven't been seeing each other very long," Reno says to me just as we cross onto 15th Avenue. He is clean shaven except his chin patch, and his shoulders look particularly broad in his structured peacoat. "But my parents are visiting Seattle, and they would like to meet you."

Reno's uncharacteristic nervousness makes him fidget. "No pressure, I'd completely understand if you think it's too soon," he adds before I have a chance to say anything. It has only been a couple of weeks, but it's been enough time for me to feel like myself again.

"I'd love to meet them." My smile widens. I have no hesitation.

I wear a powder-pink embroidered button up and dark bootcut jeans with red ballet flats, striking the balance of softness and spunk. My kind roommate nods in approval of my outfit before I leave for dinner.

At a Lower Queen Anne restaurant, Reno's parents greet me with open hugs. Both down-to-earth Midwesterners, I am instantly taken by their warmth. As the evening wears on, I feel Reno relax next to me. After dinner, they hug me goodbye, even tighter than before.

Reno and I saunter away holding hands. "You are amazing," he says. "They love you."

I can't believe how easy it is. No stress about my weight or what I need to change. They welcomed me instantly as the person who makes their son happy. Reno's parents were riveted by my stories of my work in nonprofit and my childhood working with my parents at our restaurant—really, they were interested in everything I shared with them. Already, after one meal, I feel loved.

When the splendor of Seattle summer arrives, I am ready to rest and replenish without the demands of the MBA program. Living in a new city while in graduate school is like living under a rock. I rarely have the headspace or time to explore. Summer is my chance. Though I intern at a small creative agency specializing in sustainable brands as well as at the Nonprofit Assistance Center in the International District, there is far less pressure and a lot more time than during the school year.

Summer also means that, for the first time in our months-long relationship, Reno and I have ample time to spend with each other. Rich on time but poor on cash, we make an adventure of hopping on random city buses to see where they take us. Using our free student bus passes, we climb on to see which cranny of Seattle the bus will take us. Excited to explore Seattle and happy to be together sitting as closely as possible, we don't care where we end up.

One such ride stops suddenly in the middle of a quiet, hilly neighborhood.

"Are you two getting off?" The young driver smiles at us. "This is my break." He removes a paperback from his backpack.

From all the way in the back of the bus, Reno and I smile at each other. "Oh, um…can we wait and keep riding when you're done?" I respond, a bit embarrassed, chuckling at our predicament.

"Sure, we'll start again in fifteen minutes," he says, sinking into his seat and escaping into a thick sci-fi novel.

Reno and I link arms and lean closer, admiring the pretty little houses outside and the flowering trees here and there. The bus becomes warm in the summer heat, but nothing bothers us. We wait for the empty bus to splutter back to life, all the possibilities still ahead of us.

I belong here. I belong here.

Silently, I chant to myself at The Fairmont Olympic, the fanciest hotel in Seattle, trying not to feel out of place in my grey suit from the clearance section at Ann Taylor Loft. I kick myself for throwing on woolen stockings under my skirt at the last minute, making me look like an overgrown toddler. Being a Phoenix girl though, my fear of the cold wins over fashion every time.

Breathe.

I am at the Puget Sound Business Journal awards banquet to receive the 2008 Women of Influence Scholarship. The Italian Renaissance-inspired architecture and the glamor, wealth, and ease of those around me screams old money. I try to stay strong.

At the Flinn Scholarship banquet at the Arizona Biltmore nearly a decade ago, the glitz and glamor of my surroundings had similarly bowled me over. Back then, I stood tall, believing I'd made my parents proud, only to find a very frustrated Baba at the end of the evening.

This time, when I go on stage to accept my scholarship, Reno beams at me from the audience. After I stumble through my acceptance speech, he stands up, cheering loudly. His unabashed pride steadies me.

Reno is never threatened by what I can do. Instead, he celebrates how well-matched we are intellectually. Identifying as a proud feminist, his progressive beliefs align with my own. Though he plays drums in two bands and gigs regularly in town, despite our behemoth workload, Reno also finds time to serve as a founding board member for Rain City Rock Camp, a nonprofit whose mission is to empower girls and gender non-conforming youth through music. I love Reno's passion, steadfastness, and confidence. He is composed in what he says but never afraid to speak his mind or from his heart.

"I love you," I say to him before I can catch myself. We are cuddling on the couch at my house in Sandpoint, watching the presidential election results late into the night.

I can't believe we have our first Black president. Reno and I are both overjoyed.

"Thank you," he says to me in response, kissing me.

I am careful not to say those words again, as much as I can help it, but it's hard.

Our first Valentine's Day together, almost a year after we'd started dating, I prepare us a romantic dinner of seared salmon on puff pastry over wilted spinach—a tribute to a dish I love at a restaurant in Tucson. Reno shows up at my door with a gift of small, handmade soaps from Ten Thousand Villages, a fair-trade nonprofit gift shop on whose board he serves as an intern, and a card which reads "Wo ai ni" inside. The character for love is a hybrid of the two Chinese symbols for "to receive" and "heart." Reno had enlisted the help of a Taiwanese international classmate for help to write it.

"It's perfect," I beam.

After dinner, we walk to Matthews Beach and sit on an old wooden bench by the turtle pond, relishing the celebration.

In the midst of the recession in 2009, when the unemployment rate in the U.S. is the highest it's been since 1982, Reno and I graduate from the MBA program. Reno is elected by our class to give a speech at our graduation, which helps win my parents over. My parents' first meeting with Reno goes smoothly, as I had given them a heads up about the tattoos and piercing. Reno's parents are in town too for the graduation, of course, so we all meet for lunch at Duke's Chowder House in West Seattle, followed by a walk down the beach promenade. All is peaceful and well, a respite from the stress and pressure for Reno and me about what's to come next now that grad school is over.

Half of the graduating class struggles to find jobs while staring down student loans nearing six-figures. We are both unemployed at the time of graduation.

By the following month, however, I am hired as the Fund Development Manager at the Girl Scouts of Western Washington. I make plans to move out of the house I share with three roommates into a small apartment of my own, closer to my new job.

Reno is taking his lack of job prospects hard. This economy is not what any of us expected. He is at the UW Career Center almost every day and doing everything he can, but it is a struggle. One night, Reno and I are hanging out in his studio. I have my laptop in front of me at his desk. I am apartment hunting and busy making plans for my upcoming transitions. He is looking at me from the bed. I look up to see that he has a dreamy look in his eyes.

"Michelle, do you want to move in together?" Reno asks me shyly.

I smile, pleased. But I have been giving this idea a lot of thought on my own, and I am ready with an answer.

"No...I don't think that's a good idea." After all, I'm still a Chinese daughter. I have been raised and conditioned that this is a stupid thing for a girl to do if she wants a future with her partner. "I don't believe in moving in together before marriage."

Reno is shocked, speechless for once.

I move to his side on the bed. "I promised myself," I add.

Confusion crosses his face. "It's just...it will take so much longer for us to get to know each other to be ready for marriage if we never live together."

I am undeterred.

After all the warnings from Baba about living with a boyfriend, and after what happened with Zach, I am determined to be smarter this time. I want to safeguard this relationship. I am not in a rush to get engaged, but I also don't want moving in together to prevent marriage from ever happening.

Reno is blindsided by my response. Society conditioned him to believe that women always want to move in together.

A week or two later, I find the perfect, affordable one-bedroom apartment on top of a steep hill in lower Queen Anne, very close to my work. I move in, get settled, and immediately realize that Reno is missing.

Reno is not Zach.

I trust him and want him to live with me.

Sheepishly, I bring up the topic next time Reno comes over.

"Um...I changed my mind," I say with a mischievous smile. "Do you want to move in with me here?" I gesture to the space around us with my arms.

"Oh my god, you!" Reno replies, laughing, knocking me over in a sideways hug.

When I tell Baba about our decision, he threatens to fly to Seattle to throw Reno out of the apartment. It is another empty threat, but I still feel the chill of fear in my bones as he roars through the phone.

Reno gives up his studio near campus, and our cohabitation goes smoothly and unremarkably for the next six months. He and I decide that we will switch back and forth on whose family to visit each holiday season. This year, we go to Phoenix for Christmas, which, in retrospect, is a funny idea as my parents never celebrate the holiday. Later, I will learn Baba and Mama stressed and worried about gifts and what foods to serve.

Reno and I have a good time in Phoenix. I show him around my old high school and middle school, and we enjoy down time and being taken care of by my family, and we relax. On day three, however, Baba solemnly tells Reno and me that he needs to speak with us.

"Uh oh," I turn to face Reno. "I have a feeling what this is about." Baba had warned me that now that we've been living together for months, he expects an engagement.

"But I think it will be fine," I say to Reno. "At this point, he is all talk."

Nevertheless, Reno leads us to the room we're staying in my parents' house. "We should pack," he says, nervous but focused. "Just in case."

"What?" I chuckle. "What do you think is going to happen? He's not going to throw us out."

"Still, I would feel a lot better if we are prepared for anything."

I kneel down on the ground by my suitcase and pack up everything, just in case.

Soon, we are seated across from Baba and Mama in our formal dining room. My mother pours us hot tea from a small, white teapot I haven't seen used in decades. My parents have so many things stashed away everywhere, especially in the kitchen and dining area.

"You know what I need to talk to you two about," says Baba in his serious voice. His back is straight, and his shoulders are rounded. "You've lived together. I will not let you leave this house without a promise that you will get married."

"We are not ready, Baba," I answer. "We will let you know when we are."

Baba shushes me.

"I'm talking to Reno," he says. "Reno, can you promise me that you will marry my daughter?"

"Dr. Yang, I love your daughter," says Reno. "But I cannot promise you that right now. When we do decide to get married, we want the decision to be ours alone."

An awkward stare down ensues, neither side relenting until it becomes dark outside and is time for dinner. I am not sure how we get out of that one, but we do.

The final day of our visit passes calmly. Baba and Mama drive us to the airport, and we hug each other goodbye. Reno and I both release a sigh of relief.

Back in Seattle, I thrive in my new career, both working full-time and volunteering for special troops after work in programs like "Girl Scouts Fostering a Future" and "Girl Scouts Beyond Bars."

Reno begins working at a creative agency where his talents are quickly recognized. He is happy.

It is September, just over a year after we moved in together. Content in our little apartment in Seattle, all the puzzle pieces feel as if they are fitting together.

"I have a special idea for a date night," says Reno. We are sitting on my hand-me-down red couch.

"Oh yeah?" I ask in my pajamas, perking up. Who doesn't love a good date night?

"I met someone who can set us up with a private tour of the downtown Seattle Central Library for us. What do you think?"

"You had me at library!"

Reno seems uneasy that evening, stuttering and walking in circles when we are getting ready.

When we arrive at the pyramid-like glass and steel structure downtown, a bespectacled librarian with salt and pepper hair greets us.

"You are Reno? Then you must be Michelle!" He is seriously beaming at us. His smile lingers over us for an unnaturally long moment before he rushes us around the library.

The tour seems very hurried, and I am a little disappointed the guide hasn't shown us anything I hadn't already known about or seen. Then he leads us to the atrium floor, often referred to as the heart of the library. Its walls, ceiling, floor, and doors are all a shiny, bold red. I love the idea that this library has a beating heart.

Once in the heart, the librarian opens a door I didn't realize was there. He ushers us into a stark white conference room and says, "I'll let you two hang out here for a moment to look at the photos here. I'll be back in a few minutes." He subtly nods at Reno.

"Well, that's a little strange that he just left us here," I say, obediently studying the black and white prints on the wall of Seattle architecture.

Reno clears his throat, "Michelle…"

I turn around and see him untuck a tiny bit of floral purple cloth from the front zipped pocket of the camera bag he is carrying. Reno unwraps a ring and launches into a grand, prepared speech, but I don't hear any of it except, "Everyday, for the rest of my life, I choose you."

I squeal. I can't help it.

Reno slides the ring on my finger. The ruby, my birthstone, is at the center with two gracefully carved pieces of black jade on either side of the silver-colored band. "The jade is from my pendant from New Zealand," he explains. The beautiful spiral carved pendant had been a parting gift from his bandmates when he lived on the island before graduate school. "It is said to absorb the soul of the wearer, so this ring, with your birthstone, connects us."

I am taking everything in silently.

"Well?" he asks again, grinning. "Will you marry me?"

"Yes!" I exclaim.

Relief washes over Reno's face.

He does not get down on one knee. We are not that kind of couple. We want to enter into this partnership on equal footing.

CHAPTER 51: Promise

SEATTLE, WASHINGTON

In a dusty makeshift dressing room, I marvel at my reflection in an old-fashioned standing mirror. For the first time, both my hair and makeup is done professionally. I cock my brow, turning my face from side to side. As if by magic, filled-in eyebrows lend power and confidence to my soft features. My nose, which may have been referred to in Korea as a garlic nose, bulbous and unattractive, shrinks suddenly into proportion. Proud cheek bones make their presence known under what my father hoped was baby fat, but never melted away. My slight lips borrow a bold pout from the coral stain, finished with a shiny gloss. The makeup artist calls this look "the fresh-faced bride," and I can't believe I am pulling it off.

A single red silk blossom adorns my black hair, expertly swept up in artful knots with more bobby pins than I can count, ensuring not a strand is out of place all day and night.

Self-conscious of my hulking shoulders and floppy, ham-like arms, I had dreaded shopping for a wedding dress. I could only imagine myself looking like a hippo in frills in the sleeveless and form-fitting gowns in magazines and movies. The message has been clear—women like me don't deserve pretty dresses, let alone true love.

But my gown's tailored bodice and full skirt work on my plus-sized body. To my surprise, every dress I try on at the generic mall bridal shop I stumble into with my parents without an appointment makes me feel beautiful.

And now, the partner of my dreams who can't wait to marry me is standing outside the dressing room door.

Nine years prior, I had been admitted to a psych ward. Worried I would never be put back together, I feared I could never be strong and happy again. I earned this rebirth through tears, pills, and thousands of dollars spent on treatment—blood drawn and tested every six months to ensure my chemistry is level. Putting one foot in front of the other, blind faith over uncharted territory led me to this dream milestone.

In direct contrast to the photos I've seen of other brides, pampered in glamorous lounges with fairytale lighting and velvet, tufted armchairs, I am standing on carpet that is old and dank. Clutter collects in corners with broken picture frames sticking out beneath heavy stage curtains meant to disguise this dusty storage room. Our wedding photographer purses her lips, attempting, but failing, to hide her disapproval, but I don't care one bit.

The Fremont Abbey, a former church that had been used as a homeless shelter, vacant in the late 1990s and reopened in 2008 after extensive, seismic renovations, is exactly where we want to be wed. Like me, the venue has been many times transformed. Its latest, unexpected reincarnation is perhaps the best version of itself yet. The red brick exterior walls and steeple brim with history of the Seattle Fremont neighborhood. The charm and glory of the tall stained-glass windows and high arched ceilings were not lost in its metamorphosis into a secular, non-profit community arts space.

Despite being initially taken aback by the humble surroundings, the wedding photographer captures one of my favorite photographs of the day in this dressing room/storage closet. My mother, aunt, and best friend Teresa each burrow a hand deep under the fluffed-up layers of my petticoat while our faces bloom with laughter. Though the details of the memory are lost, like sugar dissolved, the joy lingers.

For a long time, I did not believe I would ever be worthy of happiness, of love.

Too many times, I doubted if I was worthy even of life.

No, not a girl like me who would never be thin enough, demure enough, or sane enough.

Yet, here I am. And there he waits, with nearly two hundred boisterous guests who've traveled from near and far, eager to witness and bless our next chapter. The day is a celebration of the love I have had all of my life—the love of my parents, my brother, my friends, and even myself.

I look in the mirror one last time and step through the door.

I PROMISE . . .

To be empathetic, sincere, and passionate
To be considerate, kind, and true
To listen, to laugh, and to learn
To celebrate your gestures, both big and small

To support your ambitions, wherever they may take us
To raise a family with you, whatever form that takes
To be your sidekick, whenever you need one
To remain true to myself even as we grow together

To amplify your emotions whenever you want it
To balance your emotions whenever you need it

To surprise you even when you've seen it all
To fight for us even when it hurts
To appreciate you even when it's easy
To be honest with you even when it's hard

To understand what you meant even if it's not what you said
To tell you what you mean to me every day of our lives

To love you first and above all others,
With this audience as my witness,
Until puppies stop being adorable and music stops being awesome.

CHAPTER 52: Asian American Eyes

SEATTLE, WASHINGTON

"Baba, guess what?" I scream joyfully into the phone. "We bought a house!"

I am pacing with excitement in our larger Lower Queen Anne apartment. I can look out the generous windows and see the glittering lights along I-5 in the distance at night. Reno and I had moved to a two-bedroom unit on the top floor after our first year in a one-bedroom, eager for a separate office. We love this building, this location, but a year after being married, we are ready for more permanent housing.

Reno and I have been house hunting for a year in the tight Seattle housing market. We are thrilled to be making the largest purchase of our lives.

"Good," Baba grunts. "Now you must help me talk to Didi."

"Talk to Didi? About what?" I ask, jarred by the sudden pivot.

"There's an MBA program in China. You talk to him. Convince him to go. He must do this for his future."

"Baba, when will you realize that Didi will never do as you say? Whatever you pressure him to do, he will do the opposite. Why can't you see that?" Baba, caught off guard by my bluntness, is quiet, so I continue. "Didi has no interest in going back to school. He barely survived college. And he has no interest in studying in China. Remember when I offered to pay for him to do a semester study abroad, and he refused? You can't force him to do what he doesn't want, Baba. He is an adult in his late twenties."

Baba hangs up in disbelief that I will not go along with his scheme. He isn't used to being spoken to this way, but I don't care. I refuse to be his foot soldier.

Curling my knees up to my chest on the edge of our black fabric IKEA couch, I feel sorry for myself. I had called my family to share good news. A house is a big step in the life we are building, a precursor to the start of a family. I expected congratulations, a moment of celebration.

Soon, my cellphone begins to ring. It's Mama. She is his mouthpiece, and I don't feel like talking to her. I don't answer. She calls again and again that night and the next day.

"Beautiful Jade, you know how much Baba loves you. You are his favorite. How can you speak to him like that?" Mama's voice cracks in a teary voicemail. "You must call him and apologize. Okay, Daughter?"

Mama does not often leave messages crying on the phone. I call her back immediately, worried.

No answer.

I call again and again, once every hour, wanting to make sure she is okay. When she proves unreachable, I try my father's phone. Baba also does not answer. I become more worried and agitated. My parents always answer the phone. In the middle of a movie, during dinner, in conversation, it doesn't matter to them. If the phone rings, they always answer, but not now.

I walk out to the balcony of our apartment, which I've lined with pots of tomato plants, herbs, and flowers. The gentle, early summer breeze from the Puget Sound is cool and pleasant.

There is only one other person I can call.

"Didi, have you heard from Mama?"

"Not since she left me a message crying yesterday."

"Me too. You haven't talked to her?"

"No."

I try to ignore the worst-case scenarios flashing in my mind—an overturned car in the desert, a heart attack, a stroke. I have always been their translator. What if the doctors or police officers don't know how to find an emergency contact for them?

Two worry-filled days later, I am in my bathrobe and frazzled when I get through to my mother.

"Mama, are you okay?"

"I'm fine," she says, all nonchalant,

"Why did you call crying? Why didn't you answer for two days?"

"You need to apologize to Baba," she says, her tone matter of fact.

"You're okay? Nothing happened?"

"I'm fine," she says coolly. "You need to apologize to Baba."

Blood drains from my face, and fury courses through my core, down to my fingertips.

For the first time in my life, I recognize that my parents are manipulating me. With startling clarity, the patterns of their manipulation reveal themselves. My parents, who are supposed to love and protect me, had purposely caused me severe mental anguish. A tactic that has pervaded my life. Baba is the mastermind and dictator, Mama his loyal soldier. She will never disobey him, even when it means putting me or Didi in harm's way.

A few months earlier, Reno and I had begun talk of starting a family. I am unwilling to bring a child into the world without healing my wounds first. When intermittent rage toward my parents shoots out of me in uncontrollable bursts, its intensity startles me. In the past, I'd gone to therapy only as needed as a supplement to my short appointments with a psychiatrist. My therapy appointments were often months apart, but sometimes years passed without an appointment at all. This time, I seek weekly intensive therapy for myself and for my future child.

"I don't expect this to take very long," I explain at my first appointment. "A few weeks maybe. I just don't know why I get so furious at my parents sometimes, even though, overall, we have a great relationship. I just want to work through it. I don't think it's anything major."

"Do you have a history of childhood trauma?" my new therapist asks. Her chestnut-brown hair is pulled in a high ponytail. Her immaculately tailored pencil skirt and expensive-looking blouse gives her an Audrey Hepburn vibe.

"Childhood trauma?" I repeat. "No...I don't think so. My father hit us growing up, but I don't think that's uncommon for Chinese immigrant families. I'm sure it wouldn't qualify as trauma. Other people have it much worse."

My therapist looks at me as if she is not convinced.

What I can't know is that I am describing only the tip of the iceberg. Not only that, I am a ship colliding into the iceberg with crushing force, without comprehending the extent of the damage or the enormity of the obstacle.

Throughout these sessions, I describe the memories haunting me out loud, translating the events into English for the first time, providing them a new context. What seemed perfectly normal inside my head all these years in Mandarin, spoken aloud through an English filter is crushing. Re-examining every punishment, beating, and insult through an American lens turns everything I've normalized inside out, gutting me. For the first time, incidents like Baba ramming my head into the wall when I was sixteen years old no longer seems like an acceptable punishment.

My therapist advises, "I want you to travel back in time in your mind and be an adult advocate to your child self. What would you say to her?"

Shaking, I can't speak. A dam has broken. I weep for my child self, I weep for my adult self.

After over a year of psychotherapy sessions, I reach out to Didi. We aren't the closest, in childhood or adulthood, but as my healing begins, there is so much for us to discuss.

I call him from the desk in the office of our new house in the Lake City neighborhood of Seattle, reflecting on all that we've been through together. The house is on a split lot, and I can look out the window on my left to see my neighbor's house. I play with my hair, now cut into an edgy inverted bob. I even do the unthinkable by my parents' ordinances and bleach and dye pieces of my bangs.

"You have to admit, though, I was a pretty bad kid," Didi jokes on the phone.

He expects me to laugh, but I am serious.

"No kid deserved that, no matter what you did," I reply solemnly. I am still riddled with guilt for my past inability to protect him, for never being on his side when we were kids.

"Yeah," his voice cracks. "I guess you're right."

Neutralizing the aches from past traumas commands a high price. Time and space to heal is the minimum payment. For over a year since Mama's voicemail, I cannot talk to either of my parents. I refuse all attempts from them to reach me.

"Congratulations," says Didi in a merry 'I-told-you-so' tone. "You finally stopped drinking the Kool-Aid."

I hear his smile. He is happy to be no longer alone, no longer the black sheep. I am now by his side, where I should have always been.

On my therapist's advice, I write a letter to my parents recounting every significant hurt they'd caused me. When I finish, the letter is nearly ten pages typed. My therapist has me read it aloud to her, and again, I am shocked how much worse the stories sound in English. I sob so hard I can hardly breathe.

I mail it, nervous for the ensuing conversation, readying my arguments.

But Baba and Mama never read the letter.

When we get on the phone for the first time in over a year, all they have to say to me is "We can't read it, it's in English. We don't understand."

All those years I translated for them as a kid. I thought this time they would be able to find someone else to help them understand. Instead, I am dismissed.

"Where is all this coming from, Beautiful Jade?" asks Mama.

"What do you mean, Mama? You were there all the time that Baba has been cruel. Don't you remember all of the times he terrorized and hurt us?"

"No, that didn't happen," she says.

"Yes, it did. Didi and I both remember." And we both had bruises to show for it, on the inside and out.

"Even if it did ... Maybe I have a vague memory ... Just put it out of your mind. It is better to forget the bad and only remember the good. Don't hold onto all these unnecessary things."

This is Mama's key to survival. This is how she's been coping all of her life. Blocking out the trauma and burying her head so deep that her ears fill with sand. Pretending bad things never happen. Not to herself. Not to her children.

"Fine, fine. Everything is my fault," Baba offers disingenuously. "I'm no good. Forget the past. Can we move on now?"

But I can't forget and move on.

I am still angry.

I am stuck.

CHAPTER 53: *Body*

SEATTLE, WASHINGTON

"You look beautiful. Like a pregnant model," says Reno as I pose for a photo in the sun, a hand resting on my baby bump.

I've never loved my own body more than in those nine months. I am growing life. My body is powerful. During pregnancy, I treat myself with extra love and tenderness, protect myself from uninvited gazes, Eastern or Western, male or female. My body is mine, and during this incubation, my baby's cocoon.

Something finally changes in my thinking as I mature, as I learn to fight for myself.

Being fat is not a crime. Loving food is not one either. Why are we trained from a young age to fight our bodies? To change them into what they're not? Like Lindy West, I realize I can't advocate for myself if I don't first admit what I am. For too long, I have been conditioned to believe that my value as a woman would be in slightness, my ability to take up less space.

On a visit to Korea when I was sixteen, I was crossing a crowded street, arm in arm with my beloved grandmother when an old man I didn't know stopped me, "너 살 좀 빼야 돼. Nuh, sha jum be ya deh! You need to lose weight!"

"아저씨 뭐 보태준 거 있어요. Ahjushi, mo bo te june ge i se yo?" I retorted with all the uncharacteristic sass I could muster.

He didn't expect this insubordination and gulped like a fish for words.

As soon as the snark left my mouth, I worried about my Lao-Lao, hoping I hadn't embarrassed her. But when I looked to her, she chuckled, eyes twinkling.

In that moment, I loved her more than ever. It was the first time a family member had come close to standing up for me.

Fat is something I have always been and likely always will be, so I decide to let myself be. I free myself. I don't deserve shame or disrespect because of my body, because it doesn't fit a society constructed Asian ideal of slightness or a Western ideal of hourglass voluptuousness. My body demands that I prioritize my mental health over my physical one when needed. My medications cause weight gain, but my mental stability is far more critical than extra numbers on the scale.

Above all, I know I am beautiful. I have always known, even though the world has tried to convince me I'm not. I never stopped seeing who I really am, even when I believed no one else could.

I am a fighter, a friend, a lover, a sister, and a soon-to-be mother.
The fight is not over.
I'm still working on my issues.
But I am worthy.
I am enough.

CHAPTER 54:
Thirty-Eighth Parallel

INCHEON, PHOENIX, AND SEATTLE

The Korean War has not ended, despite the cease-fire in 1953. The North and the South are frozen in the conflict, trapped in a war which has claimed three million lives, including more civilian deaths than World War II or the Vietnam War. At the signing of the armistice agreement, the two Koreas were divided along the thirty-eighth parallel buffered by a demilitarized zone.

The battle between me and my parents also remains frozen. I refuse to forget the past. They refuse to acknowledge any wrongdoing.

"You'll understand what's in our hearts, Beautiful Jade, when you have a child of your own," Baba and Mama have said since I was a child. With every punishment, the intangible idea that someday, when I became a parent, my childhood suffering will make sense. Only then, will I truly understand.

When my body begins to grow new life, my heart breaks all over again. I desperately want to believe Mama and Baba—that having my own child will allow me to forgive and understand them. Instead, I became angrier and more inconsolable over the way Didi and I were treated. Seeing my childhood through my soon-to-be mother's eyes is too much to endure. I will never allow my child to live through the daily terror and manipulation that Didi and I endured.

"Without you two, I would be so free. I could do whatever I wanted," Baba loved to say to Didi and me. "I sacrificed my life to take care of you two. You must work hard for the rest of your life to repay me, to make it worth it."

Baba drilled into us since we were small that Didi and I owed him and Mama our lives. "Shengming zhi en, the debt of life, is something you can never repay. You must dedicate your life to trying."

After holding my baby in my arms for the first time, I cannot disagree more with Baba. Becoming a parent was my choice, something I wished for with all of my being. A child is a gift that I hoped I'd be worthy of receiving. I prepare as much as possible to be a nurturing, intentional, and patient mother. I want to do right by my child. Having a child is the opposite of a sacrifice. He will not owe me any debt for giving him life. Reno and I chose to bring him into the world. Because of our choice, it is our responsibility to give him a loving and stable start in life.

I vow to break the cycle of yelling, beatings, and manipulation— to break the cycle of verbal and physical abuse, to protect my baby above all else.

Our Seattle house in Lake City is modern with striking clean lines and huge windows. I fill our home with round objects and neutral tones to try to soften the look. By the time we adopt a dog and then, a year later, when our child arrives, the house is definitely a home.

Our Baobe thrives, playing in the park down the street and chasing chickens at our neighbor's yard. He sings constantly in English and the Mandarin and Korean songs I've taught him. He becomes grumpy, though, when at age four and half, we start having him attend Mandarin class at a tutor's home nearby.

"Why do I have to go to Mandarin class?" Baobe whines.

"You'll want to know how to speak Chinese one day. You'll thank me then."

"Hating Chinese class is like Asian American indoctrination," I explain to Reno who is very supportive of Mandarin lessons. "When Baobe gets older, he'll want in. He'll be able to commiserate over it with other Asian Americans."

My child will yearn for his Asian heritage to feel whole. I never want him to feel that void. My duty as a mother includes helping him feel connected. I, too, need to better embrace my roots to stand tall. For decades, my culture had been taken hostage by abuse and trauma, preventing me from celebrating my heritage wholly. For decades, I believed that being Chinese equaled a life of abuse and trauma. But I am liberated by the truth, by my ability to sever the artificial link between trauma and culture. The two are no longer intertwined in my heart, my skin. Only with this severance can true progress and healing be possible.

Every Lunar New Year, Baobe—who can eat his weight in dumplings—dresses up in Chinese silks. We take the light rail to Chinatown to watch the lion dance in the International District in the freezing cold.

"Say hi to Lao-Yeh and Lao-Lao." I cajole my child to talk to my parents on regular video chats, though he's always wiggling away. The language barrier and distance forms an obstacle too great to capture a preschooler's attention.

Since Baobe came into our lives, I've built a truce with Baba and Mama. It's a stalemate with clear boundaries. I will not allow myself to be lured into their manipulations, though sometimes they still try. The frequency has decreased, as it has not worked in years. I reject their Mei ban fa and so they have found other ways to work things out themselves.

Instead, I have constructed a bridge of love and affection, one of nurturing and goodwill for Baobe to access his Lao-Yeh and Lao-Lao. With this bridge, he can explore the Chinese side of his heritage. I hope he can love all of himself, embrace his culture and relatives, without the shadows of trauma from generations past.

CHAPTER 55: Progress

INCHEON, SOUTH KOREA

I am flanked by Reno and our exhausted but excited five-year-old, buzzing from the unlimited screen time on a long flight and hardly any sleep. This is my first time back in Korea in eleven years. But it doesn't feel at all foreign. A part of me has always been here.

Incheon International Airport is impressive, gleaming and marbled. I smile, taking in my surroundings, thinking of all the finales in K-dramas that end in airport chases. Looking at my beautiful family, I can't wait to introduce them to my extended family.

My twenty-year-old self would never believe this is my life. Though I still struggle at times, my bipolar disorder is well-treated and has been in remission for years. My mental illness does not hinder my career or any other part of my thriving life. I wish I could tell my younger self that everything would be okay.

Favorite Uncle and his two teenage sons welcome us with enthusiastic, awkward hugs. They greet Reno and Baobe with exaggerated English hellos and herd us into their Kia Minivan. My aunt is waiting for us back at their home with a cake.

The next day, my first request is to visit the school for the Chinese that I attended as a child. My cousins, who are seventeen and eighteen years old, both recently graduated from there.

We arrive at the school as the final bell chimes. From the outside, the buildings look the same, but the interiors are modernized. The new principal greets me kindly. I remember him from my childhood. He is a nice teacher whose wife taught me piano lessons. I smile, thinking of their spoiled chubby son. Old memories sweep over me in Technicolor from all directions. Children spill out into the schoolyard, playing tag and bouncing basketballs. Baobe runs among them, giggling.

Reno is comically hanging back under a tree, trying not to startle anyone as a foreigner at their school. I'm standing at the edge of the basketball courts with my cousins, keeping an eye on Baobe.

"What's it like going to school here now?" I ask my cousins. Then, I add with an uncomfortable laugh, "Do they still beat the students with big sticks?"

"No way!" they scoff in disbelief. "They wouldn't dare. We'd report anyone who tries!"

"Really? They stopped?"

"Yes, ages ago. Over ten years ago, the Korean government passed restrictions on corporal punishment in schools, and our Chinese school was included. They'd never do that now."

Last I'd heard, Teacher Wong had become principal. I had worried the little Chinese school might have been overlooked or exempted from any such legislation. I breathe in deeply and exhale slowly, expelling the weight I had carried. Another part of me is freed. I brim with pride and validation. Culture can be separated from trauma.

After letting Baobe play a while, I catch up with him and point out a small, grey roof-top structure, which looks just like I remember. "That was Lao-Yeh's office. Mama used to play there."

Baobe obliges me in posing for a photo at the stoop where I used to sit all the time, waiting for Baba. Then I take him by the hand and lead him to the old atrium. I kneel behind him, my breath warming his tiny right ear. I point to a large wooden placard with columns of names in calligraphy gleaning in dedication. I whisper, "Yang Fu Jio. See? That is your great-grandfather's name. He helped build this school. He made things happen. Isn't that cool?"

My son nods his adorable, bobbly head, grinning with pride, then runs back out into the warm summer breeze blowing from Incheon Harbor to play alongside the other children.

THE END

Acknowledgments

This memoir wouldn't exist if not for librarians. My deepest gratitude to all of the keepers of the books, especially Erin Helmrich and Emily Murphy. Thanks to Fifth Avenue Press for giving stories like mine a chance to reach readers in the world. I'm forever grateful to Fifth Avenue for allowing me to work with editor extraordinaire Hannah Beresford and my dream cover designer Yvonne Chan (thanks for the referral, Carole Guizzetti).

To all of my English teachers who nurtured my love for the written word: Mrs. Yip, Mr. Sabel, Mr. Hrovat, Mrs. Moore, and Mr. Lee—thank you for seeing the sparks in my writing.

To my agent Kat Kerr, for never giving up on me. I can't thank you enough.

To Alice Martell, for being the first literary agent to believe in my work and making this journey real.

Thank you, Shirley Roberson, for watching out for me!

Much love to Tria Wen, my first writing partner, I can't wait to hold your beautiful memoir in my hands.

Thank you to all my beta readers: Melody Ip, Sarah Park, Julie

Story, and Joanna Mei Fang, for giving so generously of your time and trudging through my first drafts.

More gratitude to Mochi Magazine for giving my start and amplifying my voice.

I owe a great deal to Eileen W. Cho for showing me by example publishing my writing is possible and for introducing me to the Binders community. Thanks especially to Tamara Gane, who taught me so much about the freelance writing business when I knew nothing.

Thank you Lauren Hough for teaching me to fight back and showing me the power of the writers community.

To all my freelance editors who supported my writing: Laura Norkin, April Hussar, Lara Eucalano, Sheri Reed, Jane Carr, Amber Leventry and so many more—Thank you!

To my dear friends Teresa Zhang, Lauren Hall-Lew, Shermayne Brown, Jennifer Lee, and Fadi Musleh—I don't know where I would be without you. And to all my new hometown friends (A.H. Kim, Kyunghee Kim, and Shirley Ma to name a few), thank you for helping me spread roots and for all of your support.

So much love to my Didi. I wish you all the good things.

And to Reno and Baobe, you inspire me every day.

Mental Health Resources

By no means a comprehensive list, this is meant to help those who are just beginning their mental health recovery journey.

A special note of gratitude to all the doctors, psychiatrists, psychologists, therapists, nurses, and researchers who truly care and perform their immensely challenging jobs with dedication and empathy.

ORGANIZATIONS AND SUPPORT GROUPS

NAMI
Heinz C. Prechter Bipolar Research Program
International Bipolar Foundation
Youth Mental Health Project
Bipolar Online Support Group for Perinatal Moms & Birthing
DBSA Support Groups
Mental Health America
Asian Mental Health Collective

BOOKS

What My Bones Know by Stephanie Foo
Permission to Come Home by Jennifer T. Wang, Ph.D.
Inferno: A Memoir of Motherhood and Madness by Catherine Cho
I'm Telling the Truth but I'm Lying by Bassey Ikpi
Tastes Like War by Grace M. Cho
The Body Papers by Grace Talusan
I'm Not Your Perfect Mexican Daughter by Erika Sanchez
The Magical Language of Others by E.J. Koh
Speak, Okinawa by Elizabeth Miki Brina

PODCASTS

Embodied on NPR
Healing the Tigress
Asians Do Therapy
Giving Voice to Depression

About the Author

Michelle Yang is an advocate whose writings on the intersection of Asian American identity, body image, and mental health have been featured in NBC News, CNN, *InStyle*, and *Reader's Digest*. Michelle has also been featured on NPR, *Washington Post*, and *The Seattle Times* for her advocacy. She loves exploring new parts of her new home state of Michigan with her

PHOTO BY JOSH BARNHART

family and smoking up the kitchen with spicy recipes. You can find her on michelleyangwriter.com or on Instagram @michelleyangwriter.